D0983080

CLASSROOM DYNAMICS:
Implementing a Technology-Based Learning Environment

CLASSROOM DYNAMICS:
Implementing a Technology-Based Learning Environment

WITHDRAWN
ENGLAND LIBRARY, USF

Ellen B. Mandinach
Hugh F. Cline
Educational Testing Service

PHILA. COLLEGE PHARMACY & SCIENCE
J.W. ENGLAND LIBRARY
4200 WOODLAND AVENUE
PHILADELPHIA, PA 19104-4491

LAWRENCE ERLBAUM ASSOCIATES, PUBLISHERS

1994   Hillsdale, New Jersey   Hove and London

ACD-6701

Copyright © 1994 by Lawrence Erlbaum Associates, Inc.
All rights reserved. No part of the book may be reproduced
in any form, by photostat, microform, retrieval system, or
any other means, without the prior written permission of
the publisher.

Lawrence Erlbaum Associates, Inc., Publishers
365 Broadway
Hillsdale, New Jersey 07642

Library of Congress Cataloging-in-Publication Data

Mandinach, Ellen B.
    Classroom dynamics : implementing a technology-based
learning environment / Ellen B. Mandinach and Hugh F. Cline.
        p. cm.
    Includes bibliographical references (p.) and index.
    ISBN 0-8058-0555-9
    1. Educational innovations—United States. 2. Classroom
environment—United States. 3. Computer-assigned instruction—United States. 4. Learning. I. Cline, Hugh F. II. Title.
LB1027.M3176 1994
371.3'34—dc20   93-13183
                                                              CIP

Books published by Lawrence Erlbaum Associates are printed
on acid-free paper, and their bindings are chosen for strength
and durability.

Printed in the United States of America
10 9 8 7 6 5 4 3 2 1

LB
1027
M272c

To
Gloria and Whitey
and Lynn and Hugh,
with loving gratitude.

And to
Drs. Joyce Glazer and Gary Karpf,
without whose expertise, assistance, and support
this book would not have been possible.

Table of Contents

Preface

School administrators often cite the apocryphal analogy of elephant mating behavior and educational reform. Both are accompanied by a great deal of noise and dust, but nothing happens for a very long time. In the case of elephant mating, the calf typically arrives in 24 months. In the case of educational reform, it is usually a much longer time before anything is even noticeable. From one perspective, this book is about much noise and dust with very little happening for a long time. It is the report of an attempt to introduce change in schools using a computer-based curriculum innovation for teaching higher order thinking skills to middle- and high-school students. A *leitmotif* of this volume is the extraordinary complexity and difficulty of facilitating such change in schools.

A corollary of the complexity and difficulty theme is that if one wants to promote or study change in schools, it is imperative that patience be an integral part of the strategy. Innovations in any institution, but particularly in schools, require an extraordinary length of time. Therefore, any attempt to draw conclusions prematurely from the study of planned innovations is likely to be misleading. In the project reported in this volume, it is expected that data collection, analysis, and interpretation will span many years to produce valid results and useful policy implications. A decade is not an unreasonable time frame for this type of endeavor.

This is an unusual project because it is planned to continue for such a long time. This is also an unusual book, for it is a report of activities during the early years of a technological innovation and research project in which the primary emphasis thus far has been on establishing the innovation. This volume focuses on describing the innovation and includes few traditional, empirical data analyses reported in the usual manner. Although the project is now more than 6 years old, it still is in the implementation stage. The research activities which will examine systematically the impact of the innovation are just getting underway. This book is an account of an ongoing process, a fascinating process; moreover, it is one that is likely to be repeated in the near future in countless schools throughout the nation.

The authors believe that the experiences gained and the insights produced in the early stages of designing and implementing this project need to be recorded and shared with colleagues in the educational research and practitioner communities. The account of the creation and implementation of this project is given in some detail in this volume. In this Preface, it is sufficient to call the reader's attention to the dramatic shifts in the scope and foci of this endeavor as it evolved in launching the project. After describing these shifts in perspectives, a preview of the volume chapters is provided.

Initially, the authors were interested in conducting field research focusing on the issues of acquisition and transfer of higher order thinking skills. This meant conducting research in schools in which teachers and the curriculum were promoting learning and the use of problem-solving skills in one subject area and the subsequent transfer of those skills to problem solving in other subject areas. Successful transfer means that the students are learning and understanding the concepts underlying the problem-solving procedures and can then apply those same procedures appropriately in a different context.

When a high school in Vermont that was just beginning such a program in its science department was discovered, the authors were delighted. The teachers in this school planned to use a recently released software package for building models and simulations on microcomputers. The software package is a microcomputer implementation of systems thinking, a dynamic, analytic, problem-solving procedure. Systems thinking is a problem-solving strategy that employs models and simulations to examine the changing relationships among the parts of any dynamic phenomenon.

Approximately half the science courses in this school were to be taught using systems thinking, and the remainder would be taught in the traditional manner. As students progressed from 9th through 12th grade taking the course sequence consisting of general science, biology, chemistry, and physics, they were equally likely to be assigned to classes using systems thinking and the computer. It appeared that a naturally occurring, longitudinal, quasi-experimental research design had been discovered. Over a 4-year period, the impact of various patterns of use and nonuse of a computer-based curriculum innovation could be observed, and at least some answers to questions concerning the acquisition and transfer of higher order cognitive skills might be forthcoming.

A cognitive analysis of problem solving using systems thinking as implemented in the software was undertaken, and an instrument to test students at the beginning and end of each academic year was created. Plans were made to use old course final examinations to assess students' substantive knowledge gains. Before and after comparisons were planned on both problem-solving skills and declarative knowledge among the various combinations of systems thinking and traditionally taught classes over a 4-year period. In addition, plans for extensive classroom observation and interviewing of students and teachers were formulated. Furthermore, a special class was offered, giving students an opportunity to do independent research on an historical or contemporary conflict situation and to build models simulating these events. Extensive observations and interviews with the teacher and students in this special class were planned as well.

All these research plans were delineated in the fall of 1986 when the project began. It took only several months before all confidence in the quasi-experimental design vanished. It became clear that the computer-based curriculum innovation of systems thinking could neither be quickly nor comprehensively applied in the courses. The teachers were in the process of learning systems thinking and the software. They were gradually designing modules of instruction to use the system thinking perspective and the computers. The process of implementing the curriculum innovation was time consuming, and it took more time for some teachers than others.

It became clear increasingly during the fall of 1986 that it would take at least several years after the innovation was initiated for the research design to detect any impact on student-learning outcomes. The classroom observations and in-depth interviews with teachers and students revealed that the computer-based curriculum innovation would occur gradually and in a nonlinear progression. There would be advances and setbacks. The technology-based innovation would occur slowly, but only if carefully nurtured by the project staff as well as the teachers and administrators. The process was analogous to organic growth rather than a dramatic overnight transplant.

Experience with this project transformed the authors' conceptions of the appropriate perspectives, methodologies, and expectations relevant to research on computer-based innovations in schools. As shown in the following chapters, some organizations and individuals tend to resist change. Research projects that focus only on studying change and do not provide support for the innovation are likely have very little to observe. The contributions of such projects to policy formation relevant to educational improvements will be meager. Investigators must become change agents as well as students of the transformation process.

Under these conditions, the traditional conceptions of objectivity as promulgated by the positivist scientific approach must be modified. Dispassionate data collection and analysis are less significant than understanding the perspectives of the participants. Indeed, the most fruitful methods in this kind of research are the ones employed by field anthropologists rather than those used by experimental psychologists. The emphasis in this research is not on sound psychometric instruments but on developing a global understanding of the processes of change at both the individual and organizational levels.

Work on this project thus far has provided an enlarged view of the appropriate tasks, possibilities, and responsibilities involved in evaluation research. These themes have been described in the educational research literature, but work on this project has concretized and amplified them. For these reasons, it is useful to record as systematically as possible all activities in the projects to date.

For some time now, educational psychologists and cognitive scientists have been interested in the development of critical thinking skills among students. The rate at which new factual information is produced in our rapidly changing society is overwhelming. Teaching students all the facts necessary to prepare them for their various roles in the adult world of work has become an impossible task. There is simply too much new information generated every single day in our data-rich society to justify maintaining an educational system that emphasizes teaching facts and declarative knowledge. Rather, there is a growing recognition that students need to learn procedural skills and the underlying concepts that allow them to identify, retrieve, and use information from a variety of sources to deal with a broad range of problems.

The emphasis on problem-solving skills is not new in educational research and practice (e.g., Polya, 1957). However, this perspective is neither widely understood nor appreciated by most practicing teachers and school administrators. When the decision was made to establish a school-based project focusing on the development and transfer of higher order thinking skills, these skills were expected to be unfamiliar to most students and teachers. Therefore, this project was designed to encompass multiple research foci, thereby insuring that a broad and comprehensive examination of both the short- and long-range consequences of the innovation would be captured in the investigation.

The project was designed to include three foci. The first focus would be on learning outcomes among students. Here the project staff would look for evidence of the acquisition of declarative knowledge. More importantly, they would seek evidence relevant to the understanding and acquisition of procedural knowledge, problem-solving skills, systemic thinking, and the use of those skills in new content areas. The second focus would be on classroom dynamics. Here the investigators would collect information on changes in teacher behavior while organizing and conducting their classes. Descriptions of practical applications for systems thinking and the microcomputer software package for different subjects can be of great value for cognitive analysis of teaching. They also can provide demonstrations of models and teaching strategies that could be applied by other teachers in their courses. The third focus is on changes in the school as an organization. Here the interest is in the changes that might occur in the structure and functioning of the school as a consequence of introducing the curriculum innovation. Issues such as patterns of communication, influence, power, and authority would be of interest.

The three foci of the systems thinking project, student learning processes and outcomes, teacher behaviors and classroom activities, and organizational changes, have resulted in a division of labor among the authors. The first author, Ellen B. Mandinach, is a psychologist. As project director, she has responsibility for all activities. She also directs that part of the implementation and research efforts which deals with learning outcomes. The second author, Hugh F. Cline, is a sociologist. He has primary responsibility for the organizational aspect of the study. Together, they have joint responsibility for the research focusing on changing teacher behavior. Thus, the intellectual perspectives of psychology and sociology jointly are brought to bear on this project.

As mentioned previously, this book is a preliminary report on an interesting technology innovation project. Descriptions of the project include an account of the innovative curriculum stressing the learning and transfer of higher order skills, the development of new methodologies of evaluation research, and the study of change at many different levels, including student learning, teacher behavior, and organization structure and function.

The transformation of the research design from a quasi-experiment to the multiple perspectives and their corresponding methodologies has made the authors realize that the teaching and learning activities that occur embrace what is known as the *constructivist perspective* (e.g., Cognition and Technology Group at Vanderbilt University, 1992). This pedagogical philosophy is discussed at some length because it is one of the major unifying themes of the implementation and research activities reported in this volume.

Chapter 1 presents an historical account of the design and implementation of the systems thinking project in a single high school in Vermont. Chapter 2 provides a description of the expansion of that project to include a network of two middle schools and four high schools in California, and subsequently an additional high school in Arizona. It also gives an account of the research methods employed in the project. Chapter 3 then describes the trio of components of the systems thinking approach, including the theory, the hardware, and the software. The chapter first recounts the development of systems thinking as a conceptual and heuristic tool. It also presents a brief history of computer and microcomputer usage in schools, ending this discussion with a description of a particular type of computer, graphical user interface (GUI). This type of microcomputer is especially appropriate for the systems thinking curriculum innovation. Finally, the chapter introduces the software package that implements systems thinking. An example provides the reader with some feel for the potential of this software package.

Chapter 4 reviews the problems, issues, questions, and dilemmas encountered in the project to give a clear sense of the variety and complexity of issues involved in creating and evaluating a computer-based technology innovation such as systems thinking. In Chapter 5, a matrix of teacher patterns of adaptation to technology is developed, and vignettes of prototypic project participants are presented, detailing the ways they employ systems thinking in their instructional activities. Chapter 6 then explores the future research agenda for the project and suggests that the methods will continue to undergo change and refinement. Finally, the last section draws out some preliminary policy implications from the project for the future of the teaching profession.

The volume has three appendixes. Appendix A includes descriptions of the eight schools participating in the project. These are the first drafts of case studies of each school. Appendix B uses the tool of systems thinking to focus on the analysis of computer-based, educational technology innovation projects. The perspective of systems thinking is used to shed light on the very object of inquiry of this investigation. The intent in this appendix is to share with readers the process employed in modeling complex, multilevel, interacting systems over time. The appendix includes a first draft of a system thinking model of change in schools resulting from a computer-based innovation. The model is multilevel, multifocus, and multimethod; and it provides an opportunity for more systematic review of both the anticipated and unanticipated consequences of promoting computer-based change in schools. Appendix C contains a list of all the teachers and project directors who have thus far participated in the STACI[N] Project.

At several points during the preparation of this manuscript, colleagues and reviewers asked the authors why this volume was prepared at such an early point in the life of the project. Researchers usually delay publishing books and articles on their projects until they have reached a stage at which they can report the analysis and interpretation of empirical data, hypothesis testing, or address questions about the impact or effectiveness of a program. So, why publish now? The authors have learned a great deal about educational research and reform in the process of launching this project, and they think it is important to share what they have learned with the larger educational research and practice community. This volume is a description and analysis of those many varied and rich experiences.

ACKNOWLEDGMENTS

The contributions of many persons and institutions made the STACI Projects possible. The initial STACI Project was conducted under the auspices of the Educational Technology Center, Harvard Graduate School of Education, and was supported by the Office of Educational Research and Improvement under contract number 400-83-0041. We gratefully acknowledge the substantive support and assistance provided by the co-directors of the Educational Technology Center, Charles Thompson, Judah Schwartz, and Martha Stone Wiske. Research during this project was conducted at Brattleboro Union High School, Brattleboro, Vermont. We would like to thank the administration and faculty at Brattleboro for their cooperation and continued collaboration.

The STACI[N] Project is being conducted under the Secondary School Mathematics and Science Grant Program, Secretary's Discretionary Fund, in the U.S. Department of Education, award number R168D90006, under the Innovation in Education Program, award number R215A00154, and under the Eisenhower Program for Mathematics and Science, award number R168C10031. We would like to acknowledge the administration and faculty of the following schools and districts: Brattleboro Union High School and Windham Southeast Supervisory Union, Brattleboro, Vermont; Hillview Middle School and the Menlo Park City Elementary School District, Menlo Park, California; Menlo-Atherton High School and the Sequoia Union High School District, Atherton and Redwood City, California; Mountain View High School and the Mountainview-Los Altos Union High School District, Mountain View, California; Sunnyside High School and the Sunnyside Unified School District #12, Tucson, Arizona; and El Camino High School, South San Francisco High School, Westborough Middle School, and the South San Francisco Unified School District, South San Francisco, California. In particular, we would like to thank all the dedicated teachers with whom we have had the privilege to work, including the local project directors and their colleagues for continued efforts, hard work, and commitment to STACI^N. We especially would like to thank Stan Ogren for his sage counsel on this and many other projects.

We most gratefully acknowledge the contributions and support provided by Dr. Barbara Bowen, Manager of External Research, Apple Computer, Inc., and her staff, Denise Coley, Julie Lieber, and Teri Stover. The generous hardware contributions provided by Apple have made the STACI Projects possible.

We also acknowledge the systems expertise provided by High Performance Systems, Inc., and in particular, the project teacher trainers Barry Richmond, Steve Peterson, and Lyn Swett Miller. Without their support and expertise the project teachers would likely be mired in an infinite feedback loop. We also would like to thank David Kreutzer of the MIT Systems Dynamics Group for his contributions and efforts in working with the students and teachers at Brattleboro Union High School.

Many people at Educational Testing Service have provided support and contributions for the STACI Projects. Foremost, we would like to thank Dr. Henry I. Braun, Vice President for Research Management, and Dr. C. Victor Bunderson, formerly Vice President for Research Management, who have provided internal funding for the STACI Projects to insure their survival. We also would like to acknowledge the following ETSers for their contributions to STACI and STACI^N: Nancy Benton, Pam Bowski, Colleen Lahart, Beth Mowery, Bill Senior, Peggy Thorpe, Corrine Cohen, and Kay Tyberg. Finally, we especially wish to thank Ruby Chan, Gene Horkay, and Mimi Perez for their many contributions to this manuscript as well as the STACI^N Project.

Richard Ruopp, formerly President of Bank Street College of Education and currently at TERC, provided invaluable feedback on the manuscript. We also thank ETSers, Randy Bennett, Larry Frase, Lori

Morris, and Karen Sheingold, who generously agreed to review the manuscript.

Finally, we would like to thank family and friends who supported and sustained us while we were in hibernation working on the book. The first author wishes to thank Julie, Ed, Chris, June, Helen, Lydia, Joan, Meg, and Jane for their friendship, patience, and understanding. The second author wishes to thank Hilary Hays for her support and his late wife, Pat, for her longstanding support, encouragement, and love.

Ellen B. Mandinach
Hugh F. Cline

1

The Systems Thinking and Curriculum Innovation Project

GENESIS

Educational Testing Service (ETS) was one of several collaborators in the Educational Technology Center (ETC), located at the Harvard Graduate School of Education. Founded in the mid-1980s, ETC was funded initially by the Office of Educational Research and Improvement (OERI) in the U.S. Department of Education. Its mission was to examine the impact of technology on science and mathematics education. ETS's original role was to provide dissemination services for ETC. After 3 years the directorship at ETC changed and so too did the personnel and focus of ETS's participation. ETS then began an examination of the acquisition and transfer of higher order thinking skills in classroom computer learning environments. This particular emphasis was not novel, for substantial earlier research had focused on the cognitive effects of learning in computer environments. Such research was carried out in many places, including the University of California at Berkeley (Dalbey & Linn, 1985; Linn, 1985; Mandinach & Linn, 1986) and the Center for Children and Technology at the Bank Street College of Education in New York (Pea & Kurland, 1984; Pea & Sheingold, 1987).

Most of the early research projects yielded inconclusive results on the impact of programming or learning from cognitively engaging software on students' acquisition of content knowledge and higher order thinking skills. Two special issues of the *Journal of Educational Computing Research* documented these discrepant results (Mandinach, Linn, Pea, & Kurland, 1986-1987). The issue of transfer was at the heart of many of these studies. The assumption was that learning to program was particularly likely to foster generalizable skills across domains. Some of these projects also highlighted the many problems associated with implementing new technologies in classroom settings and attempting to examine their impact. Although the results from many early studies were discordant concerning the effects of programming and the use of software on cognition, they did provide direction for ETC, ETS, and other organizations conducting additional research on these issues.

Numerous reasons can be cited for the ambiguous pattern of results, including inadequate hardware and software, untrained teachers, inappropriate support materials, weak links to the curricula, premature examination of impact, and inappropriate research methodologies. The rationales put forward for the use of computers for instructional purposes were varied and often unspecified. There seemed to be a widely held belief that microcomputers were powerful machines, but neither manufacturers, educators, nor researchers were certain sure how they should be used in schools.

Perhaps the foremost impediment to effective computer implementation facing both teachers and researchers was the quality and objectives espoused by much of the early educational software. These programs often were targeted to lower order skills and domain-specific tasks. They were largely drill-and-practice, used by teachers as adjuncts to instruction rather than integrated into ongoing classroom activities. They became known as "drill-and-kill" activities that were nothing more than electronic problem sets. There were no explicit ties to the curriculum, thereby making much of the software difficult to apply and therefore pedagogically disappointing. The nature of the software made implementation problematic due to some basic incompatibilities with the structure of most classrooms. That is, programs often were designed for a single student-to-computer interaction rather than small group or whole class activities. Students had to be "pulled out" of ongoing classroom activities to use the computers, which often served the role of baby sitters. With relatively large student-to-computer ratios, the early classroom uses were highly rigid and virtually untenable.

In 1986, ETS staff attempted to identify some examples of promising commercial software that could be used to study the cognitive impact of learning with computers in classroom settings. The focus was on both higher order thinking skills and content knowledge. ETS staff wanted to work in the classroom and examine software as it was implemented naturally, in contrast to a more contrived laboratory setting.

Project staff surveyed commercial software producers, educators, researchers in the field, and industry or academically based developers. The outcome of this extensive search was distressing. It became clear that a software package appropriate for this project did not exist. Furthermore, discussions with software developers, both commercial and nonprofit, did not provide any confidence that such software would become available in the near future. Therefore, the authors decided to pursue a slightly different approach to the examination of a computer-based curriculum innovation. There was a growing appreciation among science and mathematics teaching experts that modeling and simulation should play a major role in enhancing learning among precollege students (National Council of Teachers of Mathematics, 1989). The application of system dynamics then became a logical focus of this project.

Initial Exposure to System Dynamics

Because of the increased focus on simulations, guidance was sought from the System Dynamics Group at the Sloan School of Management at the Massachusetts Institute of Technology (MIT). As is described in chapter 3, the Systems Dynamics Group had constructed and worked with simulations for many years (see Forrester, 1961, 1968, 1969). In August, 1986, the project staff visited MIT to consult with the staff in the System Dynamics Group. An event occurred that indicated the vast potential of using modeling and simulation software for the research.

That event happened during a visit to a small summer workshop for high school students being conducted by a member of the MIT System Dynamics Group. The students were being introduced to the principles of system dynamics and the software package Structural Thinking Experiential Learning Laboratory with Animation (STELLA) (Richmond, 1985). The visit occurred in the middle of a 2-week training session. The participants were average, inner-city high school students who were paid volunteers. The instructor was engaging the class in a discussion of factors that influenced the varying levels of automobile registrations in the greater Boston area since the 1920s. The students were debating the shape of a graph depicting rising rates of registrations. When the instructor asked what might be the trend during an economic recession when fewer people were able to buy new cars, an extraordinary event happened. A young woman who previously had been less than engaged in the discussion and more interested in the neighboring boys, announced to the class that the automobile they were discussing was comparable to the trend in the size of her personal wardrobe. Her wardrobe was usually increasing in size as purchases and gifts normally exceeded discards. However, the rate of growth of her wardrobe was frequently affected negatively by fluctuations in her own financial status. The wardrobe, with its inflows and outflows of items, was indeed a system similar to the population of automobiles. She had generalized her understanding of a concept in one setting (i.e., fluctuating numbers of autos) to another setting that had great relevance for her (i.e., the size of her wardrobe). System dynamics had provided the means by which she could draw parallels among disparate phenomena and understand in each how the variables were interrelated.

The basic principles underlying this demonstration are the same ones that underlie general systems theory and are the foundation for constructing simulations in a wide variety of settings. It was obvious from that session and subsequent discussions with the staff from the MIT System Dynamics Group that the potentials for using systems theory and simulation-modeling software to create a cognitively engaging and demanding learning environment were enormous. Thus, began the exploration into the application of system dynamics into precollege classroom teaching and learning activities.

Project Planning

As the authors began to consider a research project that was based on the implementation of system dynamics in precollege instruction, they learned that a small high school in southeastern Vermont was beginning to introduce system dynamics in several classes. A local corporate executive, who had been trained in system dynamics while an undergraduate at MIT, had stimulated interest among administrators and faculty at Brattleboro Union High School (BUHS), Brattleboro, Vermont. Sufficient interest had been sparked, and several workshops already had been conducted for students, faculty, administration, school board members, and the general public. These workshops were conducted by the staff of High Performance Systems (HPS), the software company that produces STELLA. HPS is located only an hour and a half drive from Brattleboro. One BUHS teacher had previously used a sabbatical leave at Dartmouth College to enroll in classes on systems theory taught by Barry Richmond, President of HPS. Four BUHS teachers already had applied for a Discretionary Grant from the Secretary of the U.S. Department of Education to support their efforts to implement systems thinking in their courses. The grant was approved for one year, and $20,000 was awarded in the summer of 1986. BUHS was embarking on an exploration of the potentials of systems in several courses.

After receiving approval from ETC and OERI in August, 1986, the authors met with relevant faculty and administrators at BUHS to explore the possibility of a collaborative implementation and research project. The systems thinking group at BUHS consisted of four teachers who enjoyed support from their principal and superintendent. However, they had only three Macintoshes for the project. One was donated by the community member who introduced systems thinking to the school; the district supplied a second; and the third was purchased with funds secured from a local foundation. However, it soon became clear that it would be nearly impossible to implement systems thinking with only three computers to be shared among four teachers and their students. Not only would students have little time on the computers, but there would never be sufficient on-line time for teachers to develop curriculum materials.

Through ETC, ETS was able to secure from the External Research Group at Apple Computer, Inc., a donation of a classroom set of 15 Macintoshes to facilitate the integration of systems thinking into the curriculum at BUHS. The funds provided by OERI made possible the payment of small stipends to the four teachers, the hiring of a paraprofessional to eliminate the need for teachers to assume nonacademic responsibilities, and funds for other miscellaneous project-related expenses. In return, BUHS promised to provide a forum in which ETS could conduct research on the impact of using systems thinking in student learning. Thus, was born the Systems Thinking and Curriculum Innovation (STACI) Project.

THE STACI PROJECT: DESIGN AND IMPLEMENTATION

The STACI Project was a 2-year research effort conducted by ETS under the auspices of ETC, with funding from OERI. The intent of the project was to examine the cognitive demands and consequences of learning with the systems thinking approach and the STELLA software.

Project Objectives

The original purpose of the project was to test the potentials and effects of using the systems approach in existing secondary school curricula to teach general problem-solving skills as well as content-specific knowledge. The research focused on the learning outcomes and transfer that might result from using such an approach and software in classrooms. The primary research question focused on the examination of the extent to which students could acquire content knowledge and higher order thinking skills through exposure to and interaction with curricula infused with systems thinking and subsequently generalize knowledge and skills to problem-solving tasks in other substantive areas.

The instructional perspective espoused here is termed the systems thinking approach. The approach consists of three separate but interdependent components. The first is system dynamics, the theory on which the instructional perspective is based. The second component is the Macintosh microcomputer on which the STELLA software runs. The third component is STELLA, the software package that is used as a tool to teach systems thinking, content knowledge, and problem solving.

Site Description and Design

BUHS serves a rural five-town district in southeastern Vermont whose population is approximately 20,000. The school has roughly 1,600 students and a faculty of 80 teachers. Brattleboro has an interesting population composition. On the one hand, there are many native New Englanders who make their living farming or in other small local industries. On the other hand, the area surrounding the community has become a region to which many ex-urbanites have escaped. The area has attracted artists, authors, and culturally minded former city dwellers who believe deeply in providing progressive and quality education for their children.

Four teachers formed the systems group at BUHS. All were trained to use the systems thinking approach through workshops, and in one case in college courses. When the STACI Project started in the summer of 1986, curriculum development was just getting underway. Very few precollege systems applications existed at that time. It was the teachers' intent to identify particular parts of their curricula, especially those dealing with dynamic phenomena and others that heretofore had been difficult to teach, and apply the new instructional perspective to those targeted areas. Four courses in the sciences—general physical science (GPS), biology, chemistry, and physics — were taught using an integrative approach with systems. The approach was integrative in that the teachers identified concepts where instruction could be enhanced by the use of systems principles. Rather than teach those concepts as they had in the past, the systems teachers explicitly emphasized the systemic and dynamic nature of the topics, noting such ideas as causality, feedback, variation, and interaction. The courses covered the same body of knowledge taught in the traditional curriculum, but specific topics were addressed from a systems perspective.

In contrast, a new, experimental social studies course entitled War and Revolution was created in the 1986/1987 school year that implemented the systems approach in a manner different from the integrative strategy employed in the science courses. War and Revolution was conducted as a college seminar, for the teacher rarely lectured. Through class discussions and independent research projects, students analyzed dynamic historical situations from the perspective of decision makers. The course provided a unique approach and structure to the examination of historical events. Systems thinking formed the basis of inquiry for the course in which students examined the genesis and progression of a variety of conflicts throughout history including coups d'état, revolutions, and wars. The intent was to develop both analytical skills and an appreciation of the complexities and importance of policy decisions in conflict situations.

TABLE 1.1
Enrollment and Class Figures

Course	Systems Thinking		Traditional	
	Classes	Students	Classes	Students
1986 - 1987				
GPS	3	47	3	69
Biology	4	82	4	94
Chemistry	3	63	3	64
Physics		Not included this year		
TOTAL	10	192	10	227
War/				
Revolution	1	8		
1987 - 1988				
GPS	2	41	3	47
Biology	4	80	5	104
Chemistry	3	66	4	93
Physics	3	65		
TOTAL	12	252	12	244
War/				
Revolution	1	10		

In the 1986/1987 academic year, systems thinking was integrated into three GPS, four biology, three chemistry classes, and the War and Revolution seminar. An equivalent number of traditional classes were taught concurrently by other members of the faculty. Some 200 students were exposed to the systems approach in the first year (see Table 1.1). In the project's second year, the systems approach was used in two GPS, four biology, three chemistry, three physics classes, and War and Revolution, with approximately 260 students receiving instruction using the systems approach.

Data Collection

A variety of methods and procedures were employed to assess the outcomes of introducing the systems thinking approach, including course grades, standardized tests, classroom observations, interviews, and specially created instruments. Performance on course examinations, quizzes, and exercises were the measures of content knowledge.

As is commonly done in differential psychology research, achievement tests served as rough estimates of general ability, in this case, as measures of crystallized ability. Crystallized ability reflects the long-term accumulation and organization of knowledge and skills, essentially general achievement (Snow, 1980). Other measures related to skills underlying systems thinking were also given. These included inductive and deductive reasoning, figural analogies, and understanding relationships. The Advanced Progressive Matrices (Raven, 1958, 1962) were used as a measure of fluid ability. Fluid ability reflects the adaptation of knowledge and skills on new and unfamiliar tasks (Snow, 1980). Abridged versions of previous final exams were administered to the systems and traditional classes in the beginning of the school year to serve as baselines of content knowledge. Teachers administered content-specific assessment activities throughout the year. These tests and exercises were roughly comparable in their subject-matter coverage. The traditional and systems teachers also prepared and gave common final examinations to their classes.

A draft instrument was developed by ETS staff to assess knowledge of systems thinking. The Systems Thinking Instrument (STI) measured a broad spectrum of skills ranging from elementary concepts to complex modeling skills. It focused on concepts such as variation and variables, causation and causality, feedback and looping constructs, graphing, and modeling. The test was administered only to the systems classes to measure acquisition of systems principles.

Classroom observations were conducted throughout the 2-year project. Project staff observed both the systems and traditional classes to obtain information about course content, structure, and classroom procedures. Systems classes were observed both when the new as well as traditional materials were presented. Observations were scheduled when similar topics were covered to see how the systems and traditional teachers differed in their approaches to the targeted concepts. For example, project staff observed how systems and traditional biology teachers presented the topic of immunology, noting differences in emphases and method of presentation.

Interviews with systems and traditional teachers were conducted on an ongoing basis to obtain additional information about the classes and curriculum materials. Emphasis was placed on gathering information from the systems teachers concerning the issues they confronted during the development and implementation of the curriculum innovation. The interviews also provided an opportunity to probe teachers' evolving perceptions of the systems thinking modules, implementation difficulties, and other issues related to the effects of the curriculum innovation. In addition to interviews with the teachers, meetings were scheduled regularly with administrators and school board members to obtain information about their perceptions of the systems thinking project.

MAIN AND ANCILLARY STUDIES

As noted earlier, the primary objective of the project was to examine the extent to which the systems thinking approach could enhance the teaching and learning of higher order thinking skills and content knowledge. The research plan was to implement a quasi-experimental design that would examine the differences between the systems thinking approach and courses taught in a traditional manner (Mandinach, Thorpe, & Lahart, 1988). In addition to the main study on impact, ETS designed and conducted three ancillary studies that were intended to address focused areas of inquiry about the impact of the systems thinking approach on various aspects of the learning process and of increasing importance, the process of implementation.

Main Study: Modes of Implementation

This section provides a brief discussion of the preliminary curricular and cognitive outcomes that resulted from the 2-year implementation of the systems approach into the science classes and the War and Revolution seminar. It is apparent that a simple description of learning outcomes would overlook the many important lessons gained from observation of how the systems approach was implemented. Thus, descriptions of the modes of implementation and the integration of the systems approach into the various courses are presented, emphasizing the types of modeling activities observed. The preliminary trends observed in the data on learning outcomes will then be described. Because there was limited implementation in the project's first 2 years, these results must be viewed as preliminary and at best tentative. The quasi-experimental paradigm used for examining differences was severely compromised, because the treatment was so restricted, thereby limiting the extent to which any definite conclusions can be drawn.

As already noted, an integrative approach was used in the science courses. This means that courses covered the same body of knowledge as traditional classes, but discussions of selected concepts and topics were supplemented with the systems perspective and illustrated with systems models. In contrast, the systems thinking approach was the conceptual and theoretical foundation of the War and Revolution seminar.

Modeling activities generally took three forms: parameter manipulation, constrained modeling, and epitome modeling. Depending on the course, students: (a) were given existing models and were asked to alter particular parameters to examine their effects on the system; (b) used modeling to solve traditional textbook problems; or (c) developed their own models based on primary research. These three approaches, spanning a continuum of cognitive complexity, were likely to correspond to different outcomes in terms of the acquisition of content knowledge and problem-solving skills.

The least complex and cognitively demanding use of systems thinking is parameter manipulation. It is assumed that manipulating parameters in an existing model promotes basic inquiry skills (e.g., the understanding of causality and variation), and might influence directly the acquisition of content knowledge. Originally this form of modeling activity was thought to be most appropriate for younger or lower achieving students because of its possible explicit links to the curriculum and less demanding cognitive requirements.

In contrast, model building was expected to promote more general problem-solving skills and the transfer of those skills to other areas of inquiry. Two levels of model-building activities were identified. Constrained modeling occurs when students are assigned traditional textbook problems to which systems thinking can be applied as an alternate solution strategy. Traditional methods (e.g., mathematical solutions) might be one strategy, but the systems approach might serve as another, more dynamic and thus potentially more effective means by which to solve the problem.

Finally, the most complex application of the systems approach is what is termed epitome modeling. Here, students construct their own models, based on their individual research and conceptualization of the given phenomena. The models constructed by the students in the War and Revolution seminar are examples of epitome modeling. Many higher order thinking skills must be applied in epitome modeling. These forms of systems applications will be described in more detail in chapter 5.

The application of the systems approach in the science curricula differed across specific disciplines, with several trends emerging as the teachers adapted the approach to their courses. Implementation also varied across courses depending on whether the approach emphasized individual, small group, or class activities.

In GPS, which is a general freshman course, the teacher introduced systems with causal loop diagrams and graphing concepts. Simulation was a recurrent theme throughout the course, as it was used to highlight many concepts for which students were asked to develop simple models. There were no overall differences on the STI between students in the treatment and control classes. In-depth comparative analyses of performance indicated some subtle differences in response patterns. Students who received traditional instruction exhibited greater comprehension of the scientific vocabulary. They were able to identify and define simple patterns, but they could not identify those same patterns in more complex problems. In contrast, the systems students were more adept at decomposing problems to understand better the aggregate. They did not concentrate on terminology. Instead, they provided descriptions that indicated their comprehension of patterns of change over time. These results are consistent with the emphases of the systems and traditional courses.

Biology is the scientific discipline taught in high schools that one might expect to be most amenable to systems analysis due to the large number of natural systems taught in the curriculum. Because the interrelationship among living systems is a key concept in biology, many relevant examples were identified to which the systems approach could be applied. In the biology course at BUHS, students were introduced to the fundamentals of systems, modeling, feedback, and causality. The teacher developed and presented models of such topics as oxygen production, metabolism, population, transport, and immunology. The primary learning activity in this course was parameter manipulation. The teacher presented a model to the class in a lecture format. As a class, students then worked on the models and manipulated parameters. They did not construct their own models. Moreover, they rarely even touched the computer. Most often, the teacher manipulated the computer while the students provided answers from their seats.

The biology teacher treated the curriculum modules taught with the systems approach as distinct and separate types of classroom activities. No explicit links were made to the curriculum, no rationales were provided as to why the approach was being taught, nor how it could be used to analyze biological phenomena. Instead, students perceived that they were doing something different and perhaps even detrimental to their performance in biology. They really were not so much concerned with how much or what they were learning or not learning, but where they were in relation to other teachers' biology classes. One student actually questioned what would happen to them, because they were three weeks behind some of the traditionally taught classes. A question such as this raises issues of implementation, measurement, and accountability that will be addressed in a later chapter. The teacher attempted to explain that the systems approach, used as a problem-solving tool, was an investment toward students' long-term educational objectives. He urged them not to worry about being behind the traditional classes. Few, if any, students understood this explanation.

The integration of the systems approach into chemistry was admittedly difficult, according to the BUHS teacher. The original intent was to use the approach to highlight chemical concepts that had relevance to social issues (e.g., pollution, global warming, acid rain). However, constructing models of such complex phenomena is far too complicated for most high school students and probably for many teachers as well. Consequently, this teacher revised his focus and identified a few topics in chemistry that could be modeled at a lower level of complexity, such as reaction rates and equilibrium states.

The teacher combined parameter manipulation and constrained modeling techniques within a guided inquiry format. Although students worked through structured worksheets and manipulated parameters, they also were given the freedom to conduct experiments and construct simple models on their own. Structural diagrams and models provided tools to illustrate the functions of and relations among variables. They were used also to test hypotheses and observe changes in the behavior of variables over time and under different conditions. From these guided inquiry experiences, a generic understanding of the behavior of sets of interacting variables was developed.

The chemistry teacher also adapted textbook problems for use in systems modules. Worksheets were constructed to illustrate that problem solving is an iterative process of testing, revising, and retesting hypotheses. Problems often included sequences of "what if" scenarios. Students hypothesized about what would happen if parameters were changed, provided rationales for the hypotheses, and then tested them by constructing and running STELLA models. For example, students constructed models of chemical reactions, indicating how changing temperature affects rates. They then expanded their original models to include additional factors. Students ran the model and tested hypotheses, focusing on the problem's dynamics and outcomes.

On the other hand, the physics teacher at BUHS developed and used an inquiry approach in his courses. Textbook problems were solved using systems as well as traditional mathematical techniques. Using the constrained modeling paradigm, students solved the problems with the traditional mathematical solutions in addition to systems analysis. The following acceleration problem is one such constrained modeling assignment (Miller, Dillon, & Smith, 1980).

A late passenger, sprinting at 8 m/sec, is 30 m away from the rear end of a train when it starts out of the station with an acceleration of 1 m/sec². Can the passenger catch the train if the platform is long enough? (Note: This problem requires solution of a quadratic equation. Can you explain the significance of the two values you get for the time?) (p. 52)

Students typically solved the problem mathematically, then applied constrained modeling techniques. In order to construct a model, students first needed to comprehend the problem, translate the physical concepts into systems representations, and insert numerical parameters and the scientific logic needed to run the model dynamically over time. They also needed planning, hypothesis testing, analysis, and debugging skills to identify and remediate problems for subsequent revisions.

Figures 1.1 and 1.2 represent two solutions to the acceleration

FIG. 1.1. Acceleration problem: Solution 1.

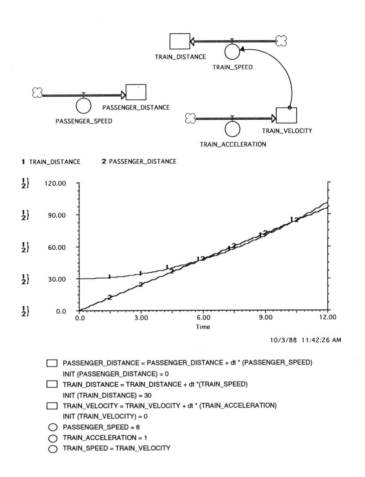

1 TRAIN_DISTANCE   2 PASSENGER_DISTANCE

10/3/88 11:42:26 AM

☐ PASSENGER_DISTANCE = PASSENGER_DISTANCE + dt * (PASSENGER_SPEED)
INIT (PASSENGER_DISTANCE) = 0
☐ TRAIN_DISTANCE = TRAIN_DISTANCE + dt *(TRAIN_SPEED)
INIT (TRAIN_DISTANCE) = 30
☐ TRAIN_VELOCITY = TRAIN_VELOCITY + dt * (TRAIN_ACCELERATION)
INIT (TRAIN_VELOCITY) = 0
○ PASSENGER_SPEED = 8
○ TRAIN_ACCELERATION = 1
○ TRAIN_SPEED = TRAIN_VELOCITY

problem. The structural diagrams, simultaneous equations, and graphic representations are presented for both solutions. It is important to note that although the two solutions are quite similar, there are some rather subtle distinctions that indicate different approaches to the problem. No judgments as to correctness can or should be made between these two situations. The basic structure of the two models is identical and reflects the students' understanding of acceleration. They simply reflect how two different students understood and conceptualized the physical phenomenon. This problem was used for in-depth analysis in the Self-Regulated Learning Substudy. Analyses of these solutions are presented in detail in the next section on the substudy.

FIG. 1.2. Acceleration problem: Solution 2.

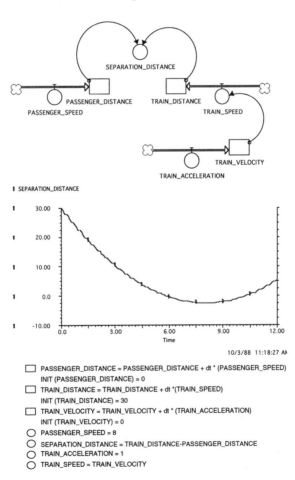

10/3/88 11:18:27 AM

☐ PASSENGER_DISTANCE = PASSENGER_DISTANCE + dt * (PASSENGER_SPEED)
INIT (PASSENGER_DISTANCE) = 0
☐ TRAIN_DISTANCE = TRAIN_DISTANCE + dt *(TRAIN_SPEED)
INIT (TRAIN_DISTANCE) = 30
☐ TRAIN_VELOCITY = TRAIN_VELOCITY + dt * (TRAIN_ACCELERATION)
INIT (TRAIN_VELOCITY) = 0
○ PASSENGER_SPEED = 8
○ SEPARATION_DISTANCE = TRAIN_DISTANCE-PASSENGER_DISTANCE
○ TRAIN_ACCELERATION = 1
○ TRAIN_SPEED = TRAIN_VELOCITY

The main classroom study provided the opportunity to examine broadly the impact of systems thinking. However, it did not provide the chance to conduct some in-depth research on the cognitive processes involved in implementing the systems thinking approach. Nor did the quasi-experimental design elicit as much information as originally anticipated due to the limited extent to which the approach could be implemented in the school year. Consequently, the substudies were conducted to provide additional insights into the impact of the approach.

The original intent of the quasi-experimental design was to compare learning outcomes that resulted from traditional and systems-based courses. The design assumed that there would be sufficient application of the systems thinking approach that could be measured. It also assumed that direct comparisons could be made between the systems and traditional classes. For a variety of reasons, the design could not be implemented in a systematic way. First, the systems and traditional teachers were not always able to coordinate their course content and assessments to yield informative comparative data. For example, if a teacher developed a systems module on a particular topic, the traditional teacher attempted, but was not always successful in teaching that topic at roughly the same time or in the same level of detail. Furthermore, when the teachers collaboratively designed their tests, only a few items could be used to measure learning of systems-based topics. It was exceedingly difficult to develop tests that would be valid measures for both systems and traditional classes.

The second and most important impediment to the quasi-experimental design was the fact that there simply was not a sufficient amount of systems applications in the courses. Teachers were developing curriculum materials, but no one realized just how time consuming and labor intensive a task it would be. A small exposure to systems thinking would have been appropriate for a formative evaluation, but not for a more formal assessment. More extensive and sufficiently refined systems-based materials were needed. Hence, valid data for the quasi-experimental design were unavailable. However, a great deal of formative information was collected, causing a refocusing of implementation goals and research objectives.

The Self-Regulated Learning Substudy

The first substudy focused specifically on the acquisition of higher order thinking skills, particularly self-regulation, among a select group of advanced science students (Mandinach, 1988a). The examination of self-regulation, general problem-solving skills, higher order thinking skills, and related constructs has been the focus of many studies (e.g., Brown & DeLoache, 1978; Flavell, 1976, 1979, 1981; Shulman & Keislar, 1966). The studies each identify a composite of skills that reflect their operational definitions of the construct.

For the specific purposes here, the substudy examinees the concept of *self-regulated learning* and uses the definition outlined by Corno and Mandinach (1983), as a student's active acquisition and transformation of instructional materials. Information acquisition processes include receiving stimuli, tracking information, and self-reinforcement. They are referred to as alertness and monitoring. Such processes are considered metacognitive, for they regulate the transformation processes that include discriminating relevant from irrelevant information, connecting new information with prior knowledge or skills, and planning particular performance routines. Planning is also considered metacognitive when a task requires higher order schemata.

Self-regulation is a level of cognitive functioning to which students and teachers should aspire. Unfortunately, few students use it consistently. Because the construct requires high levels of both acquisition and transformation processes, it is neither appropriate for nor engendered by all classroom tasks. Instead, students are hypothesized to alternate among different forms of cognitive engagement or variations on self-regulated learning (higher or lower levels of the acquisition and transformation processes), both between and within different task situations. A student who exhibits high transformation and low acquisition skills is said to be *task focused*. They activate more transformation than acquisition processes, thereby focusing almost exclusively on the specific task. Students who are low in transformation but high in acquisition skills are termed *resource managers*. These students organize information and engage acquisition processes but look to other sources for assistance with necessary information transformations. Students low in both acquisition and transformation skills are considered *recipient*. These students passively receive instruction, investing minimal cognitive effort in the learning task by permitting the instruction to accomplish much of the work for them.

The impetus of shifts among these variations may often be task demands and/or features of instruction. Some tasks may require self-regulation whereas others may demand other more efficient forms of cognitive engagement. Thus, the substudy sought to understand how the use of the systems thinking approach impacts on self-regulated learning skills and the variations among levels of cognitive engagement.

Students from traditional and systems chemistry and systems physics classes were selected for in-depth interviews that were intended to elicit information about how the systems approach influenced their acquisition of content knowledge, the use of self-regulated learning skills, and their ability to transfer those skills and knowledge across courses. In-depth, cognitive analyses of 53 students who had taken differing sequences of traditional and systems science courses over the 2 years of the project were conducted.

This substudy was designed as a follow-up to the research in the physics and chemistry classes. Thirty-one chemistry and 22 physics students participated in the Self-Regulated Learning Substudy, designed to examine how exposure to the systems approach in one course subsequently affects acquisition of content knowledge and self-regulation in other courses. Data for the substudy were collected in two formats. First, a specially designed instrument, the Self-Regulated Learning Instrument (SRLI), was used to assess the forms of cognitive engagement exhibited by students in the science courses. Second, in a clinical interview format, the students were asked to solve problems analogous to those encountered in their classes. Think-aloud protocols were collected and analyzed.

An existing instrument was modified for the purposes of this substudy to measure the component processes of cognitive engagement (Howard, 1987). The SRLI contained 16 dichotomous items, representing five subscales: selecting, connecting, planning, alertness, and monitoring. One response alternative indicated the student's preference for a particular process; the other response indicated the student's aversion to that process. Students' responses then were classified as self-regulated, task focused, resource management, or recipient, based on the pattern of scores on the subscales.

Differences in response patterns on the SRLI emerged between the physics and chemistry classes. The most common form of cognitive engagement among the physics students was self-regulation, whereas the most common in chemistry was recipience. Tracing the pattern back to the students' first year course, students who took both traditional biology and chemistry were at a distinct disadvantage with respect to the effective use of the cognitive engagement variations. It appears that not having a systems course was detrimental in that students were less likely to exhibit appropriately adaptive forms of cognitive engagement; having some systems thinking was advantageous with respect to these cognitive processes.

Many of the patterns have implications for instructional remediation. For example, students who were found to be deficient in a particular component could be provided instruction directly targeted to that deficiency rather than remediation across processes. In this way, instruction could build on cognitive strengths while remediating specific weaknesses.

The substudy also examined differences in problem solving exhibited on the assigned tasks such as the acceleration problem presented earlier. The patterns of solution observed in the substudy are similar to those that Larkin and Chabay (1989) noted with respect to learning in science. These authors differentiated between how novices and experts approach scientific problems. Experts do not rely on equations, but rather engage in scientific reasoning and problem solving. Novices, in contrast, rely on trying to generate equations that can be used to solve a problem. The position taken by Larkin and Chabay is that there is a dire need to improve learning in the sciences by increasing the use of reasoning and decreasing the reliance on equations.

The majority of the high-ability physics students chose to solve the assigned acceleration problem using STELLA and systems thinking. For example, the student who constructed Solution 1 depicted in Fig. 1.1 distinguished between the two main components of the problem, train distance and passenger distance and chose not to connect them in the model. Thus, the graphical output produced two separate function lines. The x-axis is time; the y-axis is distance, beginning with a zero point and increasing. The function lines intersect at two points, thereby yielding two solutions. These points of intersection indicate when the train and passenger are at the same place at the same time, allowing the passenger the chance to board the train.

Solution 2 (Fig. 1.2) is similar, but the student connected the two main components of the model. Train distance and passenger distance are linked defining a new variable, separation distance. According to the equations, separation distance is defined as the difference between train distance and passenger distance. Thus, when separation distance equals zero, the train and the passenger are in the same place, allowing the passenger the opportunity to board the train. Here, the graphical output produces one function line, separation distance. Again the x-axis is time. Although the y-axis is distance, there is a subtle difference. Here the zero point becomes critical. Prior to the first instance when the function line crosses the zero point, the distance between the passenger and train is decreasing. They then are at the same place at the same time until a few seconds later, after which the separation distance begins to increase. Note that the only difference in the equations produced between Solutions 1 and 2 is the inclusion of separation distance.

In-depth analyses of exercises like the acceleration problem were conducted in physics and yielded interesting information about the ways students approached physics using systems thinking. Many students reported that the mathematical solutions failed to provide concrete representations of the problems and physics concepts. Instead, the numbers had only abstract meaning that they could not link to real-world phenomena. Students who used STELLA to model the problems were unable to alter parameters and demonstrate both theoretical and practical understanding of the problem and solution. In contrast, several students expressed a preference for the mathematical solutions. Some of these students were confounded by the structure of STELLA. What they perceived as simple problems were made overly complicated by modeling. The traditional solutions were more straightforward for some of the mathematically sophisticated students. Two students used only equations to solve the problem. One of these students reported that the problem was concrete enough for her using only the quadratic equations. She felt that unless the problem was especially complex, STELLA was unnecessary. In her opinion the assigned problem was not sufficiently complex to warrant such analysis with modeling. Another student used systems principles (i.e., causal loop diagrams) but did not implement them with STELLA. She reported that although the mathematics was logical, the systems approach enabled her to organize and check her work mentally and focus on the important concepts.

On the whole, most of the students agreed that they achieved a better and deeper conceptual understanding of the physical phenomena and the processes by which they obtained their solutions through the use of systems analysis. Those students who chose to use STELLA said that the problem was made easier and visually more concrete with the use of systems principles. The multiple visual representations in the STELLA diagrams, graphs, and tables, allow the students to see relationships among variables. Such representations are important aids to help students link the real-world phenomenon to the physics and mathematics.

Several students cautioned that although the systems approach is a helpful perspective for some physics problems, it is not appropriate for all. They also cautioned that there is a need to have sufficient knowledge of the content area. Without the domain-specific knowledge, students would not have been able to apply STELLA as a problem-solving tool. Several of the lower achieving students had trouble solving the problem with or without STELLA. However, those who had been exposed to systems thinking in their chemistry course were much more at ease in attempting to apply STELLA to solve the problem.

Students' perceptions of the approach's impact on their learning were quite varied and differed in the chemistry and physics courses. Applicability depended, in part, on the complexity of the assigned problems. Traditional methods were seen as more useful and efficient for simpler problems, but the students reported that the systems approach was more effective for those that were complex and dynamic. Some, but not all chemistry students agreed that systems thinking was a useful problem-solving tool that helped them better to understand the content of their course. They were much less specific and articulate than the physics group in describing the approach's possible applications. This finding is quite possibly due to the fact that most chemistry students are in the 11th grade and most physics students are in the 12th grade. It also is possible that the implementation was different in the two courses. However, both chemistry and physics students saw the approach's applicability to other academic disciplines, particularly history and social studies.

The War and Revolution Substudy

The second ancillary study was a case study of the War and Revolution seminar (Mandinach, 1988b). This study focused on the 18 students who enrolled in the experimental course during the 2 years of the project. The purpose of the substudy was to collect in-depth information about the thought processes, performance patterns, general problem-solving skills, and knowledge of students who were exposed to a seminar infused with systems thinking and the simulation-modeling software.

The seminar provided a unique approach and structure to modeling and the examination of historical events. It illustrated how modeling and inquiry skills can be applied to subject areas that are less readily defined in quantitative terms. The course was conceived as a means by which to use modeling to gain a more thorough understanding of sociopolitical events. The unique aspect of the course was the prominent role given to systems thinking in the study of history.

In a seminar format, the teacher used historical conflicts to introduce students to systems thinking as a strategy for analyzing the dynamics of past events. They studied conflicts, reviewed existing models, and experimented with constructing their own models. Each student selected a particular historical conflict, which became the basis of a year-long independent study project. Using a variety of reference and historical materials, they fully researched the topics, preparing many iterations of their models. At the end of the school year, they also were asked to develop a model of the Zimbardo Prison Experiment (Haney, Banks, & Zimbardo, 1973; Zimbardo, Haney, Banks, & Jaffe, 1973) to demonstrate their modeling capabilities on a topic containing analogous systems. The students were given background materials that described the Zimbardo Prison Project as a study in which college students were assigned randomly to portray either the role of a guard or a prisoner in an experiment simulating a correctional

FIG. 1.3. Structural model of the Zimbardo Prison Experiment.

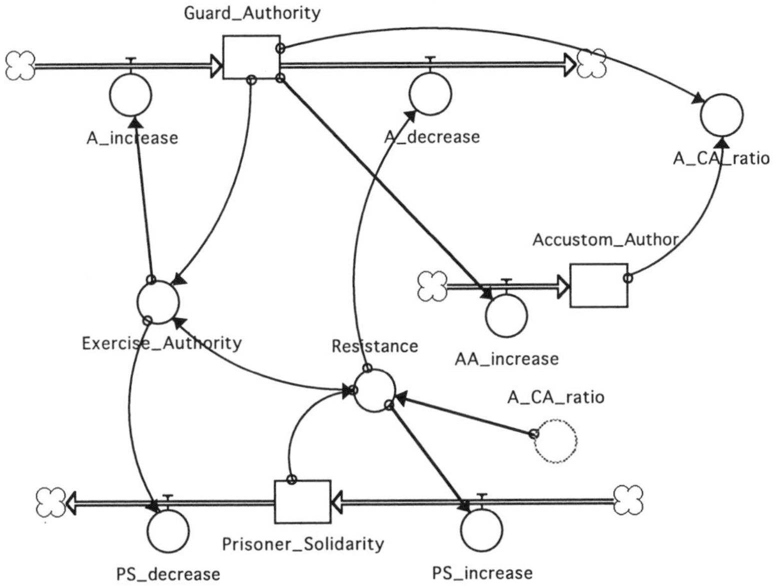

institution. The independent projects and the Zimbardo exercise are examples of epitome modeling (see Fig. 1.3). Although the topic of the Zimbardo exercise was somewhat removed from the course content, students were acutely aware of the similarities between the experiment and their projects. More importantly, they were able to apply the analytic and problem-solving techniques engendered in systems thinking as they modeled the Zimbardo exercise.

Student projects included such topics as the Iranian Revolution (see Figs. 1.4 and 1.5), the U. S. Civil War, the Falklands War, South African race riots, and the 1956 Hungarian Revolution. Students carried out their own primary research on the selected topics. The teacher and other students supplemented the basic research with articles or suggested readings as discovered. Students worked independently and in small groups. Frequently, the entire class was brought together to exchange ideas and discuss specific historical events. Several times during the year, students were required to present to the class the current versions of their models. They were expected to provide supportive evidence for their models. Thus, classroom sessions allowed the students to experience the sequence of activities commonly employed in scientific inquiry: hypothesize, tests, revise the hyphothesis, and retest. The sequence is particularly salient in model building. The classroom sessions also allowed the teacher to map the development of students' mastery of their topics.

FIG. 1.4. Model of the Iranian Revolution: First iteration.

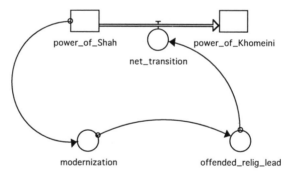

Students first prepared causal loop diagrams, off-line flow-chart-like visual representations, of their topics and provided written documentation about the history, theory, and logic on which the models were based. They then prepared structural models that were run dynamically with STELLA. Clear progressions in students' thinking about their projects could be discerned from the iterations of documentation and models. Students identified critical variables and hypothesized the relations among the variables. These hypotheses were modeled on-line iteratively. That is, students tested several versions of their models, revising sets of parameters and examining how those changes might affect outcomes.

FIG. 1.5. Model of the Iranian Revolution: Final iteration.

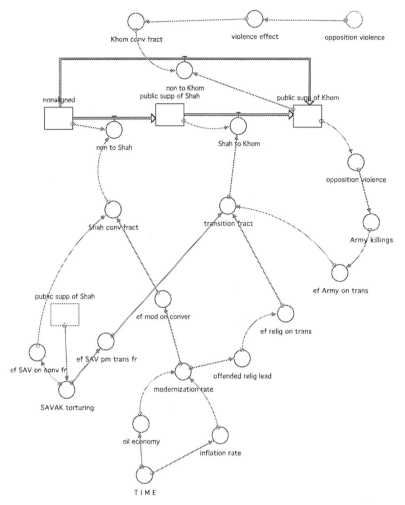

The iterative process helped students develop and refine their models. The process required them to focus on the systemic nature of the problems. To understand the historical phenomena, they could not look at only one isolated incident. Rather they had to examine the relationships among many variables. STELLA facilitated the iterations by allowing the student to focus on a subset of relations at one time and then subsequently observe the combined effects. Thus, students were forced to ask questions they might otherwise not have considered; they had to define and redefine questions and focus on the system as a whole. The students viewed the systems approach as a technique to help them analyze problems by requiring them to specify more clearly the structure of their historical event.

The systems thinking approach also was used as a tool for comparative analysis. Class presentations and discussions provided opportunities for students to identify similarities and differences among their projects. The generalizability of analytic skills was evident as students consulted with each other on their projects.

Students' critiques of the seminar provided insights into perceptions of how the systems approach affected their thinking. They saw that the approach was a technique that could be used to analyze problems, formulate research questions, examine and organize information, and focus on essential factors and relationships, especially in dynamic situations. It helped them structure their thinking and specify more clearly the historical phenomena. As one student said, "I found that using modeling not only widened the range of my exploration, but it redefined my original question. It didn't change the question, but caused better understanding."

Despite the many positive comments about the approach's impact on learning, students criticized the systems approach implementation, particularly in the second year. A discussion of this and related implementation issues are addressed in chapter 4. However, one problem specific to this social studies course was observed as students constructed their models. Students sometimes resorted to unsystematic testing when they assigned numerical values to qualitative variables in order to make the model run. Although the relations among the variables were specified logically in the causal diagrams and the students understood how to quantify numerical variables, they still had difficulty with the less quantifiable parameters. As one student noted, "People were too hung up on just trying to get a desired graph of their situation, and not trying to see what happened if they changed some things around." Another student stated, "Overall, I think that system dynamics is a very good learning tool. Still I have to question the validity of assigning values and equations to valueless concepts and unequationable events. But I think that if the conclusions reached from system dynamics are not taken too seriously, the process of creating a model can ultimately benefit the modeler immensely."

The Organizational Substudy

The third ancillary inquiry was an organizational case study of the impact of the computer-based curriculum innovation at BUHS (Cline, 1989). The primary methods of data collection for this substudy were in-depth, focused personal interviews conducted with teachers, students, administrators, district-level staff, school board members, parents, and several influential community members. The case study focused on changes in the structure and function of the organization that might be attributable to the introduction of the systems thinking approach. The interviews focused on such topics as changes in work assignments, patterns of authority and influence among faculty and administrators, changes in communication networks, and the impact of the computer-based innovation on satisfaction, productivity, and morale among members of the school community.

Organizational changes are usually difficult to discern as they rarely happen quickly or with dramatic impact. Consequently, interviews need to be repeated with many individuals over time to document small but continuing changes. During the first 2 years of the STACI Project at BUHS, the systems thinking approach was struggling to become established and, therefore, the consequences for organizational change were just beginning to take place. Nevertheless, several noticeable patterns were beginning to emerge. For example, the assignment of teachers to courses was influenced by the fact that three science teachers were using systems thinking and the other members of the department were not. In an attempt to maintain traditionally taught classrooms for the purpose of comparisons, several shifts were necessary in course assignments. Some of the science teachers who were not involved in the project were particularly unhappy with these rearrangements.

During the first year of the STACI Project at BUHS, a new wing for the Science Department was under construction. Although the computers arrived in school in late fall, they were placed in a temporary location in the main building until March when the new wing was ready for occupancy. In the earlier location, teachers outside the science department had access to the computers. By the time they were moved to the new wing, which is somewhat isolated from the rest of the school, this access was denied. Because easy access to the machines was no longer possible, some unhappiness was created among teachers who were not part of the project. The systems thinking project became viewed by the rest of the faculty as a small and exclusive activity that did not have much relevance for the rest of the school. The frequency and intensity of interaction and communication among the three science teachers in the project was increased substantially. Also, communication with other teachers in the science and other departments diminished somewhat. It is possible that patterns of interaction are finite for most individuals, and increases in one area must necessarily result in decreases in another.

Almost all teachers in the project at BUHS reported experiencing a decrease in their productivity and an attendant drop in job satisfaction and morale as a result of their initial participation. Working with systems thinking was demanding, and these teachers already had little or no spare time to devote to this new effort. Consequently, they each added new burdens to their already heavy schedules. One teacher in particular was terribly frustrated that students in his class did not show remarkable learning improvements by the end of the first academic year. In his opinion student achievement was lower than in previous years, and the teacher felt that the entire experience was very frustrating for him and the students. At the end of the second year, this teacher dropped out of the project. At the same time, the teacher who had been conducting the War and Revolution seminar decided to retire. It was clear that the initial efforts required to develop the expertise to use the systems thinking approach effectively were substantial and caused a clear and steep drop in perceived productivity, satisfaction, and morale.

Despite all the initial turnover in the BUHS project, systems thinking still established a strong foothold in the science department. A new superintendent, a new science department chair, and the continuing principal all provided moral and financial support for the project. As a result, the satisfaction, productivity, and morale began to rise as the project moved ahead. The organizational substudy had few general findings to report at the end of the first 2 years at BUHS due to the fact that organizational change tends to lag behind the changes in student learning and classroom activities. Nevertheless, the case study provides baseline data for future comparisons.

CONCLUDING COMMENTS

Substantial progress was noted at BUHS during the 2 years of the STACI Project. Although the systems thinking approach was implemented only to a limited extent during that time, the teachers, ETS staff, and other observers all agreed that the perspective showed a great deal of promise. It was originally anticipated that the quasi-experimental design would yield systematic and informative data that would be used both for course improvement and research purposes. Hindsight now indicates that even if there were more intensive and extensive implementation of the systems approach, a quasi-experiment is not the an appropriate research paradigm. The formative experiment (Newman, 1990) seems much more suitable for such implementation and research projects. Curriculum development and implementation needed to be nurtured. A learning outcome is not simply one isolated event and cannot be detected with one single measurement. Instead, implementation is a dynamic, evolving, and continuous sequence of events that must be studied longitudinally.

The work at BUHS highlighted the need for a new and flexible research methodology, one in which the researcher must function in several roles beyond that of the impartial observer. BUHS also served as a signal for the potentials of the systems thinking approach. Both teachers and researchers gained a better understanding of the implementation process and the attributes that either facilitate or impede that process. The work at BUHS laid an essential foundation for the ensuing extension of the STACI Project to other schools.

2
The Systems Thinking Network Project: STACI[N]

GENESIS OF THE NETWORK

Rationale

In February, 1987, 6 months after the inception of the STACI Project, ETS staff met with the manager of External Research at Apple Computer, Inc., who had made possible the donation of the classroom set of computers for BUHS. She was briefed on the project and informed as to how the systems approach was being implemented. It was pointed out that although the curriculum innovation was evolving slowly, a number of interesting and promising developments had already been observed. Despite the initially slow progress, she was nevertheless impressed with the potential that the systems thinking approach provided for effective computer uses in schools. What ensued was an intriguing suggestion. She asked if it would be possible to transport the systems thinking approach to a school in the San Francisco Bay Area to determine if it might succeed when teachers did not have such ready access to the developers of STELLA at HPS and the experts in the Systems Dynamics Group at MIT.

The frustrations and delays in curriculum development that the four BUHS teachers experienced while working in isolation indicated that it would take an exorbitantly long period of time to develop a critical mass of materials that would elicit significant changes in teaching and learning outcomes. The teachers at BUHS needed not only expert consultation but, more importantly, colleagues with whom they could collaborate on the development and implementation of curriculum materials within their specific subject areas. One isolated teacher in a given subject area simply does not have sufficient resources to call upon in a labor-intensive endeavor such as curriculum development, regardless of the amount of energy, enthusiasm, and motivation he or she might have. Two teachers in the same discipline, but separated by 3,000, miles also might not make a difference. However, several teachers working together within a discipline to implement systems thinking in their classes might make a critical mass. Thus was born the concept of a network of teachers devoted to using the systems thinking approach in several content areas. The superscript N was added to convey that the project now included a network of schools, and STACI[N] came into existence.

It was suggested to Apple that perhaps a consortium of schools that varied with respect to socioeconomic characteristics (e.g., size, student population, administrative support) might be the most informative organizational scheme for the newly conceptualized project. Thus began the exploration of the possibility of establishing a network of schools in California and Vermont to work collaboratively on the implementation of systems thinking. At Brattleboro there were a number of fortuitous events that made the implementation of the systems thinking approach possible and ultimately resulted in the STACI Project. The foremost of these was the sequence in which one parent and one high school teacher initially promoted the use of systems thinking. Four teachers then started the project, and ETS came in to observe the process and facilitate its development. A different strategy for launching a systems thinking approach in the California schools was needed.

ETS staff were faced with decisions concerning school selection. A first issue was to consider what characteristics might contribute to the success or failure of the curriculum innovation. These characteristics included district, school, and teacher factors. For example, how many computers per school were needed? Would the provision of dedicated computers for each teacher participating in the project make a difference? For what types of schools, teachers, courses, and students might the approach be most effective and provide an informative experience? At what grade levels should the expanded project be targeted? How much and what kinds of support would be needed for the new teachers and schools? An additional set of issues involved appropriate selection criteria for districts, schools, and teachers. Perhaps the most important issue was how to obtain the financial support necessary to make the network a reality.

Launching the Project

Initial contacts were made with school systems and teachers that had histories of effectively using technology in their curricula. First contacts were made at a variety of organizational levels. Sometimes the entry occurred with the superintendent, building principal, computer or curriculum coordinator, and frequently with a well-respected teacher. These initial discussions led to the identification of several potential sites.

Ultimately, four high schools and two middle schools on the San Francisco Peninsula were identified. The Director of Apple External Research agreed to donate for each of the six new schools a set of 20 Macintoshes, three printers, a modem, and an AppleLink account to support an electronic mail network. Because it was anticipated that collaboration and communication among participating teachers would be vital aspects of the project, proximity was a critical characteristic. All six schools in California were within a 1 hour driving distance of each other. Consequently, the burden of traveling to any other school for a meeting, conference, consultation, or classroom visit was minimized. Furthermore, the geographical propinquity reduced the costs of using commercial telephone lines for the electronic mail network.

In March, 1988, each school was visited to introduce the proposed project. Many teachers attended the introductory meetings. Some expressed interest and volunteered, and others were nominated for participation in the project. Usually the building principals and other administrators also attended. During the visits the proposed project, its structure, and objectives were described. Issues of management, possible risks and benefits, potential sources of support, and research plans also were discussed. The teachers were introduced to STELLA at these meetings. They were shown a simple model building exercise in population dynamics, and given the opportunity to examine some previously constructed simulations. Many teachers became excited about the potentials for their specific curricular needs. Tentative dates for the first training session in the summer of 1988 were discussed. During these visits separate meetings were held with each superintendent to discuss the formal arrangements for the implementation and management of the project.

The configuration of schools for the newly established Systems Thinking and Curriculum Innovation Network (STACI^N) Project included: (a) the original group of four teachers from BUHS; (b) Mountain View High School, serving an ethnically diverse community in the Silicon Valley; (c) Menlo-Atherton High School in Atherton, a school with a striking bimodal population (students from the affluent communities of Atherton and Menlo Park and those from the poor, at-risk, primarily minority city of East Palo Alto); (c) Hillview Middle School located in Menlo Park, which feeds into Menlo-Atherton High School that serves the affluent communities; (d) South San Francisco High School, South San Francisco, and (e) El Camino High School, South San Francisco, institutions with high proportions of Asian and minority students (some 26 languages and dialects are spoken in the district) from a primarily industrial, lower-middle-class city; and (f) Westborough Middle School, a feeder to the two aforementioned high schools. These schools are described in more detail as evolving case studies in Appendix A.

It was suggested that each school appoint 5 teachers to the project. Although Menlo-Atherton High School did not ask for additional support and resources, the administration requested that 7 teachers participate. Thus, at its inception, the STACI^N Project consisted of 32 teachers in California and 4 in Vermont. In the two middle schools there were 4 mathematics, 3 science, and 3 social studies teachers. In the high schools, including BUHS, there were 16 science (5 general science, 4 biology, 4 chemistry, 3 physics), 3 mathematics, 3 economics, and 4 social studies teachers.

The first official meeting of all project participants occurred in July, 1988, during which time HPS conducted a 2-week summer training program. Apple External Research arranged for the delivery of 30 Macintosh microcomputers for use by the teachers. The training was held at the

Stanford University School of Education, where teachers from the Bay Area schools received intensive instruction on systems theory, principles, and STELLA modeling. Due to the unfortunate lack of resources, the Vermont teachers could not attend this first STACI[N] training session.

The training contained three major components. First, background and theory sufficient for understanding systems thinking were provided. The second focus was hands-on instruction in how to use the Macintosh computer and STELLA, targeting relevant pedagogical applications. Third, teachers collaboratively began to develop introductory instructional modules that could be integrated into their classes.

The training assumed two forms. For a brief period each morning, HPS provided information about systems concepts and modeling. The remainder of the sessions were devoted to on-line, hands-on interactions with the computers. Teachers spontaneously formed into content-specific working groups called task forces. Consequently, most of the subsequent interactions were conducted in small group format, corresponding roughly to discipline.

By the end of the 2 weeks, most teachers had acquired a basic working knowledge of systems thinking, the Macintosh, and STELLA. Each of the content-specific task forces had developed curriculum materials that could be integrated into their classes upon returning to school. Other potential topics for systems modules were identified, with plans for lesson development during the academic year. Several of the groups scheduled meetings for continued collaboration after the workshop concluded.

A retrospective analysis of the summer training and ensuing few months yielded several observations. The first was the striking pedagogical and philosophical differences between the California and Vermont teachers. Although the teachers from Vermont were not observed as they were introduced to systems thinking, there were opportunities to witness curriculum development and subsequent training activities. Perhaps due to the fact that the California group was eight times as large, the four Vermont teachers did little in the way of collaborative curriculum development. The California teachers, in contrast, were more receptive to small-group, collaborative efforts. They readily shared materials and ideas and were in no way hesitant about presenting those ideas to the entire group, even at the risk of receiving preliminary but explicit criticism. This may be due, in part, to the structure of the workshop. It is unclear the extent to which HPS fostered a similar perspective when conducting the Vermont training. The purposes were quite different and for different audiences. HPS created a learning environment in California in which the teachers understood that insights and progress occurred though collaboration, including joint, critical examination of ideas and constructive feedback. In contrast, the Vermont group at that time felt the need to anticipate all possible questions and answers before they risked presenting materials to either students or colleagues. It was not until the composition of the group from BUHS changed and the new teachers were introduced into the STACI[N] culture that collaboration began among all the sites.

At the time of the initial training, this dichotomy was merely an interesting observation. However, it now appears that the combination of collaborative and risk-taking behaviors are important distinguishing characteristics among the more and less effective users of the systems thinking approach. Related characteristics include willingness to take risks, relinquishing classroom control, supporting the interactive exchange of information between student and teacher, sharing responsibility for learning, becoming a facilitator of learning rather than a transmitter of knowledge, and an increasing inclination toward a constructivist philosophy.

A second observation was that in many respects the summer training was analogous to the activities that would occur in the classroom when the teachers began to integrate the systems thinking approach into their curricula. As students in the summer training, the project teachers had a general idea about the utility of the approach as an instructional tool. They also had strong incentives for learning the approach. However, much of the initial training material that HPS presented in the first week was highly theoretical and based on examples previously used at the postsecondary level. There were few topics immediately relevant for precollege instruction. The teachers tried to understand and adapt the materials, but they grew increasingly frustrated during the first week. HPS staff subsequently changed the second week's materials in an attempt to make them more salient. During the second week, the teachers' enthusiasm returned as they saw the increasing relevance and applicability to their courses. HPS, too, was learning, as they had limited prior experience instructing middle and secondary school teachers.

This cycle of striving for relevance, feedback, and subsequent revision of materials is much the same pattern the teachers encounter in their own classrooms. The cycle of frustration and enthusiasm also is mirrored by students as they seek to understand information whose relevance to the curriculum is not immediately obvious. The interactive perspective and the shared responsibility for learning are often observed in project classes. Thus, the teachers' behavior as students during the training serves as predictors of activities in their own classrooms. Correspondingly, the pedagogical style of HPS is one that could successfully be emulated by project teachers.

Project Resources

Apple intended to deliver the donated hardware in time to launch the project in the beginning of the 1988/1989 school year. As indicated earlier, the hardware configuration for each school included a laboratory set of 15 Macintoshes, three ImageWriter printers, and a modem. Project teachers received a Macintosh for individual use at the summer training. Apple also established accounts for the schools and ETS on AppleLink, the company's electronic mail network.

Unfortunately, Apple had difficulties delivering the hardware as intended. The first pieces of the laboratory configurations arrived at the schools in November. Because of hardware shortages, delivery was not completed until January. The original plan was to donate Macintosh Plus computers, but these machines were in short supply at the time. To eliminate further delays, Apple sent Macintosh Plus computers to three schools, and the remaining three schools received Macintosh SEs. Apple also provided external hard drives for each project teacher.

The difference in type of Macintosh computers shipped prompted some logistical and parity problems. Teachers from the schools that received the Pluses quickly became disappointed with what they perceived as less desirable hardware. To allay these problems, equipment transfers were arranged to insure that all project teachers had a Macintosh SE for their individual use. This mixed hardware configuration did cause some incompatibility and networking problems. By the summer of 1989, hardware bugs, repair problems, and incompatibilities still were being resolved.

The project participants met for a second intensive weekend workshop in February, 1989. All California teachers attended this workshop, but only the physics teacher from BUHS traveled to Stanford. The trip proved to be a valuable interaction for him as well as for the California teachers. The workshop was an important refresher both intellectually and emotionally. The teachers gained additional training in systems thinking and STELLA. They also were introduced to STELLAStack (Richmond & Peterson, 1988), the HyperCard interface to STELLA. Some of the teachers began to make extensive use of STELLAStack, which enables the creation of comprehensive learning environments, using more graphics and limited animation. The winter workshop clearly reignited the teachers' enthusiasm for the project. However, it was clear that they were frustrated by the delays in launching the project. Several schools and districts also sought local funding from individuals, corporations, and foundations. A grant from a local source was secured by one district, contingent on raising matching funding. This district provided professional development funding to participating teachers to support their work with systems thinking. The district also provided stipends for the teachers to attend the weekend workshop.

For the first year, much of the financial responsibility for the project fell on the schools and ETS. Although proposals for funding the project were enthusiastically encouraged by several private and public funding sources, the initial search for funding proved to be fruitless. ETS insured the project's survival, supplying funds to support 1989 winter and summer workshops.

With ETS support, a 6-day summer training session was conducted by HPS in June, 1989. Convened immediately after the school year concluded, the training was again held at the Stanford University School of Education. The chemistry teacher from BUHS was able to attend this workshop, and the experience broadened his perspective on how systems could be used. It also strengthened his enthusiasm for the project. A few teachers withdrew from the project, whereas several new teachers were added, particularly in high-school mathematics. The configuration of teachers resulting from these changes included 5 mathematics, 4 social studies, and 1 science teacher at the middle-school level. At the high-school level there now were 6 mathematics, 5 physics, 4 social studies, 3 biology, 3 chemistry, 3 general science, and 3 economics teachers. There were now a total of 37 project participants.

The second summer training was structured much more to meet the specific needs of individual teachers. New participants were provided an introduction to the systems thinking approach, and some of the original teachers requested reviews of these materials. Others were able to move right into curriculum development activities. The primary focus of this training was to provide the support necessary for each teacher to develop readily usable curriculum materials for their courses the following year.

Lectures and didactic instruction were minimized; hands-on small group collaborations and guided modeling by HPS were emphasized. Some teachers created animated learning environments using STELLAStack; others prepared STELLA models and accompanying curriculum materials. Thus, a diversity of activities were ongoing, based on the individual needs of the project teachers. HPS staff were most effective in responding to the diverse needs. Teachers and trainers together struggled with many difficult pedagogical issues concerning the use of the systems thinking approach in precollege instruction, a topic with which no one had a great deal of experience. By this time the workshops had evolved into interactive learning experiences for all participants.

In August, 1989, ETS was notified that the U.S. Department of Education Secretary's Discretionary Grants Program had awarded a 2-year grant to the STACI^N Project. The award enabled the project to conduct the first component of a planned two-phase implementation and research agenda.

Part way through the first year of this award, Apple asked the ETS staff to identify possible project teachers who might participate in a large conference of educational administrators. Apple wanted to identify teachers who were experienced with technology-based curriculum innovations involving special populations. The ETS staff recommended a mathematics teacher from Sunnyside High School, a barrio school in Tucson, Arizona, who had attended several STACI^N workshops as an informal member of the project. With only his personal Macintosh, he was implementing with phenomenal success the systems thinking approach with his students.

Apple invited this Tucson mathematics teacher to make a presentation at a major computing conference for educational administrators from large urban districts. The teacher insisted that several students accompany him to enhance the presentation. Apple agreed and funded a cadre of enthusiastic students to come to the conference in San Francisco. The students and the teacher were so effective and articulate that the national press reported on their presentation. Apple subsequently agreed to donate a laboratory of Macintoshes to Sunnyside to enable them to implement systems thinking on a broader scale. Sunnyside thus became the eighth school in the STACI^N Project during the spring of 1990.

ETS was able to secure additional funds from the U.S. Department of Education Innovation in Education Program to support the project's expansion in Tucson. In the summer of 1991, STACI^N was awarded a second-year extension of the Innovation in Education grant. The extension award enabled the project to continue in all eight schools for another year. At the same time, ETS was notified that a 3-year proposal to the Eisenhower Program for Mathematics and Science also had been approved. By the time the Eisenhower award is completed, the project will have received 8 years of funding from the U.S. Department of Education. These monies allow the project to continue to sustain teacher support activities for further curriculum development and implementation efforts. The resources also provide for a substantial expansion of research activities. Teacher support and research are the two major phases of the STACI^N Project.

TEACHER SUPPORT ACTIVITIES

The STACI^N Project consists of two overlapping phases to facilitate the implementation of teaching and learning activities using the systems thinking approach. The first phase is devoted to providing the support necessary to enable teachers to develop curriculum materials and instructional strategies with systems thinking. This phase focuses on training that assists teachers in developing and infusing the technology-based curriculum innovation into their courses. The inservice programs provide teachers with a new method by which to use technology effectively to improve instruction and learning. The second phase is discussed in the next section. It is devoted to research on the cognitive, instructional, and organizational impact of the curriculum innovation.

Provision for Expertise

In the teacher support phase, the first activity is extensive inservice training. Because systems thinking and the STELLA software require an understanding of the theory and concepts that underlie the approach, it has been necessary to provide ongoing training in general systems principles. Thus, the workshops have enabled project teachers to acquire sufficient knowledge to explore the potentials of the approach, develop curriculum modules, and begin to implement them in their classes. The emphasis in the workshops has been on providing competent, practicing professionals with a new, interactive instructional tool to be used to facilitate learning. This learning focuses on dynamic problem-solving techniques, rather than on simply transmitting information.

As already mentioned, project teachers are exposed to the instructional approach in workshops twice each year. Additional training sessions have been distributed throughout the duration of this multiyear project. The importance of bringing the teachers together for periodic training and collaborative working sessions cannot be overstated. Because of the intellectually demanding and labor-intensive nature of curriculum development, teachers need blocks of uninterrupted time in which to work. Consequently, these workshops are scheduled when they are likely to be maximally productive with a minimum of interruptions. The training sessions emphasize hands-on participation by the teachers. The model of instruction espoused is to simulate an interactive and constructivist perspective that they can apply in their own classrooms. The guiding principle is to allow teachers to learn how to use the systems thinking approach so that they can readily infuse it into their curricula.

Task Forces, Networking, and Collaboration

Another important source of support for teachers is sharing knowledge, experiences, and perspectives with others who have similar interests or instructional problems. For this reason, teachers and schools in the project have been organized into a network. The promotion of effective uses of computer-based teaching innovations in the schools can be enhanced greatly by providing access to that network. Using a variety of modes of operation, including electronic mail, regular meetings, frequent conferences, reports, and a quarterly newsletter, the network provides many opportunities for the teachers to interact and share experiences concerning effective practices for computer-aided teaching with systems thinking.

Because it is critical for teachers to be able to seek assistance easily from experts and other teachers, an electronic mail network on AppleLink was established among the eight schools, HPS, and ETS. Thus, when teachers experience successes or difficulties with any phase of curriculum development or implementation, they can use AppleLink to seek feedback from colleagues, HPS, and the ETS project managers.

More importantly, the electronic mail network also enables teachers to transmit and share curriculum materials. Unlike many traditional curriculum materials that can be prepared as final products, systems models are never absolutely complete or definitive. Each teacher imposes his or her own theoretical and instructional perspective on the model. Consequently, continuous revisions of the materials are necessary and can be made by simply accessing the network, which facilitates wide dissemination and sharing of the systems modules. Each school maintains a log recording use of the electronic mail network. Examination of the logs monitors the patterns and uses for both consultations and materials dissemination.

Another support activity in the first phase of the project is the provision for collaboration and expertise through disciplinary task forces. Teachers within a content area are able to garner only so much substantive assistance for curriculum development from the training sessions, HPS, and network activities. Face-to-face interactions and specific support for curriculum development within the disciplines also are needed. Dissemination of teaching strategies and curriculum development has been aided by the creation and implementation of disciplinary task forces.

Each teacher initially was assigned to one of the following task forces: general science, biology, chemistry, physics, economics, social studies and humanities, high school mathematics, middle-school mathematics, middle-school social studies, or middle-school science. It was anticipated that greater productivity would result when teachers in the same discipline work collaboratively with input from substantive experts on the production of curriculum innovations. Thus, the project was originally organized to create and capitalize on a disciplinary division of labor.

The task forces were scheduled to meet three times during the school year to share information about the use of systems thinking in their courses. Each teacher was provided three release days for these task force meetings. The meetings were to focus on discipline-specific curriculum issues, with a goal toward the development of new materials. The task forces also were to meet during the summer and winter workshops to share further experiences and strategies for curriculum development and implementation of the systems thinking approach.

However, as the project has evolved, several of the task forces have addressed their objectives, whereas others have not functioned as effectively. Consequently, the teachers requested in the February, 1990, training that a slightly different organizational scheme be put into place, focusing on maximization of the productivity of collaborations and release time. The teachers pointed out that the concept of a content-specific task force was not appropriate for all disciplines or all grade levels. For example, the chemistry teachers noted that they each had different pedagogical styles and instructional objectives, with slightly different course content. Consequently, a task force devoted specifically to chemistry did not necessarily make sense. Instead, several of the chemistry teachers are collaborating with project biology teachers and attempting to bridge the conceptual gap between the disciplines by creating cross-course applications. Their goal is to introduce more biology into chemistry and more chemistry into biology.

Interdisciplinary working groups have been particularly effective at the middle-school level, in part because there are less rigid disciplinary boundaries.

Time and Money

Some teachers also suggested that release time could be used more effectively by meeting as a school group, rather than as a disciplinary task force. Particularly at the middle-school level, teachers wanted to work with colleagues from their own schools, focusing on core curriculum issues. An alternate suggestion proposed that each teacher use the three allotted release days in any way that effectively would facilitate their work on systems thinking. Many teachers simply wanted uninterrupted work time. The project has incorporated these suggestions. Several task forces do remain. However, the teachers determine how they use their release time, working in disciplinary or school-based task forces or perhaps in isolation.

Changes in the use of release days reflect the collaborative nature of the STACI^N Project. The project is a product of all the participants, including the teachers and ETS. The structure of the project will continue to evolve as teachers and researchers recognize the activities and configurations that are more effective for particular purposes.

Another extremely important type of support provided to the teachers are the $3,000 stipends to reimburse them partially for their work on the project. Although the stipends do not adequately compensate the teachers for all their hours of work on STACI^N, the money does serve very important functions. First, a stipend communicates to the teachers that their expertise and services are critical to the accomplishment of the objectives of the project. Second, stipends recognize that they are professionals and should be compensated as such. Third, stipends also provide a small source of support for individuals in an underpaid profession.

ETS staff interviewed project teachers and asked what role stipends play in their participation and what would happen if there were no stipends. In every instance, the teachers stated they that were not involved in STACI^N because of the money. However, the stipends were appreciated for several reasons, foremost of which was that the compensation conveyed a sense of professionalism. In some cases, the stipends help to justify to spouses and families all the additional time spent on the project, particularly during the winter and summer vacations.

Prior to receiving government funding, it was the project's intention to provide stipends for all participating teachers. However, the Department of Education awards restricted the use of funds to mathematics and science teachers. There were originally 11 social studies and humanities teachers participating in the project. The ETS staff did not want to abandon these teachers for two primary reasons. First, ETS felt obligated to find a way to fund all participants. People should not be eliminated from a project simply because the funding agency was emphasizing science and mathematics. Second, one of the reasons the systems thinking approach was so intriguing was its potential to stimulate cross-disciplinary collaboration. It was important not to sacrifice that opportunity.

The approach to this problem was to seek assistance from each superintendent. With the exception of BUHS, each district had at least one social studies teacher who was affected by the funding restriction. It was quite reasonable to anticipate that in a project involving several districts that differ in available resources, the resolutions of this dilemma would vary. At one school, the social studies teacher retired before assistance was requested from the superintendent. At a second site where there were two teachers, the superintendent immediately agreed to pay for their participation. The largest district was able to secure funding from a local foundation that paid for their six social studies teachers. At the smallest district, the new superintendent was unable to find the funds to support their only social studies teacher. Because the teacher resigned from the project early in the academic year due to other pressing demands, this funding problem disappeared. At one site the superintendent felt that without more advance notice he could not cover the cost of a single teacher. A cost-sharing agreement was negotiated in which ETS paid for the teacher in the first year of the project, and the district assumed the costs in subsequent years.

As the project has evolved over time, so too have the requisite support activities and resources. Training continues to be an important project activity, but it now fulfills different functions. Workshops are used less for information transmittal from HPS to the teachers. This form of communication is now needed only when a software enhancement is introduced. Instead, HPS now plays the role of coach and consultant, providing expertise to teachers as they experience difficulties with some phase of model and curriculum development. Most recently, the demand for such consulting has diminished substantially. As the HPS staff noted following the 1991 summer training, the queue of teachers waiting for assistance no longer exists. Similarly, the type of consultation now requested is much more sophisticated, showing evidence of the teachers' increasing expertise.

Issues raised at the most recent workshops also indicate the evolving nature of the project. Teachers are becoming increasingly concerned with the issues of dissemination of curriculum materials, sustained district-level support for their work, needed hardware and software upgrades, and the spread of the approach within their schools and districts. The concern is future oriented for sustaining the project and insuring that it will become deeply entrenched in the school and district culture. Steps are being taken to ensure this entrenchment. Currently, every superintendent has committed a line item in the budget to STACI[N] to cover various project-related costs.

Activities also are being undertaken to obtain funds to pay for upgrading of hardware to ensure that obsolescence does not overtake the project. Perhaps this is the most difficult and pressing concern the project must face in the coming years.

RESEARCH ACTIVITIES

The second component of the STACI^N Project consists of research on the impact of the computer-based curriculum innovation. As previously mentioned, the project contains three research foci: (a) the effects on student learning processes, outcomes, and transfer that result from introducing the systems thinking approach; (b) the effects of the approach on teacher behavior, classroom processes, and curricula; and (c) the impact of introducing such a curriculum innovation on the school as an organization.

Research Designs

For each of the three foci in this project, multiple research designs are employed. Student learning outcomes are analyzed using longitudinal data measuring increments in subject knowledge and problem-solving skills. These measurements, including process analyses, are recorded continuously for both content and procedural knowledge. The longitudinal design provides for continuous collection of these data. Hence, comparisons can be continuous and cumulative. It is expected that the most interesting and provocative results concerning learning will come from intensive, focused interviews conducted with students concerning their experiences in using systems thinking in several different courses. The interviews with the chemistry and physics students at BUHS are examples of this kind of in-depth cognitive analysis.

The design with respect to teacher behavior also will use longitudinal data. These data will document course organization and classroom activities in systems thinking classes. The data, collected in classroom observations and interviews, describe how teachers carry out their professional activities. The analyses will consist of comparative descriptions and the impact of systems thinking on teaching and learning activities. In many respects the methodologies used at this level are those typically employed in anthropological field research.

The third focus on organizational change explores the extent to which the technology-based innovation has an impact on the structure and functioning of the schools. The primary data for these analyses are being gathered in repeated interviews with students, teachers, administrators, parents, and school board members. A longitudinal design also is used at the organization change level, for it is planned that the interviews will be repeated many times with the same individuals. In this fashion it is possible to trace the changing perceptions of persons over time. Furthermore, the same topic will be explored with many individuals, providing different perspectives on the same phenomenon. The intent here is to produce what anthropologists refer to as the *emic* or insider's perspective (Fetterman, 1989).

This technique of asking the same question of many different respondents is referred to as triangulation. It is well known in the literature and practice of field studies. The same questions are repeated, not because the interviewer doubts what a respondent has to say, but simply to gather many perspectives from individuals who play different roles in the organization. *Triangulation* is being employed extensively in this project. The focus of the organizational case studies is on changes that may occur in the structural and functional features of the schools. Objects of inquiry include goal definition and attainment, division of labor, patterns of communication and interaction, distribution of authority, and levels of motivation, satisfaction, and productivity.

The multiple research designs and methodologies employed in this project are quite different from those typically used in a social or behavioral science evaluation. The well-known evaluations of large-scale action programs such as Headstart (Campbell, 1969), Sesame Street (Ball & Bogatz, 1970, 1971), and Negative Income Tax (Kershaw, 1976) all used some form of quasi-experimental designs with random assignments of participants to experimental and control groups. These are the methods specified in the standard references and texts on evaluation research (Campbell & Stanley, 1963; Freeman & Rossi, 1980; Rieken & Boruch, 1974; Suchman, 1967). However, these methods were found to be inappropriate for this curriculum innovation project.

In an early work, Cronbach (1963) pointed out that most evaluation designs were not appropriate devices for studying curriculum innovations. He argued persuasively that such research designs would not be sensitive enough to detect the important consequences of the innovation. He made an early and eloquent plea for the use of interview and observation methods in such evaluations. After Cronbach published this now classic paper, Scriven (1977) made the important distinction between formative and summative evaluation. The intent of the former is to help design and refine a program or intervention, and the intent of the latter is to make a global assessment as to value or worth of a program. Summative evaluations typically employ a quasi-experimental design, and formative evaluations rely more heavily on interviews and observations than quantitative differences between experimental and control groups.

More recently Newman (1990) introduced the concept of the *formative experiment*. Newman and his colleagues established a middle school science project using computers and a nationwide electronic mail network. Newman claimed that their activities encompassed some aspects of an experiment (i.e., introducing the stimulus of the computer-based curriculum innovation), and some aspects of a formative evaluation (i.e., the use of interview and the use of interview and field observation techniques to provide feedback to project participants to advise and refine the implementation process). The project reported in this volume is indeed very close to Newman's concept of the formative experiment.

Other recent publications by Salomon (1990, 1991) stressed the systemic context of any educational innovation. He pointed out that a research framework that attempts to determine the most important causes of a desired experimental outcome is naive. In any school-based curriculum innovation project, there are many causes and many effects, and these variables interact with one another in a series of feedback relationships. He uses the metaphor of studying a flute performance within the context of the entire orchestra. A legitimate analysis is to study one instrument, and an equally legitimate and more complex analysis is to study the entire orchestra, including all instruments. The project reported in this book also shares the flute and orchestra perspective of Salomon, for it focuses on the innovation as well as the contexts in which is introduced.

Multiple Methods

In this section, the methodologies employed to illuminate issues of implementation and impact are reviewed. The discussion here is not intended to be a comprehensive review of all methodologies that might be employed. Rather it is an enumeration of the methodologies found most useful to date. Undoubtedly others will be added to the project, but on the basis of experience thus far, the list is sufficiently interesting to merit discussion at this point. The methods employed are neither stable nor mutually exclusive; conversely, they are complementary and constantly under revision to sharpen the inquiries.

Although the plans to approximate a quasi-experimental design were abandoned rather quickly, information is collected on two dimensions of student performance, course content and systems thinking knowledge. For the former, quizzes, tests, laboratory reports, and examinations are used; for the latter, an instrument especially created for systems thinking was developed. The results of previously administered standardized tests were used in the past as estimates of general abilities.

Two other methods account for most data collection activities in this project. These are in-depth interviews and classroom observations. Repeated interviews are being conducted with students, teachers, administrators, parents, and school board members. Students and teachers in both systems thinking and traditionally taught classes are being interviewed. Furthermore, interviews are being conducted with all relevant school and district administrators. In most instances, an outline of topics to be discussed is prepared and shared in advance with the person to be interviewed.

For many issues, it has proven useful to give individuals an opportunity to know in advance the content of an interview, affording them an opportunity to anticipate questions and contemplate responses. When a more considered response to an issue is preferred, this is a useful strategy. During the course of the interviews, written notes are taken, and a tape recording is frequently made. In the future, it is expected that more interviews will be recorded.

Procedures are being developed for transcribing the notes taken and the content of the recordings made during interviews into machine-readable form. These data will be stored using an appropriate system for filing and retrieval. This system will allow extensive cross-indexing and facilitate retrieval and grouping of data collected during interviews into an infinite set of cross-classifications. Developing the system for the storage, retrieval, and analysis of all the data, including the numerical test score data and the textual interview data, is a potentially important by-product of this project.

The second most commonly used data collection procedure in the project thus far is classroom observation. The project staff have spent many hours in classrooms. Observations are being made in systems thinking classes and in those traditionally taught. The emphasis here has been on comparing how teachers cover materials in their courses. Of course, because the use of systems thinking is still relatively new, not all topics in the courses are taught using this new perspective. Therefore, it is possible to observe and record how teachers are handling specific topics using both systems thinking and the traditional procedures.

The classroom observations and interviews are providing rich descriptive materials concerning the teaching of a wide variety of topics in science, mathematics, and social studies in both middle and high schools. These materials will be valuable for other teachers and researchers. Furthermore, they document how the use of systems thinking can change the ways in which teachers organize their courses and present the materials. Conclusions concerning changes in the dynamics and structure of classroom operation using systems thinking will be based mainly on the materials collected in classroom observations and teacher interviews.

The data collected in interviews and observations are being organized and filed in portfolios. Eventually, there will be electronic, on-line portfolios documenting the teachers' experiences using systems thinking. The portfolios will contain examples of systems models and curriculum modules that have been developed and implemented in classes. Also included will be teachers' logs of activities as they relate to the curriculum innovation. Entries of particular interest include notations about when and how systems modules are integrated into courses, teachers' reactions, perceptions, and comments, in-person or networked interactions and collaborations with colleagues, and consultations with the substantive experts.

Similar portfolios of student performance will be created. As this project is expected to continue for many years, it will be possible to document both student and teacher progress in mastering and using systems thinking. The application of systems thinking problem-solving techniques can be documented for students as they progress through different courses. It also will be documented for teachers as they increase their expertise in the various courses they teach. The spread of systems thinking from the those originally participating in the program to other teachers throughout the school will also be monitored. Records or portfolios of these accomplishments will be kept at student, teacher, and school levels. The concept of portfolios that contain a variety of data and information documenting educational activities and accomplishments is one that is gaining a great deal of interest throughout the educational research community (Duschel & Gitomer, 1991; Gitomer, Grosh, & Price, 1992). This concept will be applied to the data collection and analyses in this project.

A rich source of data are videotapes of the teacher training sessions and classrooms. Taping has two purposes. First, tapes are available to teachers for continuing review during the school year. The tapes also are used for in-service training for other interested teachers in the participating schools. Second, the tapes serve as critical data for understanding many of the issues relating to the development and implementation of a curriculum innovation such as the systems thinking approach. Examination of the tapes provides insights into the processes of learning and the cognitive changes resultant from developing curriculum materials and implementing the systems approach.

The final source of data collected and analyzed in this project thus far has been the information contained in existing school records. All organizations, including schools, create and maintain a great deal of information as a routine part of their operations. These records document the activities of students and teachers. For example, student records on courses and grades are routinely kept by most schools. With appropriate permission from district officials and parents, these data can be used to supplement the analysis of data collected during the course of the project. In addition to data on student performance, school files and records can be sources of rich information describing the community, school, teachers, annual budgets, school board meetings, voter referendum issues, and the like. All these sources can provide important background information relevant to identifying changes in organization structure and function.

In retrospect, it is now clear that the initial anticipation of relying on one methodology (i.e., a quasi-experimental design using mostly standardized and specialized paper-and-pencil tests, was naive). The expansion of the methodologies to include in-depth interviews and field observations reflected the growing recognition of the complexities involved in a computer-based educational innovation project. It is now quite clear that the methods used in this project will undergo continual transformation and refinement.

Teachers as Research Collaborators

In addition to the aforementioned research activities, ETS and the project teachers have established a collaborative research plan that will provide feedback for instructional enhancement as well as evaluate various program components. As an initial activity in developing these research plans, all teachers prepared statements of objectives for their use of the systems thinking approach in their courses. These statements were compiled and compared to determine the nature and variety of the teachers' rationales for using systems thinking. Prior to and during the 1992 summer training, the ETS staff met with the teachers to begin to develop collaborative research designs to address their stated objectives. The designs and methodologies vary substantially. Some of these objectives require longitudinal designs; others are more constrained and short term. For example, a longitudinal study is being used to study the Sunnyside teachers' objective to improve postgraduation performance, such as employment, salary, and additional education. They will use various forms of authentic assessment such as portfolio collection to trace students' development during their academic careers. They also will follow selected students after they leave the school.

Some objectives are generic across teachers and schools, whereas others are quite specific. At almost every school, there is an expressed interest in examining the systems approach's impact on problem solving both in the generic sense as well as specific components of the construct, such as analysis of relationships or decision making skills. Some teachers have targeted particular concepts within their disciplines that they previously have found difficult to teach, such as osmosis and acceleration. In some cases, teachers have identified school-wide or departmental goals that are being addressed with broad-scale designs. Objectives have also been stated at different levels of analysis. Most teachers are using the systems approach to improve various facets of student performance. Thus, students' cognitive processes, outcomes, and performance are the most frequently cited goals. Teachers and instruction are other targets for research. ETS staff and the teachers want to know how instruction changes with the use of systems thinking. Teachers also are concerned with the need for new assessment techniques to measure processes and outcomes that result from the curriculum innovation. Given the variety of objectives and methodologies, there are a dozen or more substudies ongoing across project schools at any one time.

There are two intended purposes for these research activities. The first and most direct function is to enhance instruction. The objective of this research is to produce information on students' cognitive and conative performances that can be fed back into improved instructional strategies and procedures. The research designs will be adapted to the specifics of individual courses.

The second function of the research designs is to provide more global assessments of the impact of the systems thinking approach with respect to teacher behavior, student performance, and organizational functioning. This research will provide useful information to the participating school districts and as well as the education research community.

As previously mentioned, the STACI[N] teachers are important participants in the research phase of the project. The teachers' collaborative research is a symbol of the joint ownership of the project. Research designs are neither imposed nor mandated by ETS. However, jointly ETS and the teachers are collectors and analyzers of valuable data. The resulting information provides insights into procedures for instructional enhancement, a commonly shared goal.

The methodologies currently used in the collaborative research with the teachers fall into four categories that overlap somewhat. A first methodology is a paper-and-pencil instrument designed to assess students' understanding of simple systems concepts. It draws partially on the instrument used previously at BUHS. It contains multiple-choice, short-answer, and model-completion items that are at a fairly low level of sophistication. Several teachers are using this instrument several times during a school year to obtain a sense of their students' progress in acquiring systems skills and knowledge.

A second methodology is the administration of a series of essays that require students to use systems thinking to formulate responses. Topics have been selected that concern dynamic phenomena. For example, one essay asks students to examine the political issues surrounding an election, justify voting for selected candidates, and hypothesize about possible outcomes. Students are assigned essays throughout the academic year in an effort to trace their systems thinking progress. The essay responses are content analyzed to examine the degree to which the students' level of sophistication with systems thinking increases over time.

Another methodology is paired observation, in which several sets of teachers in the same content area observe each other's classrooms several times throughout the year. The teachers have selected certain variables or activities that might be affected by the use of the systems approach. For example, some teachers are examining the extent to which the classroom becomes more learner directed, the types and patterns of teacher-student and student-student interactions, on-task behavior, and the like. It is anticipated that the observations not only will provide information about possible areas of impact in the classroom, but they also will serve to provide insights into the enhancement of instructional procedures.

A number of teachers are engaged in exploring performance assessment as it might relate to systems thinking. They are selecting activities, amenable to the systems approach, which require active participation and performance on the part of the students. For example, several laboratory science courses are including extended, group problem-solving projects that can be approached using systems thinking. Several chemistry teachers are using what they call "black box" or "explain how it works" problems to which systems also can be applied. Two high school mathematics teachers are developing a continuum of increasingly difficult calculus problems by which they can assess their students' competence with systems. All these activities fall under the category of authentic assessment. They are concrete problems that can be readily solved using systems thinking.

These and other methodologies are being adapted to fit the objectives of the project's classrooms. The methodologies constantly are evolving as the teachers identify and further refine the topics and variables of interest. Thus, the STACI[N] Project and its research activities attempt to capture flexibly the dynamic nature of the systems thinking approach.

3
Project Components: Systems Thinking, Graphical User Interfaces, and Modeling

Chapters 1 and 2 described the history of the STACI and STACI[N] Projects. In the final section of chapter 2, a discussion was presented of the multiple methods that emerged in the process of launching and supporting a computer-based curriculum innovation. The next step in analyzing these projects requires a review of their intellectual and technical backgrounds. In this chapter descriptions of the three major independent, yet interdependent, elements of the systems thinking approach are presented. They include: (a) the theoretical perspective known as systems thinking; (b) the computer graphical user interface (GUI) as implemented on the Macintosh; and (c) the modeling and simulation software packages, STELLA (Richmond, 1985) and STELLAStack (Richmond & Peterson, 1988).

The theoretical perspective of systems thinking is a comprehensive orientation, and its heuristic value as a problem-solving technique is particularly relevant for these projects. Systems thinking is pertinent to the analysis of dynamic phenomena, especially those readily characterized by interacting components that change over time. This chapter reviews the recent developments in system thinking, especially the work conducted at the MIT. Some of the basic concepts are discussed, and the potential of systems thinking for precollege instruction are explored. The systems thinking approach is not a panacea for the myriad of problems that prevent more effective teaching and learning across the curriculum in our nation's schools. However, it is a very promising complement to the teaching methods currently employed. Anecdotal evidence already supplied by some of the project teachers suggests that the systems thinking approach may be particularly effective with those students who are deficient in basic skills.

The second major element in the STACI Projects is the GUI as implemented on the Macintosh microcomputer. The features of this interface, including icons, menus, and graphics, make it especially suitable for use by individuals who have not had substantial prior experience with computers. Therefore, it is in many respects an ideal computer interface for use by those many middle and high school students and teachers who have not yet been introduced to the world of computing. This chapter reviews the patterns of distribution and use of microcomputers in schools. It also speculates on the hardware and software features that have both facilitated and impeded more widespread and effective use of these machines. The discussion focuses on the instructional potential of microcomputers that allows students to direct their attentions and efforts more to substance rather than the technical details of computing.

Modeling and simulation software packages such as STELLA and STELLAStack, are the third major component of this project. STELLA, an acronym for Structural Thinking Experiential Laboratory with Animation, is a modeling and simulation package developed by HPS. It operates on the Macintosh and permits teachers and students to implement the systems thinking perspective in their instructional and learning activities. STELLAStack is an interface between STELLA and HyperCard, a software system produced and distributed by Apple to enhance the storage and retrieval of information. By connecting to HyperCard, STELLAStack makes it possible to create models that employ more extensive graphics and animation. In the final section of this chapter STELLA is introduced and examples are provided to illustrate its major features.

This chapter provides the reader with the basic concepts for understanding the systems thinking approach and the hardware and software environment in which it is implemented in this project. The chapter also provides a foundation for addressing the issues of design and implementation of effective computer-based curriculum innovations. Furthermore, it explicates both the theoretical and policy orientations developed and refined in the project. The theoretical perspectives encompass the teaching and learning of higher order cognitive skills, including problem-solving, self-regulation, and metacognition. The policy orientation focuses on effective use of microcomputers in schools to promote educational reform.

SYSTEMS THINKING

Systems thinking is a conceptual problem-solving technique that is a special case of the broader theory of systems analysis. Both phrases sound like esoteric high-technology concepts. This is not really the case. The basic ideas are simple, and most have been recognized for a long time. Indeed, many of the fundamental concepts can be found in our earliest philosophical and scientific writings. Understanding how things work and making predictions are examples of systems analysis. The literature of systems analysis is vast, and a thorough review is not appropriate here. An excellent overview of this literature is provided by Mattessich (1982).

Systems thinking, on the other hand, is one of the major components of this project and, therefore, of central interest in this volume. As defined in the Preface earlier, systems thinking is a problem-solving strategy that employs models and simulations to examine the changing relationships among the parts of any dynamic phenomenon. Fostering an understanding of problems that involve change over time is characteristic of systems thinking.

The students at Sunnyside High School in Arizona have developed an engaging way of conveying the essence of systems thinking with a simple exercise that everyone encounters daily. Each morning most people must decide what clothing they will wear for that day. A number of factors will influence that decision. For example, they are likely to consider the weather forecast, the day's activities, their mood, and their available clothing. Each of these factors may have some effect on their clothing selection. Considering each of these factors one at a time is known as "laundry list thinking." Systems thinkers, on the other hand, take a different approach.

Figure 3.1 shows that systems thinkers view this daily problem as a set of intricately interrelated factors. For example, the weather might influence what one wears. Also, how one feels might influence what clothing is selected. Correspondingly, what one wears might also influence how one feels. The two arrows connecting these factors indicate that the causal connection could conceivably go in both directions. However, to the best of our knowledge, what one wears is not likely to influence the weather, and the arrow goes in only one direction. The relationships depicted in Fig. 3.1 by the one-and two-way arrows show a much more complicated picture of this daily problem of what to wear than is suggested by the simple laundry list of the four possible causal factors.

FIG. 3.1. A simple systems model.

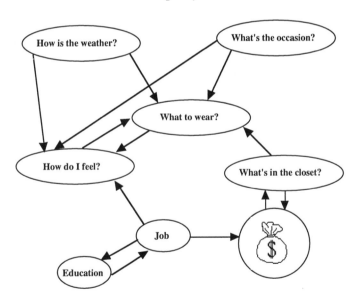

Source: Systems Thinking Club, Sunnyside High School, Tucson, AZ. Reprinted with permission.

The Sunnyside students took great pleasure extending this conceptual map by including the notion that what is in the closet is related to the amount of money a person might earn. This is depicted as a reciprocal relationship, because if one spends too much on the wardrobe, the disposable income may be severely diminished. They also point out that income is related to the type of job one holds, and that is reciprocally related to one's level of education. And that, of course, in the minds of the Sunnyside students is the point of all these activities. When students demonstrated this example to the Sunnyside Unified School District Board of Education to introduce them to systems thinking, it was enormously effective and successful, for the members voted their unanimous approval of the STACI^N Project.

As implemented in this project, systems thinking employs models and simulations to analyze phenomena that are comprised of interrelated and changing parts. The focus is usually on the simultaneous flows of inputs and outputs to and from an accumulator. A simple example is the process of accurately maintaining the balance of an interest bearing checking account. The major factors that affect the account balance are inputs of either deposits and earned interest and outputs of checks written, cash withdrawals, or service charges. At any given time, the account balance is computed by adding all inputs and subtracting all outputs. The different elements in this checking account system are interrelated. For example, the amount of money earned as interest is a function of the current rate and the account balance. Also, the service charges are usually dependent on the average daily balance and the volume of various activities, (i.e., checks written, withdrawals, or deposits). Hence, a checking account is a simple example of a system with interacting elements that change over time.

The intellectual origins of systems thinking as implemented in this project are found in the various works of Forrester (1961, 1968, 1969, 1971a, 1971b). Forrester was a pioneer in the development of servomechanisms and later of the memory components of digital computers. Following successes in these arenas, he turned his attention to the application of the principles of feedback controls in industrial settings to the broader questions of organizational management. His appointment to a professorship at the Sloan School of Management at MIT in 1956 surrounded him with colleagues who were interested in organizational problems. Forrester gathered a group of students and colleagues and began to address these issues. They intended to search for and develop linkages between engineering and management education. Forrester was particularly interested in the intersection of operations research and the newly developing field of information science. He also was interested in using modeling and simulation to explore new methods of analysis for industrial management practice and education. To promote these efforts, he established the System Dynamics Group at MIT.

Forrester and his group developed a computer language, DYNAMO, which enabled the creation of models to simulate the flow of materials and partially assembled units to an industrial production line (Pugh, 1973). This language made it possible to specify in detail the dynamics of this flow and to simulate the consequences for productivity of different levels of supply to the various points along the line. *Industrial Dynamics* (Forrester, 1961) described the models of the assembly line and presented for the first time the theoretical foundation for system dynamics.

The theoretical perspective presented in *Industrial Dynamics* was viewed by Forrester and his colleagues as a general theory applicable in a wide variety of organizational settings. The theory implicit in the DYNAMO compiler makes a distinction between two aspects of any system, structure and behavior. Of course, the two are intricately related. Forrester and his colleagues proposed that structure produces behavior; and there is an implied chronology or sequence with structure preceding behavior. The MIT group concluded that both research and education in management had traditionally been weak, because they had focused primarily on behavior and, for the most part, had ignored structure.

With the publication of *Industrial Dynamics* Forrester recognized that his focus was a too narrow. He saw clearly that the theoretical perspectives and simulation methods used in *Industrial Dynamics* could be applied to complex systems in any field. He coined the more general phrase, *system dynamics*; and this label is still used for Forrester's MIT laboratory.

It should be pointed out that Forrester and many others recognized that there is nothing really new about the use of models to represent a system. We all instinctively use mental images in every day decision making. These images are, in essence, models of our understanding of the phenomena, processes, organizations, or systems that we encounter. Selected concepts and relationships represent the mental images of our families, schools, communities, and corporations. All decisions are based on mental models. However, these models are usually incomplete and imprecisely stated.

A great deal of confusion and disagreement can result from the fact that different individuals have incomplete and divergent models of the same phenomenon. It is important that the assumptions about models be made explicit. One way to view system dynamics is that it provides both a rationale and a discipline for making assumptions more explicit. In fact, these assumptions can be stated so specifically that they can subsequently be formulated into a mathematical model and simulated on a computer over hypothetical time. Forrester conceived of system dynamics as a scientific philosophy for the analysis of social organization. He also posited that it was a body of principles that could relate structure to behavior. Through the analysis of models, Forrester intended to give organizational structure a sharper definition and a vigorous application to the analysis of collective behavior.

The theory of system dynamics, was specified by Forrester (1968) to have four components or hierarchies, which are portrayed in Fig. 3.2. The outermost component is called the *closed boundary*. This means that systems have boundaries, and models and simulations deal with components within areas defined by those boundaries. System dynamics does not ignore the fact that there are factors that cross those boundaries. It simply delineates what particular system properties are being explored within the defined boundaries.

FIG. 3.2. Four hierarchical levels in systems dynamics.

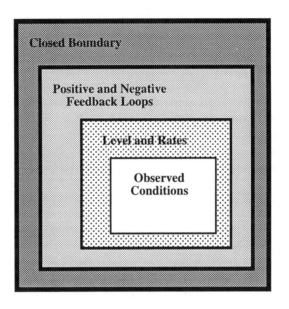

The second hierarchical level is comprised of *feedback loops*, which can be either positive or negative. A *positive loop* has a force or polarity such that any particular activity produces more activities. For example, a positive feedback loop describes the situation when a student's positive cognitive performance creates greater motivation. A positive feedback loop produces exponential growth. Feedback loops also can be negative. A positive feedback loop promotes growth, and a *negative feedback loop* promotes equilibrium. A thermostat is the classic example of a negative feedback loop. When the temperature in a room drops below the desired, preset level, the thermostat activates the furnace, which produces heat, raising the room temperature. When the temperature reaches the desired level, the thermostat turns off the furnace. All systems are composed of feedback loops. Complex systems contain many feedback loops. Most systems are composed of multilayered interconnecting feedback loops.

As shown in Fig. 3.2, the third hierarchical level of system dynamics is comprised of two the components of feedback loops: levels and rates. *Levels* refer to the states of the system and reflect the accumulations or integrations of quantities. At any given moment, levels collectively define the state of the system. Levels also are referred to as variables, because their values change or vary over time. *Rates*, on the other hand, are the activities or flows that change the values of the levels. Rates can be either constants or variables. The latter are expressed algebraically. Either singly or in combination, rates express system goals or objectives. The fourth, or innermost level of the hierarchy encompasses the *observed conditions* within any system. Inherent to the fourth level is the discrepancy between observed conditions and goals. In Forrester's view, the objective of management should be to identify desired actions that will reduce discrepancies between observed conditions and goals.

Industrial Dynamics generated a great deal of critical reaction (see Ansoff & Slevin, 1968). Many felt that the theory was naive and oversimplified. They pointed out that systems concepts had been adjusted to fit the DYNAMO compiler rather than vice versa. Forrester was convinced that the system dynamics perspective eventually would be recognized as having broad applications describing a variety of systems from industrial organizations to social, political, and ecological systems.

Despite the criticism, and perhaps because of it, Forrester was determined to explore the potential of extending system dynamics to a wide variety of settings. He began a collaboration with John F. Collins, former Mayor of the city of Boston. After leaving Boston's City Hall, Collins was appointed as a professor of urban affairs at MIT. The Forrester-Collins collaboration led to the application of the system dynamics perspective to the problems of urban growth and development. Together they created a model to represent their conception of the basic elements of urban development processes. *Urban Dynamics* (Forrester, 1969) was the product of this collaboration. Although Forrester had not previously been involved in the study of urban government, he was struck by the similarity between the work he had done in industry and many of the social, political, and economic problems that Collins recognized as traditionally plaguing large metropolitan areas.

Collecting and analyzing data covering various topics over the previous 250 years of Boston history, they examined the impact of four different programs designed to improve the city's economic and social conditions. The first program created private sector and government jobs for the unemployed. The second was a training program to increase basic skills among low-income groups. The third program provided financial aid to needy individuals, and the fourth constructed low-cost housing. The system dynamics urban model showed that in the short run, these programs produced positive results (i.e., training opportunities, more jobs, and more housing). However, in the long run, they made the city more attractive for new migrants, usually low-income and unskilled workers. Hence, the need for the same programs was increased; and the eventual outcomes of these programs was negative, usually unanticipated, and frequently counterintuitive.

Although the model constructed by Forrester corresponding to the growth and development of Boston over a 200-year period contained many variables whose interdependencies were specified in thousands of equations, the fundamental character of the system was identical to the simple example of the checking account just presented. The variables in the checking account were deposits, withdrawals, interest payments, and service charges. Each were related to the account balance in different ways, and they were all interrelated. In the urban model, there were many more variables (i.e., migration, tax revenues, social program expenditures, housing stock, and the like). Consequently, the statement of the interrelationships among these variables entailed many more equations. In principle, the structures are similar; but the urban model was vastly more complicated.

One of the urban programs that Forrester and Collins examined in some detail was low-income housing. They concluded that excess low-income housing is a basic cause of economic decay in urban areas. Among liberals, the commonly held belief at that time was that a shortage of housing was a serious problem to be resolved by increasing the amount of low-income housing (i.e., provide shelter for the poor and homeless). In many cities, legal and financial incentives encourage keeping older buildings in place. These structures become run-down and are eventually used as high density housing at low rent, which attracts more unskilled workers. Population rises, and jobs become scarce. A spiral is created that offsets any positive effects of the low-income housing program, which was designed to ameliorate the decaying innercity conditions.

In testimony before the House of Representatives Subcommittee on Urban Growth in 1970, Forrester stated some of his conclusions relating to managing social systems These comments were subsequently published (Forrester, 1971a). He said that most social systems are intransigent to any change. He testified that, based on his research, he believed that such systems are inherently difficult to change through policy formulation or modification. The dynamics of feedback loops in large social systems mask underlying causes, and policy analysts frequently focus on the more readily identifiable symptoms. Hence, the best intended policy analyses usually miss fundamental causes. In the instance of urban systems, Forrester saw excess population, particularly of low-income, unskilled workers, as the major problem.

Forrester also testified that social systems seem to have very few influence points through which any fundamental change can be introduced. In an urban system, housing is potentially such an influence point. He recommended that low-income housing should be reduced rather than increased. In his view, such a policy would make the city more attractive for all people, not only those for whom costly, ameliorative, reform programs must be launched with public funds. Finally, Forrester pointed out in his testimony that in all complex social systems, there is a fundamental conflict between short-term and long-term consequences. Short-term changes are usually more visible and therefore more compelling. They also have the potential of producing greater rewards for both office holders and seekers. Nevertheless, most actions targeted at short-term improvements usually will decrease substantially any long-term positive consequences. This example has been presented simply to convey the kind of reasoning one encounters in the system dynamics approach.

Urban Dynamics also created a great deal of controversy. It was viewed by many critics as inherently conservative and naive in its attempt to explain very complex situations. Nevertheless, proponents of system dynamics hailed it as a major breakthrough in social policy analyses. The model of the history of Boston was huge, consisting of hundreds of variables and thousands of equations. Most of the historical data fit the model well, and it suggested that the simulation might be extended and used to predict future trends for the city. The prospect of using system dynamics for predicting the future attracted great interest.

Forrester and his colleagues were encouraged by their successes in the industrial and urban domains. In the late 1960s they began to apply the techniques of system dynamics to the examination of more global problems such as population growth, natural resource consumption, and ecological balance. World Dynamics (Forrester, 1971b) summarized much of this work. Shortly thereafter, his colleagues published the controversial The Limits to Growth (Meadows, Meadows, Randers, & Behrens, 1972). This volume gained worldwide attention and was eventually translated into 19 languages. It became one of the most widely read and discussed books of its time. Completed with financial and moral support from the Club of Rome, an international group of businessmen, the book projected rates of consumption of natural resources and predicted that there would be severe shortages and chaos by the early part of the 21st century.

Understandably, this book created enormous controversy. Criticisms were leveled at the Systems Dynamics Group, both from a political and scientific perspective. From the political side, there was great unhappiness with an alleged conservative bias underlying the model. From the scientific viewpoint, many policy analysts pointed to the fallacy of using a model that fit historical data as a basis for future projections. The critics were so loud and effective that the credibility of system dynamics and, indeed, the entire field of system analysis suffered a severe blow. During the next decade, while the controversy simmered and eventually settled down, little attention was paid to predictive modeling by the System Dynamics Group.

Very recently, the use of system dynamics for predictive purposes was again brought to public attention with the publication of a sequel to *The Limits to Growth*, a new volume entitled *Beyond the Limits* (Meadows, Meadows, & Randers, 1992). These three individuals were all authors of the original volume and had continued their explorations of the consequences of further population growth and resource consumption. The new volume has already attracted some attention in the mass media. Its impact on the national and international policy-making communities in the forthcoming Clinton/Gore era remains to be seen.

Despite the new volume, Forrester and most of his colleagues have in recent years shifted their foci away from prediction and explored the potential of system dynamics in teaching. Indeed this perspective was wholly consistent with Forrester's move to the MIT Sloan School. For the next few years, attempts were made to model for the purposes of teaching students more sophisticated and explicit techniques of analyzing complex systems. System dynamics came to be valued more for its heuristic rather than predictive potential.

Until the early 1980s, all the model building and simulation activities of the System Dynamics Group were completed using the DYNAMO compiler on the mainframe computer at MIT. DYNAMO is an arcane higher level programming language. It is difficult to learn and to use effectively. Only a small number of faculty and students were adept at programming with it To capitalize on the limited expertise and create a company that could accept corporate clients interested in system dynamics, a group of Forrester's colleagues established a separate, for-profit company in Cambridge, Massachusetts, Pugh-Roberts Associates. The principals in the company were Alexander L. Pugh, III and Edward B. Roberts. As the applied section of the Systems Dynamics Group, they developed a facility and expertise with DYNAMO that was unmatched.

With the advent of microcomputers, it became clear that it would be extremely useful to create a software package that could facilitate modeling and simulation and greatly expand the application of system dynamics. However, the limited computational facilities and rigid user interfaces of the first microcomputers using the Microsoft Disk Operating System (DOS) were too restrictive to facilitate the implementation of modeling and simulation procedures. A student of Forrester's, Barry Richmond, who obtained his PhD from the Sloan School became intrigued with the possibility of creating a software package to promote modeling and simulation activities using the new Macintosh computer produced by Apple Computer.

Upon finishing his graduate work at MIT, Richmond joined the faculty of the Thayer School of Engineering at Dartmouth College. There he developed STELLA (Richmond, 1985), which implements many of the capacities of the DYNAMO compiler on the Macintosh microcomputer. It suddenly became possible to engage any student who had access to a

Macintosh in modeling and simulation activities. Previously these activities had been restricted to the small group of people who had access to a DYNAMO compiler on a mainframe computer. The implementation on the Macintosh meant that most systems analyses previously implemented in DYNAMO could now be made available to very large numbers of teachers and students.

Dartmouth College was an especially propitious institution for Richmond to choose for his first postdoctoral position. Under the guidance of first Professor, then Provost, and eventually President John Kemeny, Dartmouth College made an early commitment to provide ready access to computing for all students and faculty. Kemeny and his colleagues developed one of the very first time-sharing systems in higher education. Subsequently, they created one of the first academic computer-intensive environments by encouraging all students and faculty to purchase Macintosh computers at specially reduced prices.

When all the new microcomputers in the academic community were connected to the already existing, time-sharing system, Dartmouth's position as a leader in higher education computing was greatly enhanced. Shortly after Richmond arrived at Dartmouth, there already existed a large base of installed and networked Macintoshes and thereby potential STELLA users. To facilitate the development and dissemination of STELLA as well as future systems software products, Richmond established his own company, HPS. The production of STELLA and the creation of HPS are major points in the development and dissemination of systems thinking in educational settings.

Within a very short period of time after the introduction of STELLA, interest in systems thinking began to mount among faculty in colleges and universities throughout the country. There also were activities underway to explore the potential of systems thinking at precollege levels as well. As mentioned in chapter 1, the work at BUHS was one early development. In 1987, Apple Computer released HyperCard, a substantial extension to the storage, retrieval, and animation capabilities of the Macintosh computer. The following year, Richmond and his HPS colleagues announced the release of STELLAStack (Richmond & Peterson, 1988). This software package provides a HyperCard interface for STELLA modeling and simulation. STELLA Stack is a substantial expansion of the user interface for modeling and simulation and activities in education.

These two software packages made modeling and simulation readily available to a much broader audience of teachers and learners than had been previously possible. Recently, HPS reported that their products were installed in close to 750 colleges and universities in the United States and over 50 institutions of higher education around the world An additional 800 sites were reported in government agencies and private corporations

(Steven Peterson, HPS, personal communication, Aug. 2, 1993). However, the use of STELLA and systems thinking in schools has yet to develop on a broad basis.

Forrester has recently given additional impetus to the application of systems thinking to precollege education (Forrester, 1991). Working with colleagues and students at MIT, he is facilitating the application of systems thinking in schools. His students are developing curriculum modules using STELLA and pilot testing their use in Boston area schools. They are also working with some of the schools throughout the nation that are using systems thinking. For the STACI[N] Project, they are providing critiques of the models and accompanying materials developed by the teachers. These reviews provide a critically important quality control function for the project. Without this contribution from Forrester's group the STACI[N] participants would run the serious risk of producing inaccurate and misleading materials.

EDUCATIONAL COMPUTING

Attention is next directed to a brief history of the patterns of distribution and use of microcomputers in schools. In many respects the history of computer use in education is both disappointing and frustrating. Since the early 1960s when large-scale digital computers made their first appearance on many university campuses and in a few schools throughout the nation, a virtual armada of advocates have promoted them as the technology that would change fundamentally the nature of teaching and learning activities. Yet despite the proliferation of computers of all sizes and vintages in instructional settings from preschool through adult and continuing professional education, the impact of computers on learning outcomes is today hardly discernible in most quarters. A provocative review of the minimal effects of many educational technologies from 1920 to the present, including radio, film, television, teaching machines, and most recently computers has been provided by Cuban (1986).

During the 1960s and 1970s many large mainframe machines were donated to or steeply discounted for educational institutions by such companies as IBM and Control Data Corporation. The first large-scale mainframe computers introduced in the mid-1960s were priced in the range of several million dollars. Initially these machines were used primarily for the purposes of large-scale data processing and analyses, and mostly by scientists in research institutes and universities. However, there were several noteworthy efforts to produce computer-assisted instructional systems using a time-sharing mode of operation on these large machines. Several large systems such as PLATO (Alpert & Bitzer, 1970; Eastwood & Ballard, 1975) and TICCIT (Bunderson, 1975) were developed amid widely held expectations for extensive use in educational, occupational, and military settings.

Despite substantial investment of resources and time in the development of these systems, the extent of their use was disappointing. However, it should be pointed out that the development of these systems did contribute to the creation of a great deal of practical knowledge and experience that should prove invaluable in the design and implementation of future computer-based systems of instruction. The limited utilization of such systems as PLATO and TICCIT stemmed mainly from the fact that the systems were large and operated on machines that were too expensive for most educational institutions and therefore, simply out of question for the budgets of all but a few of the largest or wealthiest. In addition, evaluation studies of their use showed consistent but small contributions to learning (Alderman & Mahler, 1973; Swinton, Amarel, & Morgan, 1978).

The introduction of minicomputers in the late 1960s was pioneered by the Digital Equipment Company. These machines provided substantial computing power at much lower prices than the large mainframes. Initially priced around $10,000, minicomputers were certainly more affordable to some educational institutions, especially colleges and universities. However, only a few of the most affluent school districts were able to afford them. Minicomputers such as the PDP-11 and its successors, including today the powerful and more affordable VAX, eventually began to appear in some of the largest and most affluent school districts. However, the decreasing price of hardware was not sufficient to insure that computers could be used effectively by schools, for there still was very little effective software for teaching and learning activities. The microcomputer revolution, which started in the 1970s, permanently and fundamentally changed the landscape of educational computing.

During the 1970s the seeds of the microcomputer revolution were being sown in several places. The story of Jobs and Wozniak and their garage-based primitive computer factory is now legendary. In 1976, they established their own company and introduced the first commercially available microcomputer, the Apple I. Comprised of a motherboard and a collection of parts that the purchaser assembled, the Apple I attracted little public attention outside of a small group of early microcomputer enthusiasts. The next year Jobs and Wozniak, with the assistance of a newly hired financial manager, Mike Markkula, released the Apple II. This machine established a small dynasty of microcomputers that eventually included the Apple II+, the III, the IIe, the III+, the IIc, and eventually the IIgs. These machines became widely distributed in schools throughout the nation. By the beginning of the 1985/86 school year, it was estimated that over 55% of the close to one million microcomputers used in the nation's schools were Apples (Quality Education Data, Inc., 1986).

At the same time that Jobs and Wozniak were developing and distributing their Apples, other computer manufacturers were busy designing and introducing their microcomputers, including Atari, Commodore, and Tandy. The introduction of the IBM Personal Computer

(PC) in August 1981 transformed the nascent microcomputer movement into a full-scale revolution. It is relatively easy today to underestimate the importance of the introduction of microcomputers to the industry generally, and particularly to education. When IBM announced its PC, many people finally recognized that a major event had occurred in the history of technology and society.

The personal computer made available to an individual user most of the capacity of a mainframe at a fraction of the cost. The earliest personal computers sold for approximately $5,000, and they had the processing speed, memory capacity, most of the input/output options, and mean time to component failure of the mainframe computers, which in the early 1960s cost several millions of dollars. The trends of decreasing costs and increasing capacity were obvious to all. Projections of these trends made it clear that tremendous computing power could shortly be made available to teachers and students at all levels of our educational system.

In the early 1980s microcomputer prophets were forecasting the imminent production of a "3M" computer that would sell for under $1,000. This machine would have one million characters of memory, would execute its basic instructions at the rate of one million per second, and would include high resolution graphic displays on its monitor at the density of one million pixels per screen. Today the 3M machine is a reality, but its cost is still several thousand dollars, too much for schools to provide one machine for every teacher and student. However, there are now available some very small notebook computers, almost pocket-size, that possess some of the capabilities of the 3M machine and cost under $1000. Although these are not yet truly 3M computers, it is clear that the costs of microcomputers will continue to decline, although at a somewhat slower rate than previously anticipated. One can realistically anticipate that, in the not too distant future, one of these 3M computers can be on the desk of every student and teacher, kindergarten through graduate school.

The cost of all computers, including microcomputers, has dropped substantially in the last decade, and their use in schools has correspondingly increased. Surveys conducted by Becker at Johns Hopkins University have documented the proliferation of microcomputers in schools (Becker, 1983, 1984a, 1984b, 1984c). It now seems quite likely that within a decade there will be one computer on every student's desk. The widespread availability of hardware is a necessary but not sufficient condition to insure effective use of computers in schools. Experience in the STACIN Project has made it abundantly clear that software, teacher training, curriculum revision, and administrative support are all critical for the success of technology-based school reform efforts.

A growing realization of the many conditions necessary to support effective computer use in schools is leading to a disenchantment that is spreading among teachers, administrators, parents, and students concerning the undelivered promises of computers as a panacea for education. The

Cuban (1986) volume effectively documents this disenchantment. This disappointment or backlash is particularly acute in schools where substantial resources and efforts have been invested in computer-based education programs. Despite the fact that there are increasing numbers of machines available, there is very little evidence to support the claim that student learning has been enhanced. Most critics point to the lack of quality software to support teaching and learning. A review of the catalogs of the many commercial software houses that specialize in educational materials certainly confirms this impression. All too often, the emphasis is on games employing attractive features such as color and animation. Insufficient attention has been paid to instructional utility.

Despite the efforts of many government and private funding agencies to support the production of quality software, progress in this area has been slow and disappointing. Many proponents of the use of computers in education bemoan the fact that neither the design nor the user interface of most microcomputers is suitable for educational uses. Most microcomputers use DOS, which is a version of the operating systems employed on many mainframes and minicomputers. DOS is particularly difficult for beginners to understand. A newer and more powerful operating system, UNIX, is now being distributed for microcomputers. Although very powerful and flexible, it is perhaps even more difficult for beginners to learn. Many observers of the use of technology in education claim that these operating systems are a major impediment to effective use of microcomputer use in schools.

When Apple released the first Macintosh in 1984, the potential for application of computers in schools was enhanced greatly. The Macintosh was based on the GUI principles established in the 1970s by scientists working on the STAR computer at the Palo Alto, California, research facility of the Xerox Corporation (Xerox PARC). When Steven Jobs of Apple saw the STAR computer at Xerox PARC, he recognized the potential of GUI, and he was inspired to design the Macintosh. He wanted to produce a user-friendly microcomputer that would change not only the way people interact with computers but more fundamentally change the way in which people use their minds to solve problems.

The basic principles of a GUI microcomputer are really quite simple. Users interact with the computer in ways that are intuitively understandable. The design and architecture of the GUI machine departs radically from those employed in other computers, including mainframes, minicomputers, and other microcomputers. It relies heavily on pointers and graphics to issue commands to the central processing unit of the computer. The screen is portrayed as a desktop with tools displayed that can be used to accomplish a variety of tasks such as writing, editing, drawing, filing, and discarding. The tools are represented by labels or icons, which are small pictures that convey the function of a task. Tasks are identified by moving a cursor on the face of the screen with a small rolling ball, which is housed in a hand-controlled unit known as a mouse. Tasks are initiated by issuing commands to the computer via pointing with the cursor and clicking a button on the mouse.

Figure 3.3 portrays the basic screen of the Macintosh, currently the most widely used GUI microcomputer. Notice that starting from the upper left-hand corner and running across the top of the screen are a series of five labels; or more accurately, one Apple icon and four labels: File, Edit, View, and Special. These labels refer to pulldown menus, another important feature of the GUI architecture. A total of 39 different options or commands are stored under these five labels on the desktop. Any one can be made available for the user to view or initiate by selecting the label with the mouse. When the cursor, which is displayed as an arrow in the middle of the screen in Fig. 3.3, is moved with the mouse to any label, all the options under that label are displayed. For example, if the cursor is moved to Special, one finds that under that label are stored the following six options: (a) *Clean Up Desktop*, (b) *Empty Trash*, (c) *Erase Disk*, (d) *Set Startup*, (e) *Restart*, and (f) *Shut Down*. These are all housekeeping tasks concerning the desktop, files, disks, and the operating system.

An example may further illuminate: If a file is no longer needed, it can be disposed of by moving it with the mouse to the trash can, the small icon in the lower right hand corner of the screen. The mouse is used to direct the cursor on top of the icon of the file to be discarded. By clicking the mouse button on the file icon and dragging it to the trash can, the file is eliminated

FIG. 3.3. Basic Macintosh screen.

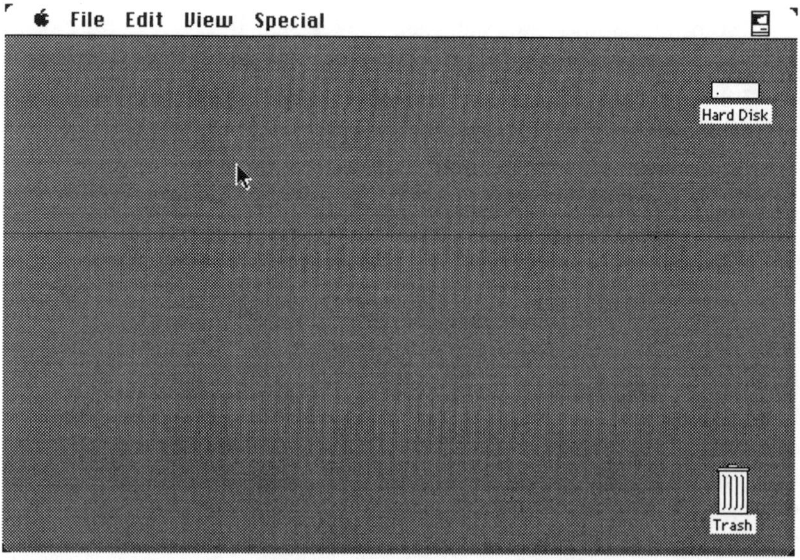

from the computer storage. At this point the sides of the can bulge slightly, indicating that some data are in the trash, awaiting final instructions to erase it from memory. These instructions can be executed by clicking the mouse on the Empty Trash option under the pulldown menu under the Special label. However, it is possible to avoid or undo the trashing as long as the sides of the can are still bulging by clicking twice or double clicking on the trash icon and moving the file icon back to a storage area. Both the undo and pulldown menus features have greatly facilitated user interaction with the GUI operating system.

Arcane control languages for operating systems like DOS and UNIX are nowhere to be found in the GUI environment. The operating system is virtually invisible to the user. Indecipherable error messages are not part of the GUI vocabulary. Although other microcomputer manufacturers, including Atari and Commodore, developed and marketed GUI machines, the Apple Macintosh was the dominant player in ushering in a new era in computing. Steven Jobs and his colleagues at Apple were successful in revolutionizing the entire computer industry with their GUI design of the Macintosh.

The Macintosh eventually became widely adopted in many colleges and universities. Faculty and students who have not previously used computers find it relatively easy to learn the system and substantially to facilitate their work. Initially, word processing was the major attraction for many college and university faculty, but they shortly began to recognize other applications, particularly those requiring enhanced graphics. As prices started dropping for the Macintosh and approached the $2,000 mark, increasing numbers of high-school teachers became purchasers, users, and proponents of GUI machines for their classrooms.

Since 1984 when Apple released the first Macintosh, the company has continuously upgraded and expanded the line. These products include a Macintosh Plus, an SE, and eventually a series of model II's, culminating in the most powerful Quadra, which is priced at over $5,000. In the fall of 1990, Apple further extended the product line of Macintoshes. Two models are especially interesting for secondary schools: the Classic and the LC. The Classic, the first truly powerful GUI microcomputer that sells for under $1,000, is particularly attractive to schools, for the price is now reaching the affordable range of many districts. The Macintosh LC is also of interest, because it incorporates a color monitor in its configuration and is priced at approximately $2000. In 1992 Apple again announced further additions to the Macintosh line. The Performa series provides three options for lower priced machines targeted at the home market. It is expected that all these prices will continue to come down to a level that is more affordable for schools. A powerful GUI machine with a color monitor priced at the $1,000 level would be a most attractive product for the school market. There seems to be consensus among computer industry watchers that the trend of increasing capability and decreasing price will continue for some time.

The Macintosh GUI design has been so widely and enthusiastically accepted by users that other major hardware and software companies are creating products with similar capacities. The recently released Windows software package created by Microsoft duplicates many of the Macintosh interface features in microcomputers that operate with DOS. In fact, intense legal battles are underway between Apple and other companies concerning ownership of the GUI design, including icons, graphics, and mouse architecture and interface.

Rather than discuss further the features of the GUI in the abstract, the next section of this chapter provides an introduction to the STELLA software package, the third component of the systems thinking approach implemented in this project. In the application of STELLA as well as the examples presented throughout the rest of this volume, specific instances of the GUI design will be further described.

STELLA

As mentioned, STELLA and STELLAStack are the modeling and simulation languages developed by HPS for the Macintosh computer. They implement the concepts embodied in the DYNAMO language developed by the System Dynamics Group at MIT. STELLA includes the major features of DYNAMO that allow individuals to make explicit their conceptual models. STELLA uses the Macintosh to transform these models into simple, logical, structural diagrams that can be run over simulated time.

Before introducing STELLA and providing an example of a model, it is necessary to discuss briefly two interrelated concepts that are fundamental to understanding modeling and simulation. The first concept is best illustrated by examining a more complex distinction between laundry list and systems thinking. Richmond (1993) used the example of analyzing the causes of overpopulation. *Laundry listing* considers such factors as poverty, lack of education, and inadequate information on birth control methods as some of the causes of overpopulation. This approach assumes that the causal factors can be weighted according to their relative importance, and empirical research can determine the accuracy of these weights. This type of thinking and research analysis are commonly expressed in multiple regression equations, in which several different variables, called causes or independent variables, are assumed to account for the effect or dependent variable. Furthermore, laundry lists promote the perception that the causality flows in only one direction. For example, in the case of overpopulation just cited, the usual assumption is that poverty is a cause of overpopulation. However, it is equally plausible that overpopulation can cause poverty. Laundry list thinking is obviously far too simplistic for most dynamic phenomena.

Systems thinking, on the other hand, offers an approach that is more appropriate for analyzing complex, changing systems; it assumes that causes and effects can be interrelated in circular processes. For example, overpopulation can both be caused by poverty as well as be the effect of poverty. Furthermore, multiple causes or independent variables, such as poverty and lack of education, can be circularly related to each other. As noted in the discussion of Forrester's work earlier, systems thinkers refer to such circular processes as feedback loops, either positive or negative. Laundry-list thinkers see the world as composed of sets of static, one-way, stimulus-response relationships Systems thinkers, on the other hand, perceive ongoing, interdependent, and dynamic processes.

The second concept relevant to modeling and simulation is the causal loop diagram. System thinkers frequently find it useful to create causal diagrams of the feedback loops they are analyzing. Causal-loop diagrams express the circular relationships among the system components. For example, Fig. 3.4 depicts two simple causal-loop diagrams, one positive and one negative. These figures illustrate the aforementioned examples on positive cognitive learning gains and the thermostatically controlled room temperature. When a student experiences a positive learning gain, the top diagram predicts that it will positively effect or increase motivation to learn; and similarly, increased motivation will lead to more learning. The plus sign in the parentheses denotes that this is a positive feedback loop promoting growth or, in the case of this example, more learning. The lower diagram depicts the negative feedback system of room temperature and the

FIG. 3.4. Causal loop diagrams.

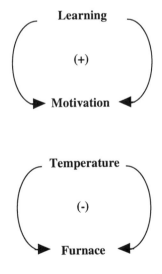

thermostatically controlled furnace. If room temperature drops below the preset level, the furnace is turned on and remains on until the room temperature returns to the desired level. The minus sign in the parentheses denotes a negative feedback loop, which promotes stability or equilibrium.

Notice that it is the reciprocal nature of the relationship that determines whether the loop is positive or negative. In the learning example, motivation and learning are related such that a change in either one will result in a similar change in the other. A successful learning experience produces an increase in motivation, which will in turn promote more learning. Similarly, an unsuccessful learning experience results in a decrease in motivation, which will in turn preclude further learning. Regardless of the direction of the change, the relationship is reciprocal. On the other hand, this is not the case for a negative feedback loop as in the thermostat example. If the room temperature remains the same or rises, the furnace is not affected. Therefore, the relationship is not reciprocal, and the loop is negative. This example could be made more complex by adding an air conditioning unit, also controlled by thermostat. However, that expansion would make the discussion more complex than is necessary at this point.

Figure 3.5 is an example of a causal loop diagram of an addiction model (Richmond, Petersen, & Vescuso, 1987). This diagram contains two loops, one positive and one negative. The positive loop specifies that as the number of cigarettes smoked increases, the need for a cigarette also increases.

FIG. 3.5. An addiction causal loop diagram.

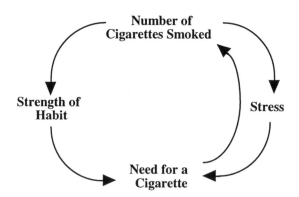

From Richmond, Peterson, and Vescuso. Copyright 1987 by High Performance Systems. Adapted with permission.

The need for a cigarette leads to an increase in the strength of the habit, which in turn produces an increase in the number of cigarettes smoked. The negative loop specifies that the number of cigarettes smoked reduces the levels of stress, which in turn reduces the need for a cigarette, weakens the habit, and therefore decreases the number of cigarettes smoked. The net effect of this causal loop analysis suggests that, in the short run, smoking one cigarette can reduce the likelihood of smoking another. However, in the long run, it increases the habit and the addiction.

Causal loop diagramming is a very effective method of illustrating some of the basic concepts of systems thinking. It is particularly helpful in pointing out the many shortcomings of laundry-list thinking. However, there are still several limitations associated with causal loops. First and foremost, they may specify relationships and predict behaviors, but they frequently do not describe the operations of systems. Without operational specification, it is impossible to understand an interactive, dynamic system. This point will become clearer when an example of a STELLA model is presented later. Furthermore, causal loop diagrams lack quantitative information; they cannot be simulated over hypothetical time; they do not distinguish between levels and rates. With these introductory comments on laundry-list thinking and causal loop diagrams, attention can now turn to the STELLA language and a model of the population example presented earlier.

Figure 3.6 portrays the basic STELLA screen. The pulldown menus are displayed across the top of the desk starting in the upper left-hand corner. Some of these menus are identical or similar to the Macintosh screen (e.g., the Apple icon, File, and Edit). However, three new menus are unique to STELLA: *Windows, Display,* and *Run*. Contained within these menus are 25 different options or commands relevant to model construction, display, and simulation. For example the Window label contains six options: *Diagram, Graph Pad, Tables, Equations, Clipboard,* and *Put Away*. The first four refer to the various modes of display of the simulation, and the last two are options for storing and retrieving models. Notice also that the cursor in STELLA is portrayed as a hand in Fig. 3.6, and the index finger of the hand serves as a pointer.

Like many GUI applications, STELLA has a toolkit. It contains the four basic building blocks for simulations: *stocks, flows, converters,* and *connectors*. These building blocks are used to create the components of a model. They correspond to Forrester's four hierarchical units, as depicted in Fig. 3.2. The toolkit is displayed along the left border of the screen with

FIG. 3.6. Basic STELLA screen.

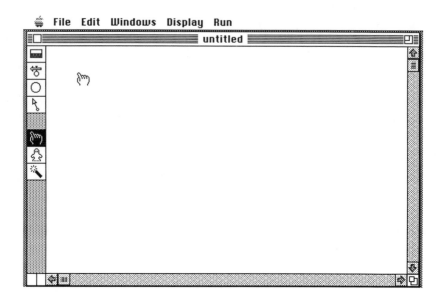

seven icons. The first four represent the building blocks, and the last three are tools used in model construction. The little ghost image and the stick of dynamite permit easy copying or removal of parts of a model.

Represented by the small boxes, stocks are accumulators; they correspond to the levels as specified by Forrester. They are the places where items accumulate. Stocks are the nouns of the structure of the model. During execution of a simulation, the values of stocks rise and fall and the animation of the Macintosh accurately depicts this by raising and lowering the contents of the box. Stocks generate flows, which correspond to the rates in Forrester's theoretical structure. In the toolkit, flows are represented by the small pipes with an arrow head denoting direction. Flows come with regulators, the small circle and valve, which connote controls on the rate of activity. Flows are the verbs of the structure. They represent activity, and they increment and decrement the stocks. They determine how quickly stock levels rise and fall.

Converters and connectors, the remaining two building blocks, are the logical units that tie the components of the structural diagram together. Converters, portrayed as the small circle, are the adjectives and adverbs. They are used to represent constants, to express relationships between variables, and to introduce external inputs to the model. Connectors, depicted as lines with arrow heads indicating direction, link stocks, flows, and converters together to form feedback loops. They represent information or logical linkages.

The STELLA toolkit is used to create models and simulations following a three-step process. First, diagrams representing the various components of the system to be modeled are created on the basic STELLA diagram screen. Using stocks, flows, converters, and connectors, the diagrams state the relationships and linkages hypothesized by the modeler. Second, the interconnections between parts of the systems are formally specified. STELLA accomplishes this specification by translating the diagrams, the logic, and the numerical parameters into a series of simultaneous equations. At this point in the process, STELLA checks to see that all components of the system are defined and that there are no missing connections between units.

The third and final step is to run the model over hypothetical time. During this step, the STELLA program offers several optional methods of display. The user selects one of these modes from the Windows menu just described. The diagram window depicts the structural diagram. During the simulation it shows the changing levels of the stocks. As the simulation runs, the graph pad can plot three variables. Furthermore, STELLA generates tables of numerical output from the model. This output is also available during the simulation. Finally, STELLA generates a listing of all the simultaneous equations created by the model.

STELLA's animation is a major factor accounting for its widespread appeal in teaching and learning activities. Capitalizing on the Macintosh's graphics capabilities, STELLA allows the user to observe parts of the structural diagram, graph pad, or numerical tables change during a simulation. This animation provides the user with an intuitive sense of how the parts of the system interact. Because STELLA provides these multiple modes of representation of the model, it is becoming widely recognized as a potentially powerful aid to learning. The reviews of STELLA in the computing and education literature have thus far been overwhelmingly positive (Jones, 1986; Robinson, 1986).

Figure 3.7 displays a STELLA diagram for a primitive human population model extending over a hypothetical 25-year period from 1990 to the year 2015. This example is one that systems thinkers find useful as an introduction to the conventions of modeling. This model has one stock, *Population*, which is influenced by two flows: one inflow, which is *Births*, and one outflow, which is *Deaths*. The direction of the flows is indicated by the arrows. In the Population stock people accumulate as the result of an inflow of births, and people decrease as the result of an outflow of deaths. Of course, in a more accurate representation of a human population, the number of people also would be influenced by factors other than births and

FIG. 3.7. A STELLA population model.

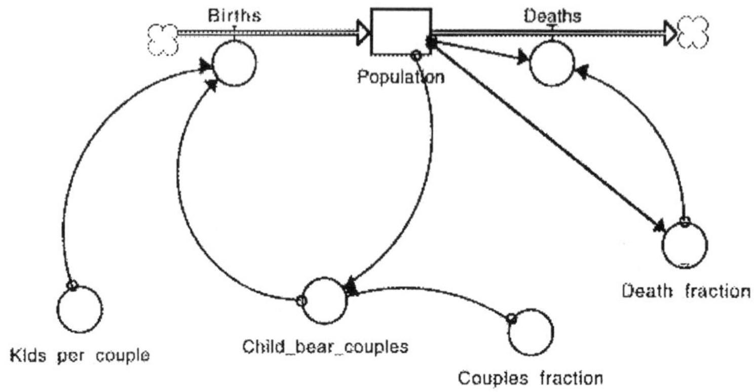

simple and ignore other factors. There is sufficient complexity in this example in defining Births and Deaths, the two major determinants of the Population stock.

Births are defined by using two converters, portrayed as small circles, *Kids_per_couple* and *Child_bear_couples*. Notice that STELLA employs the convention of linking words in labels with an underline mark. Turning to Child_bear_couples first, at any given time during the simulation of this model, the number of child-bearing couples is some fraction of the total population. In this model, that fraction is 35%. To simplify further, this fraction will remain constant throughout the simulation. A more complicated model might let this fraction vary according to the age distribution of the population, thereby accounting for the fact that only couples in the child- bearing age range can produce children. However, this complication is also ignored here for the sake of efficiency in presenting the example. Using the constant couples fraction of .35 means that at any given time it is assumed that 35% of the total population can produce children.

Turning to the second converter used in the model to define Births, Kids_per_couple, another constant is used, in this case, 10%. This constant specifies that one tenth of the child-bearing couples will give birth at any given time during the simulation. All this can be made more concrete with some hypothetical numbers. Assuming an initial population of 200, calculate that there will be 70 child-bearing couples; for the model defines Child_bear_couples as Population (200) times Couples_ fraction (.35). Therefore, there will be seven births during the first year, for the model defines Births as Kids_per_couple (.10) times Child_bear_couples (7). Notice that the arrows in Fig. 3.7 connecting the Population stock, the Birth flow and the three converters (Kids_per_couple, Child_bear_couples, and Couples_fraction) all state these relationships graphically.

Turning to the other flow in the model, an outflow from the Population stock, Deaths, Fig. 3.7 shows that it is defined by both the *Population* stock and the converter *Death_fraction*. The converter, Death_fraction, is defined with a graphical function, which allows the model builder to specify a relationship between variables as a curve. A graphical function is another special feature of STELLA. In this example, the graphical function describes the relationship between Population and Death_fraction. The use of a graphical function is noted in Fig. 3.7 by a tilde (~) within the Death_fraction converter circle.

This kind of graphical specification avoids the use of complicated mathematical expressions for the definition of nonlinear relationships. Figure 3.8 depicts the STELLA graphical function expressing the relationship between the Population stock and the Death_fraction converter. The graphical function specifies that deaths will not occur in this model until the

FIG. 3.8. A STELLA graphical function.

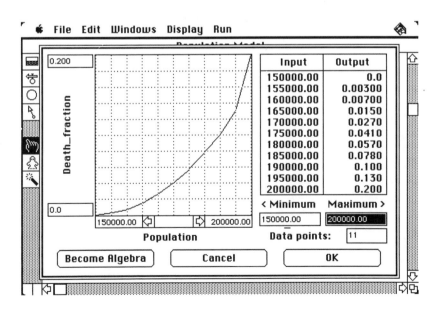

population reaches a level of 150,000. Then the deaths will rise fairly rapidly and ultimately reach a level of 200 per year when the population reaches a level of 200,000. The rate of escalation for each level of total population is specified by the curve depicted in Fig. 3.8. STELLA allows two modes of input for a graphical function. The first is to draw the curve with the mouse and cursor on the grid portrayed in Fig. 3.8. Alternately, the numerical values for the death fraction can be typed for each population level from 150,000 to 200,000 in increments of 5,000 each.

Each element, including the stock, flows, and converters in this example have now been examined and explained. STELLA automatically generates a list of the simultaneous equations specified by this model. This list is portrayed in Fig. 3.9. Note that population is defined as the integration over each year in the 25-year simulation of the accumulation of the difference between births and deaths. Also note that the population is given a starting or initial value of $1E5$, or 100,000 people. The definitions of the converters are depicted as specified above, and the values of the graphical function for Death_fraction are stated for each population level.

FIG. 3.9. STELLA equations for the population model.

Population = Population + dt * (Births - Deaths)
INIT(Population) = 1E5
Births = Child_bear_couples*Kids_per_couple
Child_bear_couples = Population*Couples_fraction
Couples_fraction = 0.35
Deaths = Population*Death_fraction
Kids_per_couple = 0.10
Death_fraction = graph(Population)
(150000.00,0.0),(155000.00,0.00300),(160000.00,0.0070
0),(165000.00,0.0150),(170000.00,0.0270),(175000.00,0.
0410),(180000.00,0.0570),(185000.00,0.0780),(190000.0
0,0.100),(195000.00,0.130),(200000.00,0.200)

When the model is run, STELLA calculates the values of stocks, flows, and variable converters for each unit of simulated time. Figure 3.10 is a table listing selected variables for each of the 25 years. Note that over the period of this simulation the population increases from the initial level of 100,000 to 172,844. Of course, the calculated values need to rounded, for the concept of part of a person is not appropriate for a population simulation. The number of births increases from the initial annual level of 35,000 to 60,049, and there are no deaths in this population until the year 2002. By the end of the simulated period, the number of annual deaths has reached 6,043. Obviously, this is a younger, healthy population at the outset of the simulation.

STELLA also produces graphs plotting the variables over the simulated time. Figure 3.11 portrays the graphical output from running the population model. The same three variables included in the table above are

FIG. 3.10. STELLA table output.

Time	Population	Births	Deaths
1990.00	100000.00	3500.00	0.0
1991.00	103500.00	3622.50	0.0
1992.00	107122.50	3749.29	0.0
1993.00	110871.79	3880.51	0.0
1994.00	114752.30	4016.33	0.0
1995.00	118768.63	4156.90	0.0
1996.00	122925.53	4302.39	0.0
1997.00	127227.93	4452.98	0.0
1998.00	131680.91	4608.83	0.0
1999.00	136289.73	4770.14	0.0
2000.00	141059.88	4937.10	0.0
2001.00	145996.97	5109.89	0.0
2002.00	151106.86	5288.74	100.35
2003.00	156295.25	5470.33	630.84
2004.00	161134.75	5639.72	1420.50
2005.00	165353.97	5787.39	2620.78
2006.00	168520.58	5898.22	3951.70
2007.00	170467.09	5966.35	4825.56
2008.00	171607.88	6006.28	5406.00
2009.00	172208.16	6027.29	5714.35
2010.00	172521.08	6038.24	5875.90
2011.00	172683.42	6043.92	5959.92
2012.00	172767.42	6046.86	6003.46
2013.00	172810.83	6048.38	6025.97
2014.00	172833.23	6049.16	6037.59
2015.00	172844.81	6049.57	6043.60

FIG. 3.11. STELLA graph output.

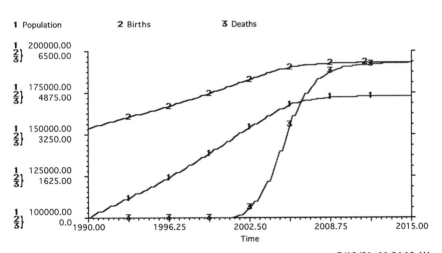

7/19/91 11:04:10 AM

71

plotted for each of the 25 years. STELLA calculates the values of these variables and plots the graphs during the time the simulation is being run. The fact that the modeler can observe dyanmic plotting of the graphs adds substantially to the attraction of STELLA for students. The graphs makes clearer than the table of values that this population appears to be reaching a steady state with respect to births, deaths, and total number of people. Such patterns are more readily detected when the model output data are presented in graphic rather than tabular form.

When simulations such as the population model are employed by teachers in schools, they can use them in a variety of ways. They can have students change parameters, such as the initial population level or the death fraction, and rerun the simulation, noting changes in the output values and graphical patterns. In addition, the teachers can have the sstudents change or extend the structure of the model. For example, they could add flows to account for migration pattersn or converters reflecting differential fertility or mortality for various age segments of the population. Futhermore, they can encourage and assist students in building models of dynamic phenomena in other substantive areas, using the insights they have gained about simulations through their work with the population model.

This example of the population model is given here to provide a concrete instance of the use of systems thinking and STELLA ana analyzing a commonly employed high school science problem. It now should be clear that simualtions and model building using systems thinking, GUI computers, and STELLA constitutes a new and exciting tool for teaching and learning activities. This tool has substantial potential for promoting kowledge acquisition, but more importantly hgiher order problem-solving skills.

This chapter has provided the background for the STACI and STACI[N] Projects. Having discussed system thinking, GUI microcomputers, and STELLA, attention now turns to the lessons learned in the STACI Projects thus far.

4
Observations, Issues, Cautions, and Lessons Learned

The first two chapters described the genesis and evolution of the STACI and STACI^N Projects. The purpose of this chapter is to extract lessons from the STACI^N experiences concerning the subtleties involved in the creation, implementation, evolution, and dissemination of the systems thinking approach as an example of a computer-based curriculum innovation. During this time, ETS staff have observed and noted many caveats, cautions, and issues from which invaluable lessons can be drawn about the various phases of a research and implementation project. Some of these lessons may not be obvious to experienced researchers or school personnel who have been involved in similar collaborative projects. Many of the issues might be perceived as trivial, but they readily can develop into bona fide problems whose resolution can be demanding in time, resources, and energy for both researchers and practitioners. Most of these issues cannot be found in standard research methodology textbooks. They are derived from accumulated experiences working with districts, schools, teachers, and students as they struggle to determine how best to capitalize on the use of technology in their institutions.

There are few textbooks that deal realistically with the practicalities involved in the conduct of research, including design, data collection, analysis, and dissemination in such complex and volatile environments as schools and classrooms. The specifics of applying research design principles are left to the common sense and good judgment of those responsible for directing the project. Furthermore, many computer-based curriculum innovations cause a role redefinition for researchers. Rather than functioning simply as impartial observers, researchers often must assume multiple roles, as change agents, implementors, facilitators, troubleshooters, fund raisers, as well as scientists. A delicate balance between the research and implementation components of a project must be struck. This chapter is an attempt to begin a dialogue between researchers and practitioners to make both parties aware of some of the difficulties and realities encountered in dual-purpose projects necessitating that researchers fill multiple roles and teachers participate often in research.

The chapter is a substantial extension of a previous discussion of issues that surfaced early in the STACI Project (see Mandinach & Thorpe, 1987). In a preliminary manner, that article explored the perspectives of both the research and practitioner communities with the intent of increasing awareness between the groups. It acknowledged the many problems inherent in implementation efforts, as well as the fact that such projects are difficult to examine systematically. Teachers who are struggling to implement a new instructional perspective must be aware of the needs inherent in research. Correspondingly, researchers must be aware of the constraints imposed by the school environment. Thus, there is a need for communication, cooperation, and recognition of both perspectives if an innovation is to evolve. As noted in chapter 2, Newman (1990) proposed the concept of a formative experiment, which is an emerging research paradigm that attempts to deal with these issues.

Two general categories of issues that are particularly relevant for computer-based curriculum innovation projects have been identified (see Table 4.1). The first category focuses on implementation issues, those factors that facilitate or hinder the evolution and progress of a curriculum innovation. The second category concerns research issues and project management questions. It includes general concerns about the design and conduct of research and the assessment of the results of the innovation by both practitioners and researchers. It also describes issues that arise concerning the management of an implementation and research project. The categories are not mutually exclusive. The inherent complexity of multipurpose projects such as STACI^N creates an interdependence among all these issues.

IMPLEMENTATION ISSUES

Within the implementation category, five general kinds of issues have been identified that projects must address as a curriculum innovation is established and evolves over time. These issues focus on (a) the district, (b) physical resources, (c) curriculum, (d) teachers, and (e) support matters. A general discussion of each issue is provided, and specific examples from the STACI^N Project are discussed.

District Issues

Motives for Participation. All districts, schools, and teachers have their individual reasons for participating in a curriculum innovation and research project. Similarly, researchers also have specific rationales for selecting and structuring projects to include particular institutions or individuals.

In the case of BUHS, the seeds of systems thinking arose from within the community and the idea commitment to use the approach already made by the four original faculty members. ETS sought an environment in which interesting and informative research could be conducted. BUHS needed the physical and financial support that the STACI Project could provide. Thus, a mutually beneficial project for both practitioners and researchers was conceived and established, although a strong sense of original ownership resided with the school.

TABLE 4.1
Summary of Issues, Cautions, and Lessons

Implementation Issues

District -Level Issues
       Motives for participation
       Administrative support
Necessary Physical Resources
       Appropriateness of hardware and laboratory configurations
       The need for teacher computers
       The need for technical expertise
       Software
Issues Concerning the Curriculum
       Theoretical foundations and introduction into the curriculum
       Topic selection, curriculum integration, and sequencing
       Curriculum issues specific to systems thinking
Teacher-Level Issues
       Changing role of the teacher
       Motivational and individual factors influencing use of the
       curriculum innovation
Support Issues
       Provision for expertise and training
       Supplementary support issues
       STELLA-specific support issues

Project Management and Research Issues

Project Management
       The need to strive toward a balance between research and
       practice
       Management issues
Research Issues
       Goals and support
       Research design issues: Addressing the research objectives
       Research design issues: Impacting on assessment

In California, ETS sought out the schools and initiated the idea for STACI[N]. It is safe to say that each school and district decided to participate for reasons specific to their own situations. There always will be some risks and benefits to incur with any new and innovative effort. Projects must be sufficiently attractive and provide benefits to the participants. However, participants must acknowledge at the inception that they also must assume certain costs and risks.

Motives for participation can vary substantially. By piecing together information from several sources, ETS staff can begin to approximate the different rationales for each site's participation. It was apparent that some schools were intrigued by the promise that the systems approach held for their students, and they were willing to assume the challenge of implementation without remuneration, either in the form of stipends or dedicated computers. The teachers' motivations to participate in these schools were primarily professional. They were interested in their own intellectual development and wanted to enhance their instructional effectiveness. The major enticements were the benefits their students would receive from the expansion of their instructional repertoires.

On the other hand, it was obvious that the incentives for participation for some schools were the computers and money the teachers would receive. In fact, some of the teachers were clearly less interested in the intellectual approach or the potential improvement in instruction that might result from participation. Rather, they saw their participation as simply a way of obtaining a small recompense and a computer that could be used for their own purposes. Although these are entirely legitimate motives, they are not quite forthright and are certainly not commensurate with the project's objectives.

The participation of Sunnyside presents an interesting example of how both external and internal pressure can influence district participation and support. As described in chapter 2 and Appendix A, one dynamic teacher at the school had been working with the systems thinking approach and experiencing remarkable success with very limited support and resources. Both ETS and Apple wanted to find a way for systems thinking to become more fully integrated into his teaching and expanded within the school curriculum. Apple wanted to donate the necessary hardware and ETS was prepared to make limited project resources available. The teachers, students, and school administration were wildly enthusiastic. Initially, the district administration was sceptical about the project. Despite the fact that it would provide numerous resources and a laboratory of computers, the district expressed two reservations. First, they were leary of any project that might make changes in the curriculum, which they had just revised. Second, because of a severe financial crisis they were unwilling to spend any money of their own on the project. In an early discussion with an assistant superintendent to explore Sunnyside's possible participation in the project, she warned, "If we have to spend one penny of district money on your project, forget it!" It was only because of a grassroots effort on the part of students, teachers, and parents that the administration acquiesced. Throughout the course of the project's first year, project participants struggled to establish the worth of systems thinking in the minds of the district administration. Eventually, the district did start to provide some minimal financial support for the project.

Administrative Support. The need for support from superiors to insure an innovation's success is not unique to schools. In all organizations, there are many reasons why senior management support is given or withheld. One contributing factor is the administrators' competence with the innovation. Technology has evolved so rapidly over the last several years that many administrators cannot be as knowledgeable or comfortable with computers as they might wish. Teachers in one school have reported that this was the case with their principal who would not support an endeavor if he did not fully understand it. This became a knowledge gap that created difficulties until responsibility and support for the innovation were delegated to the individuals most knowledgeable and closest to the project. It is precisely why in each school, an experienced teacher has been designated as local project director or project administrator. These individuals serve as facilitators between ETS and school personnel as well as substantive experts. Their leadership and advice are crucial to the success of the project.

In the four school districts represented in the California network, there have been varying degrees of administrative support from the superintendents and the building principals. Most of the superintendents not only have been proponents of the project but also have been extremely helpful in seeking local funding to provide additional support for their schools. These same individuals have been enthusiastic about their district's participation, but allowed those most closely related to the project, the local project directors, and the principals to direct the activity. During the life of this project, Brattleboro has had two superintendents, and both delegated responsibility in a similar manner. One California superintendent spent a day at the first training session to acquaint himself with the approach and provide psychological support for his faculty. He continues to attend the workshops. Another superintendent appears at every training to update himself on his teachers' activities.

The new superintendent at BUHS is such an ardent enthusiast of the project that he has had the teachers demonstrate their systems modules to him personally. He has worked with STELLA on his own to gain a better understanding of the approach. He even has a systems thinking textbook prominently displayed in his office. Even the two superintendents who were initially skeptical have become interested supporters of the project. Only one superintendent showed limited interest in the project. He adopted a hands-off policy, with no visible encouragement or support of any kind. Teachers in his district perceived that disinterest, but in this case it was perceived as a challenge and actually seemed to increase their motivation. Of the new superintendents, three are keenly interested in the project's potential and are actively supporting STACI[N] activities, one has not been in office long enough to make a determination, and another maintains some distance from project activities.

Other administrators at the district level also can influence the ease with which a project functions. One of the California districts has a special projects coordinator who has served as an intermediary and has expedited many administrative matters. This individual has assisted in seeking funding for project activities, coordinated district-wide meetings, and provided other means of support for the district teachers. However, district administrators actually can hinder project operation. One district's assistant superintendent for curriculum was opposed to the project. Another district's assistant superintendent for finance was something less than fully cooperative in facilitating the timely payment of teachers and the replacement of stolen computers, two obligations accepted by the districts and included in the initial contract letters with ETS.

Most of the principals have been extremely interested, enthusiastic, and supportive of the project. One principal attended the entire first week of the initial summer training so that he would be able to understand and converse with his faculty about the project. However, when he realized how much time it would take to understand the perspective fully, he drew back and delegated all responsibility to the local project director. Two principals have appeared at each of the training sessions to lend support and increase their understanding of their teachers' work. One California principal attended all project meetings and has spent a great deal of time in fund-raising efforts on behalf of the project. Her contribution has continued after she retired from the district. This person was an enthusiastic advocate whose interest and concern for the faculty were important factors in providing moral support and assistance for the teachers. Another principal is so enthusiastic that he could assume the title of project cheerleader. He fully supports his teachers and will do almost anything to promote their efforts.

Three other principals have shown levels of interest that span the complete range of the continuum. One supported his faculty, another remained in the background, and a third was perceived by his faculty as actively "uninterested" in the project. In fact, one principal reportedly stated that the only two reasons for allowing the project in his school were to receive the hardware donation and the subsequent positive publicity the school would reap. His style of management was perceived by many faculty as confrontational. Upon this principal's retirement, he was replaced by an individual who was keenly interested in the potential use of technology, fully supported the project, and promoted project activities. Following the announcement of his appointment, the morale of the project faculty changed dramatically to one of optimism and enthusiasm, indicating the extent to which the former principal created a pallor over the project and probably more generally over the school.

The principal who remained in the background preferred to let his faculty work independently on the project. He supported their work and was available for problem resolution. In contrast, teachers at another school perceived that their principal was disinterested. If he even knew that the project existed in his school, he never overtly acknowledged its presence to project staff or, more importantly, to the involved faculty. He did not even attend the introductory project meeting at his school. In this school, the hands-off approach was problematic, for it decreased faculty morale and motivation. These teachers perceived a severe lack of any sort of professional recognition for their project activities. The new principal of this school is one of the most ardent supporters and an active fund raiser. The teachers are appreciative of the newly found administrative support.

Of the eight original principals, only two have occupied the positions throughout the project. Both are supportive of the project's objectives. In fact, one of these suggested that STACI^N convene meetings of the principals to discuss administrative issues surrounding the use of technology. The first principals' meeting was held during the 1992 summer training. Of the remaining six principals, five are active and enthusiastic proponents of STACI^N. They all have been working with their teachers and have shown interest in and support for their teachers. They are actively engaged in fund-raising activities to upgrade the computer laboratories. Only one individual remains at some distance. He knows a good deal about the project, but chooses to remain minimally supportive and distant, a consistent pattern in his management style.

Each administrator has different motives for endorsing the participation of their schools and teachers in projects like STACI^N. There must be some minimal level of administrative support for the curriculum innovation to have a chance to take hold and survive. As noted earlier, the support can take various forms, all of which lend credibility to the project and the teachers' efforts. The absence of any administrative support can seriously hinder and undermine the innovation. For example, a department chairman in one school was on leave when the project was conceived and instituted. Because he was not consulted initially, he provided no support to his teachers regarding the project. When he returned from leave, he actually delayed progress in curriculum development because he felt the project was not of his design and initiation. To provide some chance for an innovation to succeed, there must be substantial administrative support, ranging from the district administrators to the building supervisors and to the chairpersons in whose departments the project resides. Such support can be primarily motivational and symbolic, but other forms of assistance also are needed.

Physical Resources

A second general area of concern is the provision of physical resources and facilities, without which a computer-based curriculum innovation is virtually impossible to implement. These resources include not just hardware, software, and other educational materials, but also the physical space or rooms in which the equipment will be located. Advance planning is critical because such resources generally take longer to obtain than expected. In most schools an immense amount of bureaucratic resistance must be overcome when instituting a project such as STACI^N. Fallback positions are needed when time, monetary, and bureaucratic constraints delay or hinder the implementation of the innovation. Financial constraints are usually the determining factors here, and they ultimately limit what can be done in a project.

Hardware and Laboratory Configurations. Despite the fact that the cost of hardware has decreased significantly over the last several years, the monetary outlay for a critical mass of computers continues to be substantial. Many schools purchased some of the earlier generations of microcomputers, which now have been superseded by faster and more powerful technologies. The machines donated at the earliest stages of the project have rapidly become outdated, even for the project's constrained applications. Districts cannot afford to discard the earlier machines, nor can they upgrade present configurations.

The STACI^N Project has reached the point of hardware obsolescence. As new software products become available from HPS and elsewhere that require more memory, greater storage capacity, color, and full-range animation applications such as QuickTime, the current configurations of hardware become outdated. Software advances are forcing the need for more powerful hardware in order to run the forthcoming systems thinking products. Should the project use existing technology and fall behind what others in systems thinking are doing, or should STACI^N try to remain current and on the cutting edge? Replacing 160 Macintosh computers all at one time is a fundraising nightmare, and not really practical. The project is exploring the creation of a long-range collaborative funding consortium, consisting of public and private resources, to update gradually the hardware. Federal government awards usually prohibit or restrict the purchase of hardware, so other sources must be sought. It is the project's intention to enlist the help of private individuals, local industry, and the school districts. Such fundraising efforts on behalf of the school districts are unusual activities for research organization staff members. One does not learn about such things in research methodology textbooks or graduate-school courses.

As Redfield and Steuck (1991) noted, there are major differences between the equipment researchers use and that which is readily available for school settings. Schools have limited resources and most of the purchases are low-end computers. If a collaborative project between researchers and a school is to work, there is a need for the former to supply or help obtain the requisite equipment. Yet simply providing hardware to a school is not sufficient. Each school district still needs a strategy by which to determine its computing needs and implement those requirements across grade levels and content areas. Technology is changing far too rapidly for schools to keep pace. They must expect that their purchasing decisions already are outdated even as they place their orders. What they must do is match their purchases to specific curriculum and educational objectives and available and projected applications. Primary questions for the acquisition of hardware include the type of computer, the number of computers needed, specific applications, and where the hardware physically will be located.

Decisions about these questions will influence how and to what degree the computers are used effectively (see Becker, 1983, 1984a, 1984b, 1984c). There is no one right answer with respect to how computers should be configured in a school. A laboratory setting in which a classroom set of computers is networked together can be an effective pedagogical approach for some courses and groups of students. Under other circumstances, distributing the computers across classrooms can be a good strategy. The laboratory and distributed strategies also can be combined. Such has been the case at BUHS. This hybrid strategy provided maximum flexibility for computer use. The school had three computers before STACI began. A classroom set of 15 Macintosh Plus computers were donated by Apple Computer, Inc., to allow BUHS to participate in the project. Initially, three computers were maintained in the War and Revolution seminar room. The remainder of the computers resided on transportable carts in the new science wing and moved frequently among classrooms whenever teachers conducted a systems module. Once the teacher finished a module, the machines were moved as needed to the next classroom. The portability of the Macintosh has been a definite advantage at BUHS. However, such a usage strategy required a fairly complex scheduling algorithm, a responsibility maintained by the local project director. Scheduling becomes increasingly complicated as each of the teachers requires more time with the computers and the project expands to include additional teachers.

In Arizona, the computers are distributed among the teachers' classrooms. To date, they have never been amassed in one place at the same time, although they are now considering that possibility. In contrast, all the project schools in California identified one classroom dedicated for the sole purpose of housing the project computers. Dedicated rooms solve some but not all problems. Several issues can be identified that should be noted for all rooms where computers are located, particularly for dedicated laboratories. The first and foremost is security. Schools are not necessarily the most secure institutions. Computers, particularly those as portable as the Macintosh, are easy targets for burglars. The rooms in which the computers are located must be well-secured at all times. Only a few designated individuals should have access. The rooms preferably should not be located on the first floor of a building because this would provide easier access.

Each of the schools has instituted security procedures specific to the needs of their sites. All schools maintain a limited access policy (i.e., only participating teachers have keys to the laboratory). One school even hired a surveillance company. Despite the security system in that school, two computers were stolen from a locked and monitored room. Thieves broke through a first-floor window and easily removed the machines. Although the computers technically belong to ETS, they are on permanent loan to the school. According to contractual arrangements, the onus of replacement fell on the district. However, the assistant superintendent for finance was unaware of this agreement and was unwilling to approve funding for the replacement computers. The computers were stolen in March, 1989, and were not replaced until September, only after a number of rather firm conversations with administrators. The superintendent eventually had to intercede and the replacements arrived just before school opened. The incentive for the schools is to ensure that the laboratories are secure.

Apparently the incentive was not sufficiently high because a second theft occurred in July, 1990, in which three more computers and projection equipment were stolen from the same room. It was only after this theft that the computer laboratory was moved to a more secure second-floor location. Again according to the contract, the district was responsible for replacing the computers. It did not necessarily have to replace the projection equipment, the absence of which would severely limit the effectiveness of the teachers. As noted in Appendix A, the project staff were confronted with an extremely difficult situation. The district was in severe financial difficulties, and the cost of replacement was below the deductible of their theft insurance. The teachers in this school were doing superb work with a challenging student population. The last thing anyone wanted was for the teachers to be punished for the illegal behavior of others. Yet it was important to encourage the district to take greater security measures. Apple offered to replace the computers, with the stipulation that the district had to demonstrate how it had improved security. Apple's generosity was used as leverage to encourage the district to replace the other projection equipment as well. It took over 6 months for the replacement equipment to arrive, which translated into one semester of severely curtailed instructional applications as well as some very frustrated teachers and students.

Other issues arise in physically locating the computers in a school. After a room is selected for the computers several other steps must be taken prior to placing the machines in the laboratory. Provisions need to be made for additional power and surge protection, and temperature and humidity controls should be considered. A laboratory of 15 machines requires more power than is typically supplied to most classrooms. Additional energy to run the machines must be provided. Surge protectors are essential to prevent interruptions or possible damage to the machines. Additionally, computers generate heat and do not function well in overheated or humid conditions. For schools that are located in warm weather environments, provisions should be made to cool the laboratory to protect the machines.

Another problem concerns the use of chalk in the same room as the computers. Chalk dust can do irreparable damage to disk drives. It clogs up the drives and requires costly, untimely, and unnecessary repairs. A simple way to avoid this situation is to have all chalkboards removed from the computer laboratory and replaced with whiteboards. These are safer, cleaner, and will extend the life of the hardware.

An additional problem is the physical setup in the computer classroom (see also Sandholtz, Ringstaff, & Dwyer, 1990). Computers can facilitate small-group learning. There often will be several students huddled around a machine collaborating on a problem. A traditionally designed classroom seating arrangement hinders such potentially important small group learning processes. In one of the STACI[N] Project schools, the computers were spaced on tables around the perimeter of the laboratory, with rows of desks in the center of the room. This arrangement did not provide room for more than one computer user to sit at a machine. A simple solution here was to remove most of the traditional desks and provide a flexible classroom environment in which individual, small-group, and entire class activities could be conducted. Thus, it is important to recognize that some fundamental procedural changes will occur in a classroom due to the use of the computers. If schools are to maximize the use of the technology, they will need to provide new and flexible physical alterations to accommodate the hardware.

A great deal of planning, time, money, and labor goes into retrofitting a room for computer use. Teachers and students may not be aware of the necessary precautions concerning the hardware and security. For example, if a teacher forgets to lock the laboratory, irreparable harm could occur. From the perspective of the administration, dedicating one room as a computer laboratory could be problematic, especially if project teachers do not use the room every period of the day. Space constraints are often severe. However, if computers are to be used effectively and the hardware protected, the dedicated room might be necessary. Unfortunately, in one school, there is such severe crowding that the computer laboratory is also used as a regular classroom. Although the administration acknowledges that this is an ineffective and unsuitable arrangement, there is no other immediate option.

Teacher Computers. Even with a fully equipped school laboratory, it is important to provide teachers with their own dedicated computers so that they do not have to compete with students for the use of the machines. Because a great deal of time, energy, and effort is devoted to curriculum development and revision, the teachers need to have their own computers readily available. The computer should be located in a convenient working environment, at school, home, or wherever the teacher usually works. ETS staff proposed to Apple that each of the 30 California teachers who started in the STACI[N] Project should be provided with a computer dedicated solely to curriculum development. The Arizona teachers also received their own computers. These dedicated teacher machines have greatly facilitated curriculum development. At BUHS, there is sufficient flexibility with the equipment to allow teachers to appropriate a computer for their own use.

Technical Expertise. The need for technical expertise to facilitate effective computer use is another support issue. There are many technical hardware and software problems that arise, and most schools do not have the requisite in-house expertise to deal with such issues as purchasing decisions, computer installation, and maintenance. Ideally, each school or district should have an individual who is sufficiently knowledgeable about these technical issues. The STACI^N Project is fortunate to have several teacher participants who are trained Apple technicians. They have provided invaluable assistance to other teachers. This resource person must be able to comprehend and communicate to the teachers the issues of preventive maintenance and hardware repair. This issue becomes particularly salient when networking and compatibility among different types of computers must be considered. Slightly different versions of hardware and software can create havoc. A seemingly simple task such as networking a laboratory of Macintoshes can become a nightmare if all the necessary hardware and software are not installed properly.

For example, in the STACI^N Project, each laboratory is equipped with 15 Macintosh Plus or SE computers, three ImageWriter II printers, a modem to access AppleLink, and AppleTalk connectors to create a local area network. Slight differences between the Plus and SE computers caused difficulties. In addition, problems occurred when it was discovered that a special board had to be installed in one printer so it could function with both AppleLink and AppleTalk. It took an inordinate amount of time to troubleshoot and resolve this problem. It was exacerbated because the boards in question were on backorder from Apple. Because the computers were donated from Apple, it was not practical to take the printers to an authorized dealer. Once the problem was identified and the boards were delivered, the networks functioned efficiently. Having individuals who understand basic computer operation helps the project function more efficiently.

Like many other areas of the project, having in-house expertise has both advantages and disadvantages. On the positive side, the project staff decided to increase the RAM of all project machines. It would have cost a great deal of money, not to mention time, to have each school arrange for an outside technician to install the chips in their computers. Instead, one of the certified project teachers volunteered to upgrade all the California machines. He spent 2 days doing the installations. Qualified project teachers in Vermont and Arizona performed similar duties at those sites.

On the negative side, districts can take advantage of the expertise. Troubleshooting a problem, then ordering the parts and repairing the hardware can be an extremely time-consuming endeavor, one that takes time away from other activities and is usually not compensated. The district saves money on discounted parts and donated labor, but the teacher ends up contributing many hours of time. One in-house expert has continuously balked at the request for nonproject faculty to use the hardware. The more people who use the equipment, the more repairs will be likely, resulting in a substantial amount of extra, uncompensated work on the part of this teacher. It is certainly worthwhile to try to save money and use existing talent. It is not wise to take advantage of a person's expertise without appropriate recognition or compensation.

Software. Two general issues concerning software are likely to arise in most school-based technology projects. The first is software selection. The second is software compatibility. When a school makes a decision to employ computers to enhance learning, software must be selected that will accomplish particular pedagogical objectives for specific courses and groups of students. Even with educational discounts and site licenses, software is a costly investment. Consequently, decisions should be made with caution and after careful consideration. The selection of course-specific software is likely to be complicated. Selection criteria and methods for evaluating software abound. They are generally of limited quality and utility because every school's needs are specific to their environment.

As with hardware, the software industry is developing new and expanded products at a rapid rate. These products are becoming available with faster and more powerful functions. Old products are becoming obsolete at a frightening rate. Continuity and compatibility across versions of an individual piece of software thus becomes an issue, as does sufficiently powerful hardware (i.e., more memory, additional storage capacity) to drive the updates. When updated versions of a product enter the market, they usually are not fully compatible with earlier releases. If a school has different editions, there will be access issues across updates of the software. If the new version is used to run older programs, the newly acquired power and features may be lost. Thus, consumers are forced to purchase the newer versions of products to maintain compatibility and continuity. Often this can be done at a minimal cost, but it still requires additional awareness and effort on the part of the user. Sometimes it becomes quite costly. What to do with the obsolete editions also frequently becomes an issue. Do you force everyone to make use of the updates or do you let people work at slightly different levels?

Since the summer of 1986 when STACI[N] acquired its first copy of STELLA, there have been well over a half dozen updates, some of which have included minor improvements or corrections of bugs, whereas others have required major hardware changes. Incompatibility across computers did not really become an issue until HPS released STELLAStack, the HyperCard interface, late in 1988. STELLAStack requires a 2.1 version of STELLA. Thus, if the project were to make full use of the capabilities inherent in the HyperCard interface, all the earlier versions of STELLA had to be replaced. Then STELLA II (Richmond & Peterson, 1990) was released with new and more powerful functions, but was not compatible with STELLAStack. In fact, the HPS business plan called for withdrawing support for STELLAStack, much to the displeasure of many STACI[N] teachers. Yet another version that was released in 1992 was several months late in delivery and held up progress in curriculum development throughout the project. It was expected in the early spring but was not delivered until the beginning of the next academic year, too late for the all-important timing of summer vacation curriculum development. An authoring tool due out in 1993 will replace STELLAStack by combining its functions with those of STELLA and adding many other features that require more powerful hardware. As noted earlier, these changes are so substantial that more advanced hardware will be needed to run the new products. The project must upgrade the existing hardware because this new product will not run on the current machines. There is no question that the updates are important and will provide critical enhancements to curriculum development. The STACI[N] Project is providing participating schools with these updates. ETS is working with the schools to seek funding to upgrade the hardware. However, under normal circumstances, the schools would have to assume the responsibility and burden for maintaining the current status of their software and hardware. This can become a time-consuming, costly, and frustrating activity.

Curriculum Issues

The provision of physical resources is a basic necessity and prerequisite to the development of curriculum materials. These physical resources enable the teachers to develop and implement their instructional materials. Some of the most critical areas of concern in implementing a project such as STACI[N] are the decisions that affect curriculum issues. Several caveats described are specific to the use of the systems thinking approach; others are more general.

Theoretical Foundation and Introduction into the Curriculum. Curriculum innovations often create a need for teachers to acquire a new body of knowledge and set of skills. In the case of the systems approach, systems thinking is both an instructional perspective as well as a scientific theory for analytic problem solving. Because of the dual function served by the approach, it has been imperative to provide project teachers with a good working knowledge of systems theory. Such knowledge provides the necessary foundation from which they can develop theoretically sound curriculum materials. These are the same skills and knowledge that they in turn impart to their students when they implement the systems approach in their courses.

It is not yet clear how best to introduce an innovation such as the systems approach into the curriculum. There is no simple answer, for the best strategy will depend on the course content, instructional objectives, and the level of the students. One approach is to teach the basic principles of systems thinking as a separate unit or component of a course. Such an introductory unit will provide the basic principles of systems thinking as a foundation for the infusion of the approach into subsequent classroom activities. The disadvantage of this approach is that students may perceive that the innovation is totally separate from the mainstream of the course and therefore is not to be valued or taken seriously. Systems, in this instance, becomes the focus of instruction rather than an analytic tool to be used to solve problems. When there are no explicit ties to the content, there is the potential of leaving students confused about why they are being taught the systems approach. One is likely to hear questions such as "Why do we have to know this?" or "Will this be on the test?"

An alternative strategy is to introduce systems thinking simply as a problem-solving tool that students can apply to certain learning activities within content areas. Teachers report that this perspective minimizes the risk that the approach will be seen as an independent domain. Instead, it makes the approach an additional analytic tool. Thus, the explicit ties to the curriculum become established as students are provided with a problem-solving tool that they can apply to appropriate tasks. The approach can also be introduced as an all-pervasive theoretical perspective that serves as a foundation for discussing topics within a course. Several project teachers are using this more implicit approach successfully.

Topic Selection, Curriculum Integration, and Sequencing. The issue of what constitutes an appropriate task to which the systems approach can be applied involves careful topic selection. Topics that are most amenable to the systems thinking approach are those that provide the opportunity to examine dynamic phenomena over time. An issue that was detected early in the STACI Project concerned the identification of topics or problems that are not so complex that students with limited domain-specific knowledge could create and comprehend a systems model. The example mentioned in chapter 1 involved the teacher at BUHS who intended to use the systems approach to examine the chemical components of environmental problems such as pollution and acid rain. Most students were able to understand the basic chemistry involved, but the systems models became so complex that they hindered rather than facilitated the acquisition of content knowledge. As this particular teacher gained experience with systems thinking and modeling and began to collaborate with other teachers in the project, they developed a greater appreciation of the need to limit the complexity of modeling applications.

In contrast to the cases where an intricate model is far too complex to facilitate student learning, some problems or topics may be so simple that the application of the systems approach makes things more complicated than necessary. Again, this depends on the students, the subject matter, and educational objectives. An example of how difficult such instructional decisions are was illustrated in the discussion of the acceleration problem in chapter 1. The majority of the students preferred to solve this problem with the systems approach. They reported that they achieved a more concrete, and visual understanding of the problem and its solution. However, there were a few students who elected to solve the problem mathematically, because it was quantitatively so simple that the use of STELLA would have complicated the solution process.

Once appropriate topics have been selected, there is the issue of how best to integrate the systems modules into the curricula while maintaining continuity and establishing explicit ties to the course content. If the modules are not well integrated, students will expect that less importance should be placed on the selected topics. Thus, it is necessary to stress the importance of the concepts being taught with the innovation and make explicit their ties to the curriculum. There also needs to be a strategy by which to sequence the systems topics within the overall curriculum.

These issues become all the more salient because of the limitations placed on instructional time, particularly in advanced high-school courses. Mandated curriculum objectives that teachers must address place constraints on what can and cannot be accomplished within the course of an academic year, making instructional time a cherished commodity. If teachers spend class time "doing systems thinking" rather than integrating the perspective into the courses, there might be a perception that valuable instructional time has been sacrificed in deference to systems thinking. Using the integrated approach, attention to traditional topics is not necessarily sacrificed. Instead learning may actually be enhanced; concepts are approached from a novel and innovative, constructivist, and systemic perspective. As the systems approach becomes better integrated, instructional time should be used more efficiently.

The delicacy of this issue can be illustrated in a scenario observed during the February, 1990, training. ETS staff spoke at length with one of the project teachers who had prepared a model of a generic class of problems taught in advanced placement calculus. He described how the model fit into the curriculum and how it would be used instructionally. He then mentioned that the model would not be introduced until the latter part of May, after the Advanced Placement (AP) Calculus Examination was given. Although this model was directly relevant to the course content, the pressure to adhere to the specified AP course did not easily allow for the implementation of an alternative pedagogical approach. The teacher was worried about how to fit modeling solutions into a teaching schedule that already demanded that too many topics be covered in too short a time span. Although this teacher was convinced that the systems perspective would benefit the students and was enthusiastic about introducing the approach, he could not risk the possible sacrifices to the traditional course structure and content. Several months later, he reported that he is now convinced that systems theory has permeated all his instruction. Although specific models are not always presented, the general philosophy underlies his teaching.

A positive scenario concerning the use of the systems thinking approach in an advanced placement course was related to ETS staff by a biology teacher. He reported that his students were thrilled with systems because the class had spent a substantial amount of time on a model of a particular concept that happened to be a major section of the AP Biology Examination that year. The students who had been exposed to the systems course noted that they had an unusually deep understanding of the phenomenon. Their experience with the systems approach facilitated their performance on the test. Similar comments have been made by other students who have taken advanced placement examinations. They may not know as much vocabulary, but there is a deeper understanding of topics covered with the systems approach.

Another potential issue that relates to the systems thinking approach as well as to other curriculum innovations is applicability to individual differences and specific subpopulations of students. Not all innovations are appropriate for all students, content areas, or grade levels. It is too early to determine the degree to which this analytic problem-solving tool, heretofore used primarily at the college, undergraduate, and postgraduate levels, can be used effectively in a precollege instructional setting. Nor is it known if the approach is effective with students of all ability levels or in specific grades. Individual differences will mediate somewhat the extent to which students will be able to profit from the curriculum innovation. However, anecdotal evidence indicates that students across ability levels seem to benefit from exposure to systems. Project teachers have noted some subtle differences in how students of different abilities respond to the approach. Additional research on the impact on specific subpopulations of students continues. In particular, it is the expressed intent of three schools that systems be used to assist the at-risk students. To that end, several teachers are using the approach with remedial students and report substantial success. The approach is being used successfully with some at-risk student populations in all six high schools.

Curriculum Issues Specific to Systems Thinking. Several issues specific to systems thinking and the STELLA software have surfaced as the approach has been implemented. A first issue relates to the symbol system or manner of representing phenomena within the systems thinking paradigm. As detailed in chapter 3, there are two general forms of problem representation: causal loop and structural diagrams. A causal loop diagram is constructed in terms of cause-and-effect relations among the variables in a system. Interactions among variables are denoted by the use of arrows. When a system becomes complex, it is helpful to think about it in terms of feedback loops or sequences of loops that form causal chains. It is relatively easy to trace patterns of causality among variables with causal loop diagrams. A computer is not required for such representations. Newer versions of

STELLA now include a mapping function that enables users to construct such representations on-line.

To construct a structural diagram, the computer and STELLA usually are employed. As noted in chapter 3, the fundamental concepts on which the notions of systems are based are flow and accumulation, the bases of dynamic behavior. STELLA requires the user to define these variables logically and mathematically. Some students have difficulty defining variables, particularly in mathematical terms. This problem is more frequently encountered when modeling phenomena in social studies or history than in science or mathematics courses. In the former courses, the models usually include variables that are more difficult to express in quantitative terms. Such quantitative reasoning is not usually intuitive. The project continues to monitor carefully how teachers in these disciplines choose to address this fundamental issue. Because causal-loop diagramming does not have to be a computer-based activity, care should be taken to insure that students do not perceive these as less appropriate or sophisticated forms of systems representations. Both causal-loop and structural representations are important concepts in the development of curriculum materials and the construction of systems models. They have separate but interdependent representational and instructional purposes. The task for the teacher is to identify the appropriate use for both strategies, without diminishing the importance of causal-loop diagrams simply because they are off-line activities.

As the project progresses, an increasing amount of off-line systems materials is being developed and implemented. These materials apply systems as an underlying philosophy for activities that are normal parts of the existing curriculum. These off-line activities are generally easy to integrate because they don't involve the scheduling issues that surround the computer laboratory.

Teacher Issues

Many of the issues that have been noted in the course of implementing an innovation either affect or are affected by the teachers, an actual system in action. Teachers are really the critical persons responsible for the success of an innovation. The teacher issues fall into two general categories. First, the implementation of a curriculum innovation changes the role of the teacher in many fundamental ways. Once instituted, these changes are likely to permeate classroom procedures and influence behavior with both computer-based and off-line activities. The second set of issues addresses some of the potential problems that may arise around teacher participation in and commitment to the project.

Changing Roles. Technology-based curriculum innovations such as the systems thinking approach stimulate fundamental changes in the role of the teacher and the processes by which teaching and learning activities occur in classrooms (Mandinach & Cline, 1990; Sandholtz et al., 1990). This section describes how the technology has affected teachers in the STACI^N Project. However, it is informative to discuss perspectives on teacher change related to technology. A conceptual framework into which technology-based teaching activities can be placed is presented in chapter 5. The present discussion focuses on how the use of computers has changed teacher behavior and performance in STACI^N.

There are a number of fundamental changes that occur in computer learning environments that include classroom management, the role definition of the teacher, and professional development. Teacher knowledge is one such issue. There is no doubt that teachers must have the content knowledge requisite for the delivery of both the traditional and the innovative courses. However, they also need to acquire the theoretical and technical foundations that underlie the specific curriculum innovation, in this case, systems thinking. Gaining a working knowledge of system dynamics, the STELLA software, and the Macintosh is substantially different from acquiring information about a specific topic within content areas of expertise or even another instructional approach to traditional disciplines. Systems thinking necessitates a basic understanding of the theoretical foundations on which the approach is predicated. This is not to say that teachers must become systems experts, but rather that they must have a sufficient working knowledge of and experience with the theory and pedagogical approach.

This knowledge acquisition might differ according to how the curriculum innovation is being implemented. Such differences are outlined in chapter 5 where a taxonomy for implementation is presented. In some instances, for example, using causal-loop diagrams, teachers need to acquire an understanding of the approach as an additional instructional technique or curriculum strategy. In other cases, such as building STELLA models, they also must supplement their content-specific knowledge with a more thorough understanding of the computer applications of the systems approach. They must acquire an understanding of the learner-directed pedagogical perspective, general systems theory, and STELLA. Then they must apply that knowledge to preexisting, disciplinary expertise. It is precisely for this reason that the STACI^N Project is providing continuous training and available "on call" consultants to assist the teachers. The ongoing training also serves to encourage continual progress and minimize erosion of teacher knowledge and skills.

ETS staff have observed that some teachers need to feel confident of their mastery of the systems thinking approach to use it effectively. However, basic knowledge and confidence are not sufficient conditions to insure success in implementing the systems approach. The teachers must be willing and able to share control of the classroom and learning process with the students. With traditional methods, teachers most often know what sorts of questions and responses students are likely to pose. Teachers therefore can impart knowledge and exercise control through their disciplinary expertise. This process of the all-knowing teacher controlling the flow of information is what the students at Sunnyside High School refer to as the *funnel effect*. Teachers spew information and facts into funnels attached to students' heads. The students then are expected to regurgitate these facts on tests and other assessment activities. Unfortunately, most students promptly forget the information once they have taken the test. Thus comes the plea from the Sunnyside students to eliminate the funnels.

These observations, with implications for both students and teachers, are not unlike the distinction made by Anderson (1982, 1987) between knowing what and knowing how. Students and teachers may have substantial declarative knowledge (the knowing what), but if they do not use that knowledge through active construction (i.e., procedural knowledge — the knowing how), the learning becomes meaningless. Much current research indicates that meaningful learning and, by analogy, teaching occur when some sort of action is taken on the information; otherwise it remains inert (e.g., Bransford & Vye, 1989; Lesgold, 1988). This perspective is constructivist in the sense that learning requires building knowledge structures within a context where there is active and conscious engagement in the construction of an entity (e.g., Forman & Pufall, 1988; Harel & Papert, 1991; Papert, 1991).

The constructivist perspective reflects the distinction Marshall (1987, 1988, 1992) made between work-oriented and learning-oriented classrooms, and is relevant for the STACI[N] observations. According to Marshall, work-oriented classrooms focus on the teacher's effective transmittal of information. The students' role is to complete the assigned work and be assessed. Such classrooms are static. Teachers in learning-oriented classrooms espouse the constructivist perspective whereby they facilitate the students' active construction of knowledge structures, emphasizing problem solving and understanding. These classrooms are dynamic.

With the systems thinking approach, classroom interactions change substantially. The systems approach is an instructional strategy and problem-solving tool with which students and teachers can interactively explore phenomena. Because there are generally many solution paths with the systems approach, no teacher can anticipate the range of questions and possible solutions that students might suggest. As the innovative technology, both theory and equipment, becomes a more prominent part of the classroom, the teacher no longer serves as the sole expert with absolute mastery and control. Instead, learning becomes more interactive with responsibility shared among teacher and students. The teachers no longer function solely as transmitters of content knowledge. Instead, they become facilitators of learning. As the Cognition and Technology Group at Vanderbilt (1992) noted, a student cannot learn how to construct knowledge simply by being told information. Rather, there is a need for repeated activities that actively engage students over time. Students play a more active role in their own learning. This shift often requires teachers to take risks and develop new instructional strategies to facilitate the learning process. Teachers may not be able to anticipate all students' questions, a threatening event for many individuals. They must relinquish some deeply entrenched pedagogical behaviors. This creates some fundamental shifts in the way classrooms, teachers, and students function. Observations indicate that not all teachers are interested in or capable of exploring and accepting this evolving new role.

Computer-based innovations such as the systems thinking approach also can influence communication patterns among teachers, both within and across departments and schools. When the systems thinking approach is introduced in a school, all teachers involved begin to learn the theory and application and start to integrate it into their courses. The shared experience of learning new material and using the computers creates a basis for dialogue and interaction. New patterns of communication and levels of intensity emerge. Some of this expanded communication takes place within a department to encourage the use of systems thinking in a sequence of courses in successive academic years.

For example, at BUHS, it was anticipated that the foundations of systems thinking could be introduced in a freshmen general science course, thereby facilitating its further use in a sequence of biology, chemistry, and physics courses. The intent was for teachers to collaborate to provide the needed continuity from course to course. Currently BUHS offers a systems course for those students who have had some exposure to the perspective but who seek an independent treatment. Although one project teacher is in charge of the course, the other participants consult and assist in it implementation. Collaboration might simply take the form of informal communication in which two teachers discuss issues involved in implementing the systems approach in and across their courses. More systematic interactions might be observed in a formal departmental curriculum plan or in team-taught, cross-domain classes, such as the science and technology course at BUHS. Again, one teacher is the primary instructor and the others provide input, particularly the department chairman, a former project member.

At Sunnyside, members of the mathematics department, including those who are formal project participants and those working independently, are collaborating to integrate systems into the prealgebra curriculum, a course required for graduation. At least one quarter of the course is taught using the systems approach. Currently Sunnyside is attempting to establish a mathematics–humanities connection by adding an English faculty member to the project. At Mountain View, current project teachers are working to develop and implement a special freshmen-level science course in which systems will be a prominent component. An example of formal cross-disciplinary interaction was observed at BUHS in the War and Revolution seminar. In this course, cross-listed in social studies and mathematics, one class meeting per week was team-taught by the calculus and differential equations instructors.

Other formal interactions have emerged in the California schools. At Westborough there was a working collaborative of social studies and mathematics teachers led by the project director, a mathematician. The lead mathematics teacher brought quantitative expertise to the group, whereas the social scientists provided substantive knowledge. The objective here was to have all seventh-grade students receive an introduction to the principles of systems thinking and STELLA as part of their mathematics course. This introduction also served as a basis for work in social studies courses. At Mountain View, a humanities teacher and a history teacher collaborated on themes that crossed disciplinary boundaries and used systems as the basis for joint instruction. Systems thinking was the foundation for an integrated approach in history, economics, and humanities. Another example has been noted at Hillview where two teachers team-taught an interdisciplinary curriculum that included mathematics, science, literature, and social studies. Systems thinking formed the theoretical base for these integrated courses. The Hillview teachers are collaborating with the Menlo-Atherton High School faculty to provide continuity among courses as students make the transition from the junior to the senior high school. It is likely that none of these collaborations would have been established if the teachers were not participating in the STACI[N] Project.

Informal interactions also cross departmental and school boundaries. It was reported on a number of occasions that students in the science courses or the War and Revolution seminar at BUHS often used their models as topics for essays in English composition classes, thereby exposing teachers in other departments to the notion of systems. This was an unexpected application and satisfying interdisciplinary consequence of implementing the systems approach. Also unexpected has been the formation of a science task force made up of STACI[N] teachers from several schools whose goal is to increase cross-course applications between biology and chemistry. As a result, more chemistry will be presented in biology classes and more biology will be taught in chemistry.

Another form of cross-departmental interaction has been noted in the STACI[N] workshops. Teachers naturally formed disciplinary task forces to enhance collaboration on the development of curriculum materials. Much of this work occurs in small-group settings. However, ETS staff often observe that teachers seek advice or expertise from other task forces whose content areas are relevant to their curriculum modules. For example, the mathematics teachers often are asked to serve as informal consultants on procedures for quantifying parameters in model development. These interactions have carried over into the academic year, when the task force members are working in their own schools. Thus, it is safe to say that one of the unforeseen but positive outcomes of using the systems thinking approach is increased interdisciplinary communication. These patterns of communication cross academic departments, school and district boundaries, as well as the STACI[N] task forces.

Participation and Commitment. A number of motivational issues have been observed to influence how teachers adapt to a curriculum innovation. A first issue concerns the expectations held by the teachers about the innovation and their own performance within the project. A range of expectations has been noted. At one end of the continuum, a few teachers hoped that the systems thinking approach would be a panacea, the answer to all their pedagogical problems. These teachers have been disappointed when their expectations fell short. A few teachers entered the project with a perspective that almost stated, "I dare you to prove that this stuff works." This attitude could become a self-fulfilling prophecy. That is, if they so desired, they could destine their part in the project to failure. One wonders why an individual would enter a project with an overwhelmingly pessimistic outlook. Fortunately, these individuals have gradually left the project, either at their initiation or at the request of ETS staff. Curriculum innovations need a fair test, one that is sufficiently long, well-supported, and staffed with people who will make an effort.

Perhaps the fairest test occurs when the participating teachers show a healthy skepticism yet also are willing to develop curriculum modules and assess their impact on student learning, instructional activities, and classroom processes. In most instances, the STACI[N] Project teachers fall into this middle category. Teachers do need positive attitudes to maintain motivation for their activities. All project participants, whether teachers, researchers, or administrators, must be acutely aware of striking this delicate balance among skepticism, optimism, and reality.

Interrelated issues that correspond closely to teachers' expectations are acceptance of and commitment to the project. In most instances, teachers participate in a project such as STACI[N] because they believe that the curriculum innovation will likely enhance or facilitate student learning. These projects are labor-intensive and require a great deal of commitment on the part of participants, particularly because the benefits are not likely to be manifested in the short run. Nor is progress unidirectional, as teachers experience both successes and failures along the way. One way to reward teachers' accomplishments is through the payment of stipends. As noted in chapter 2, teacher stipends are only a token gesture and partially reward commitment and effort. The amount of money provided, $3,000 per year, by most standards hardly compensates teachers adequately for the amount of work, time, and effort they are likely to devote to the project.

In the course of the systems thinking projects, ETS staff have encountered a few examples of individuals participating for what can be considered inappropriate reasons. The most egregious example was one teacher who made no effort to do any work related to the project. He reportedly never took his assigned computer out of the packing box, a machine that could have been used fruitfully elsewhere. After this teacher acknowledged that he was participating in the project only for the small stipend, he was urged to resign and was replaced with an appropriately interested and focused individual. Unfortunately, the timing of the negotiations was such that the replacement had to wait several months before the next workshop.

Another unfortunate example was the result of one principal's misunderstanding of the project's intent. As mentioned above, ETS permanently loaned each participating school 20 Macintosh computers supplied by the donation from Apple Computer, Inc. Of these, 15 computers were for the laboratory and 5 for exclusive use by the project teachers. It has always been ETS's intention to leave the machines on permanent loan with the schools to be used primarily for the STACI^N Project. If a teacher withdraws from the project or leaves the district, the computer must be reassigned to a replacement teacher. If a suitable replacement is not immediately available, the computer reverts to the laboratory as part of the network of machines. This particular principal did not understand the intention and tried to entice his faculty to participate in the project by promising them personal and permanent ownership of the computers. Unfortunately, a few teachers joined the project expecting that the computers would become their personal property and could even be disposed of as they desired.

ETS discovered the problem only after a teacher in this district announced his intention to take his computer with him upon retirement. Several rather tense, face-to-face meetings between ETS and the teachers were convened to clear up the misperception. There was no doubt that some of the teachers were very disappointed. No one withdrew from the project because of the issue, but it most certainly stretched the limits of diplomacy on the part of all involved parties. Straightforward and frank communication is essential to making a complicated project such as STACI^N work.

Related to level of commitment is the degree to which the teachers are productive and contributing members of the project. Just as level of commitment varies across individuals, so too does level of productivity. The STACI^N Project is set up in such a way that all teachers are equal members of the group and all are expected to collaborate, contribute fully, and therefore operate at roughly equivalent levels of performance. Unfortunately, equal productivity among project participants is virtually impossible. Some teachers spend hours working and produce extensive sets of curriculum materials that are delivered in a timely manner. Other teachers put forth less effort and tardily produce materials limited in both quality and quantity. A very few people are even reluctant to share their work, a basic underlying philosophy of the project.

Another issue concerning commitment to the project has arisen and focuses on activities that are more central to the research than the implementation component of STACI^N. ETS has always maintained that STACI^N is a collaborative effort, not a project administered from Princeton. Most major decisions have been made collectively. It quickly can become a nightmare trying to reach a consensus among all 40 individuals. In the 1991/1992 academic year, the project began to activate its research component. Initially, ETS staff intended to invite any teachers who wished to participate in the research activities. The intent was to enlist only interested teachers. Most teachers expressed the feeling that participation in research should be mandatory for all, a sign of further commitment to project objectives. Almost all teachers decided to engage in research activities for the 1992/1993 academic year. The others have promised to become involved in the near future. The commitment to research technically remains voluntary. However, there is subtle peer pressure within the group of teachers for all-inclusive participation.

Working in collaborative settings such as the STACI^N task forces necessitates shared responsibilities, both intellectually as well as professionally. If one teacher fails to meet a deadline or a commitment, that individual betrays the commitments to other group members. It has become necessary for each task force, school, and ETS to establish minimum standards of performance for all participants. Standards and expectations for project participation have been specified to maintain a level of excellence in performance and productivity, while also maintaining harmony and equivalence among project members.

As the project has progressed, it has become clear that a very small subset of teachers are attempting to "get by" with little or no work and effort. In some instances, there have been valid and extenuating circumstances. For example, one teacher lost his home in the Loma Prieta earthquake of October 17, 1989. Although the project computer was unharmed, he lost most of his possessions. It was difficult for this teacher to participate fully in project and school activities while dealing with more pressing personal issues. In contrast, there were three individuals who were asked to resign from the project because other commitments prevented them from doing an adequate amount of work. Their continued participation in name only was a source of frustration and disappointment to other teachers in their schools. One teacher voluntarily stepped down. The other two teachers were reluctant to resign, thereby necessitating a series of delicate negotiations. Discussions with the teacher, project director, principal, and, ultimately, the superintendent ensued until a mutually agreeable solution was found in each case, one that allowed the teacher to resign gracefully. It has been necessary for ETS staff to be fair but firm arbitrators in these instances, as the integrity of all participants and project must be preserved.

Another set of relevant issues is the teachers' approach to the curriculum innovation, technology, and the project's implementation. A first problem to be considered is that not all teachers are equally willing to use technology in their courses. Computers are attractive, but they also can be threatening. ETS staff have seen teachers' hesitance and reluctance to use computers manifested in a number of ways. Perhaps the most striking example was the one teacher who used a series of peer tutors to mask the fact that he did not even know how to turn on the Macintosh. The most frequent result is foot dragging. Like any task for which there is a certain amount of anxiety, individuals will delay because of concerns or fears. Computer-phobia has been minimized in the STACI^N Project because the Macintosh is so user friendly.

Some of the project teachers did not feel confident working with the computers. They wanted desperately to acquire a working knowledge of the hardware and software, and have spent many hours on their own initiative taking courses or receiving assistance from other project members. Several project directors have been particularly helpful, serving as mentors and in-service instructors to assist their less experienced colleagues. Consequently, these teachers have put forth significant effort and are increasingly able to implement the curriculum innovation effectively.

A slightly different manifestation of the hesitance problem has been observed in teachers who do not have full confidence in their ability to use the computer in their courses. The result is often an application that implements the technology at only a minimal level. In one case a teacher lectured with the computer in the front of the class in a completely teacher-directed, information-transmission manner. The computer simply was used as piece of audio-visual equipment that was never touched by the students. The students never got a chance to work on-line and interact with the computer. They sat passively in their seats, ignoring what the teacher was saying, and were turned off to the concept of systems thinking. The teacher did not know how to integrate the technology into his course to enhance instruction and stimulate student learning. He did know that the students were supposed to be using the computers. Consequently, he developed his lecture technique, which was more of a disservice to the curriculum innovation and to his students.

A final set of teacher-related issues concerns the curriculum innovation's organizational impact on the project teachers. The implementation of a highly visible project in a school definitely influences the content and patterns of interactions between project and nonproject faculty. The nonparticipating faculty may perceive that project teachers are receiving special treatment. In some schools, project teachers may get relieved of undesirable duties such as hall monitoring or lunchroom duty. They may receive stipends, additional privileges, opportunities to travel and interact with colleagues around the country, and have access to a variety of additional resources unavailable to the rest of the faculty. In particular, they may have priority use of a classroom set of computers to which many other faculty members would like access. Project teachers are also the focus of substantial administrative, school board, and perhaps media attention. All these factors can contribute to collegial jealousy. Interdepartmental competition also might appear, producing both positive and negative outcomes. In one school, several departments were stimulated to seek external funding and launch similar projects. There must be a willingness on the part of project and nonproject faculty to create a delicate balance between perks and equity.

Participation in a project such as STACI^N can be a roller coaster of emotions for teachers. It is likely that there will be countless delays and frustrations experienced by the teachers. There also will be many emotional highs, as teachers successfully complete a difficult instructional module or students develop an intricate model. Such peaks and valleys should be anticipated and tolerated as a normal part of a sustained effort toward a worthwhile objective.

Support Issues

To facilitate the implementation and success of a computer-based curriculum innovation, it is critically important to provide a variety of support activities for the teachers. Two general areas have been identified thus far in the STACI^N Project, where the provision of appropriate forms and levels of support can make a substantial difference in a project's outcomes. The first general category is the provision for expertise through training, networks, and communication among participants. The second category consists of specific actions that can be taken to assist the teachers in daily activities and functioning.

Provision for Expertise and Training. As described previously, training teachers in the new instructional perspective is of paramount importance. It is not sufficient simply to provide declarative knowledge or a theoretical understanding of the curriculum innovation. Regularly occurring integrated workshops are needed to provide instruction on the theoretical foundation of the innovation and, more importantly, to provide the opportunity to apply that knowledge in specific curriculum development efforts. The teachers need to experience a training situation that is analogous to what their students will encounter when the innovation is implemented in their classrooms. When the STACI^N teachers first joined the project, almost all were complete novices with STELLA and systems thinking. They acquired a working knowledge in the same manner as would their students.

Because systems thinking curriculum development is a gradual process, it is necessary to provide not just one, but an ongoing series of workshops and support opportunities. Models are rarely complete; there are always changes that can be made to enhance the materials. It has been the project's experience that teachers can progress at a reasonable pace until they are confronted with a problematic theoretical or technical principle, such as how to quantify a variable or use a STELLA built-in function. In a workshop, a trainer can troubleshoot such a problem, allowing the teachers to continue until they encounter another obstacle. If expertise is not readily available, progress is thwarted as the teachers try to troubleshoot on their own. This is precisely why the STACI^N Project has made provisions for various types of expertise. There is the need to maintain a balance with respect to the extent to which teachers become experts in systems theory. On one hand, they need to have enough experience and knowledge to troubleshoot common problems that they and their students will encounter. On the other hand, the teachers are not systems experts nor should they be expected to solve sophisticated theoretical problems. There has been a steady progression in the teachers' level of facility with STELLA. With each workshop comes a decrease in the need for consultation and assistance.

Several peripheral issues relate to training and the provision of expertise. A major problem is the scheduling of training sessions. Teachers' calendars are always full during the academic year, making it almost impossible to schedule a meeting of all project participants. Even trying to arrange weekend workshops and after-school meetings is extremely difficult. Summer workshops are more easily accomplished, but they run the risk of other conflicts such as jobs, summer school, vacations, or differing district schedules. Early scheduling is essential.

The STACI[N] Project has adopted a perspective that attempts to maximize attendance by meeting the scheduling needs of the majority of the participants. This task is made particularly difficult because there are four districts in California, one in Arizona, and one in Vermont. All schools function on slightly different academic calendars for vacations, examinations, and activities. The midyear training sessions have been held in the early part of February, after most of the schools have completed fall term examinations and before winter or spring vacations. After spending substantial time and effort trying to accommodate all schools' and teachers' calendars, a few teachers still have conflicts with the workshops. The 1993 workshop had to be shifted to early March due to conflicts encountered by several schools.

Scheduling the summer workshop entails slightly different constraints. In the first year, the workshop was scheduled for 2 consecutive weeks in the middle of July. Most teachers strongly recommended that subsequent training be held immediately after the school year ends. In the second year, HPS and ETS had a computer conference that conflicted. Thus the training convened on the Thursday following the close of the school year. It ran for 6 consecutive days, with prior understanding that some people might not be able to attend all parts of the workshop. Most teachers attended all or a substantial part of the workshop. However, one teacher failed to attend any of the training sessions and subsequently withdrew from the project. Training sessions for the summers of 1990, 1991, and 1992 were held the first week after school finished and ran for 5 consecutive week days. Future training sessions will follow the same schedules, beginning the first Monday after the last school finishes. Teachers have 1 year of advance notice to arrange their schedules. Attendance at the training workshops is now mandatory for continued participation in the STACI[N] Project.

Another related issue is the replacement and training of new project participants. As outlined in Appendix A, several teachers resigned and were replaced for various reasons. Some teachers have retired or moved to other districts. Further, some teachers resigned on their own volition, and others were asked to withdraw. One teacher took a leave of absence from her district, but specifically requested that she be allowed to continue in her role as local project director. A few other teachers have remained consultants to the project after they left positions in the participating districts.

Thus, the complement of participants continues to change, according to the needs of the teachers and schools. In many cases, these changes and resignations reflect the full set of commitments most teachers juggle. They also reflect the priorities that teachers have to make about their project participation in relation to other activities to which they are committed and their instructional objectives. On the other hand, a few teachers have found, after being trained and attempting initial implementation, that the systems thinking approach was not compatible with their courses or pedagogical style. Continued participation simply was not sufficiently attractive, of interest, or worth the time and effort. Thus, they resigned in favor of replacements who might be better served by their participation.

The changes in personnel make it difficult to maintain continuity within a project, particularly with respect to training new teachers. The combination of ongoing training and consultation with HPS and mentoring within schools helps to circumvent this problem to some extent. In Arizona, the time it has taken for the teachers to learn systems thinking has been minimized in part because of the project director's prior experience with the systems approach and the technical expertise of another participant.

Teachers may be thwarted by a number of obstacles. One such impediment is their initial lack of knowledge of systems thinking and STELLA. HPS staff serve as the project's teacher trainers. They provide expertise during the training sessions and are otherwise available through communication on the AppleLink electronic mail network. Hardware expertise is somewhat more difficult to obtain. The External Research Group at Apple Computer, Inc., who provided the computers, could direct the project to appropriate resources only while the hardware was under the 1-year warranty. ETS has passed on the responsibility for maintenance, security, and hardware problems to the districts. This shift in responsibility creates a host of problems, the first of which is the onus placed on the project director to arrange for timely repairs. Districts usually do not facilitate the logistics or financing of such maintenance.

In a project involving collaboration between a research organization and school districts, there always will be a question about the allocation of responsibility for certain activities between the project management team and district personnel. The acquisition and maintenance of hardware is an example. Undoubtedly, a hardware donation is likely to benefit schools. In the STACI^N Project, the contracts with the districts specify that the equipment is to be used primarily for systems thinking. However, other use is encouraged. The district assumes responsibility for the maintenance and security of the computers. The intent was for this transfer of responsibility to result in more timely and cost-effective maintenance and replacement of the hardware. Unfortunately, as noted earlier, it is difficult for many districts to attain this goal. Repairs and replacements have often been delayed and in many instances have been accomplished only after extensive administrative hassle.

Shifting the responsibility for teacher stipends, however, does present a management dilemma. ETS intends to provide stipends for teachers as long as possible to compensate them for their long hours of work on the project. At some point, resources for stipends likely will not be available because funds to support STACI^N will not last forever. At that time the districts may find the resources to reward the teachers; such is the case in the mentor teacher program in the South San Francisco schools. Alternately, districts may seek funding from local businesses or foundations. Ultimately, the activities that teachers undertake in implementing the curriculum innovation will have to become an integral part of their normal responsibilities that no longer deserve exceptional rewards. It is possible that some teachers may choose to abandon the systems approach. Eventually others will consider the perspective as a part of their regular instructional strategy, and the question of additional compensation will disappear.

When ETS staff interviewed project teachers about the necessity and adequacy of stipends, an interesting range of responses resulted. Not one teacher reported that they participated in the project because of the stipend. Some did, however, comment that the stipend was important symbolically. For example, several teachers mentioned that it helped assuage spouses who expressed concern about the number of hours they were devoting to the project, especially during summer vacation. The teachers could then hold up a check and say, "See, I have been paid for my efforts." Other teachers felt that the amount of the stipend was irrelevant. The fact that there was a stipend instilled a sense of professionalism among many project participants. Other teachers said that they would participate with or without a stipend. Money was not the rationale for their participation.

When asked what would happen if there were no stipends, most teachers were realistic. They thought that most people would continue working with systems; others, by necessity or due to lack of interest, might stop using the approach. Many teachers qualified their predictions. The stipends might make a difference in curriculum development efforts. Without remuneration, they predicted that there would be fewer materials developed. However, they also thought that most people would continue to implement existing materials in their curricula. Most felt that the approach would continue to be used to some extent, regardless of the level of support and resources available.

Supplementary Support Issues. As discussed earlier, the implementation of new instructional methods and curriculum innovations are labor-intensive and demanding efforts. Curriculum development and the subsequent in-class implementations require a significant amount of time over and above that which teachers normally devote to courses taught traditionally. Anything new requires change, and that requires both time and effort. The project teachers and administration readily acknowledged these facts at the inception of STACI^N. However, there are specific support activities that can be undertaken to help alleviate some of the pressures related to the labor-intensive demands of implementing the innovation.

Because of the very nature of a teacher's environment, free or discretionary time is a scarce resource in schools. Teachers' time is restricted in a variety of ways. The daily academic schedule provides very little time for innovation or reflection. Teachers usually are given short preparation periods, but these do not provide the necessary dedicated time and privacy to accomplish substantial work. Students and colleagues constantly fill preparation periods with appointments, conferences, and meetings. After-school and evening hours are generally devoted to grading and preparing for the next day's classes. There is little concentrated time for creative thinking and curriculum development activities.

The issue of time is at the very heart of any innovation project. Lack of time is one of the most pressing issues that teachers face, whether using traditional instructional or computer-based techniques. A teacher's work time is extremely limited and constrained by a host of factors (Morris, 1989). The academic calendar restricts opportunities for teachers to acquire and integrate new techniques into their courses. Implementing curriculum innovations is labor-intensive and demanding. It is unrealistic to expect such innovations to be implemented in a single academic year. They require several years to establish and refine.

One partial solution is to provide release days when teachers can devote uninterrupted, concentrated efforts to the curriculum development. In the STACI^N Project, the weekend and summer training sessions accomplish that objective to some degree. The project provides each teacher with 3 release days per academic year. Teachers can use these days in any way they think will facilitate their project work. They may consult with an expert, collaborate with colleagues, or simply take a day off from school to work in isolation on STACI^N activities. The teachers coordinate their release days with their department chairs, and the STACI^N Project reimburses the districts for substitutes. It is hoped that eventually the districts will provide for additional release time to enable the teachers to work on collaborations, curriculum development, and implementation. Some teachers have taken professional days to work on various aspects of the project, including presentations at professional meetings. Some teachers prefer not to use the release days and instead convene extra task force meetings on weekends to avoid missing a day of school.

PROJECT MANAGEMENT AND RESEARCH ISSUES

The conduct of a multifaceted project such as STACI[N] requires not only expertise in research but also experience in managing an incredibly complex undertaking. In this last section of this chapter, management issues are discussed first. Then issues involved in the conduct of the research component are described, including goal setting, support, design issues, and assessment.

Project Management

Many of the issues discussed earlier also can be considered part of project management. A major function of management is maintaining the delicate balance between the research and practice sides of the project. A second set of issues focuses specifically on activities that influence the curriculum innovation through project management.

The Balance Between Research and Practice. The introduction and implementation of a project that contains a research component brings to a school certain activities and burdens that are not normal tasks and that might interfere with instructional, administrative, or organizational procedures. It must be understood and acknowledged at the inception of a project that the perspectives of researchers and practitioners are different due to the fundamental nature and foci of their respective roles. Practitioners are in the trenches, developing and implementing the curriculum innovation, but at the same time juggling the many other duties of a classroom teacher. In contrast, researchers want to observe and document the processes by which the innovation takes hold and the subsequent outcomes. Such different perspectives provide an opportunity for a potentially fruitful collaboration. This is the case in STACI[N], where teachers are serving as research collaborators. The teachers are at the forefront of implementing new and innovative instructional techniques, and researchers are helping to facilitate and document the effects of that innovation. The researchers bring to the project the resources that make the innovation possible. Both parties provide valuable services to the other. Without the teachers' efforts, there would be no innovation to examine. Without the research, the practitioners would not be able to determine the impact of the innovation.

It is important for researchers and teachers to acknowledge that both benefits and difficulties are likely to arise from the collaboration. It is realistic to expect that conducting research in a constantly changing setting such as a school will impose limitations and demands on both parties. The study of school-based innovations requires a mutually accepted set of rules by which the collaboration is to operate — a balance of needs that is not always easy to maintain. The teachers are likely to be asked to do things that are not part of their normal responsibilities or routine. Researchers must be cautious and sensitive not to make unreasonable requests, such as scheduling events during examinations or setting deadlines in conflict with the many other responsibilities in the normal academic calendar. Teachers also must be sensitive and recognize that to conduct valid and sound research, they must attempt to meet the researchers' requests to the best of their ability, given the many constraints under which they must work. If a funding agency makes reasonable requests for certain data, the schools should attempt to comply.

A by-product of a successful project is the notoriety and attention it generates. Hundreds of requests are made each year to speak with teachers or observe classes. If the project acquiesced to all requests, the teachers would be functioning in a veritable fishbowl, accomplishing less work but spending more time responding to public inquiries. Project staff have attempted to protect the teachers as much as possible by screening inquiries to decrease interference with their classroom work.

Management Issues. The goal for project management is to facilitate and provide the support necessary to introduce, implement, and maintain the curriculum innovation over time. A primary function is to serve as liaison or communication link among the many components of the project. ETS staff play the liaison role among teachers, schools, districts, hardware and software experts, substantive consultants, funding agencies, and the media.

In addition to serving as the facilitator of communication, ETS staff also attempt to maintain a balance within the project and maintain support for all necessary project activities. These points have been elaborated in earlier sections. A project such as STACI^N is a collaborative effort and most decision making resides with all participants. However, it often becomes the ultimate responsibility of the project management staff to make decisions that affect the project as a whole or individual components of the project. In many instances, this takes the form of problem resolution. The management team is really the only entity that has a sufficiently broad picture to be able to weigh all factors. It takes patience, cooperation, coordination, communication, and judgment to achieve acceptable and reasonable decisions that are fair to all participants.

A final management issue, as noted earlier, is the eventual shift in responsibility for project activities to the districts and schools. Longitudinal commitments from funding agencies are rare and always finite. Ultimately, a transfer in responsibility from funding agencies or the research organization to local sources of support for the project must occur. The school districts might assume that responsibility or they might identify local businesses or benefactors who could assist in this mission. Analogous comments can be made about support for other costs that eventually can and should be incurred by the schools. This includes the maintenance of the hardware, updates for the software, and even the cost of an electronic mail account. This shared responsibility means providing the districts with budget estimates with sufficient lead time so that the figures can be included in annual budget negotiations. As one project director expressed, it is critical for the district to understand that the externally provided money eventually will disappear, but the teachers and the need for support will remain. The districts need to make standing commitments to supply some of the resources that must be covered in order to make the project a long-term success.

The fundamental issue here is continuous and longitudinal support by the district. It is remiss for researchers to introduce a curriculum innovation and not see it through. Yet it is also remiss for researchers to abandon the district with the onus of support. A gradual shift of financial responsibility should occur. There must be commitment on the part of the researchers, schools, and districts to assist in every way possible the gradual assumption of the responsibility for continuing support. This is an increasingly difficult task, given the nature of the funding for education.

Research Issues

Goals and Support. One of the most difficult aspects of conducting a curriculum innovation project such as STACI^N is the problem of obtaining funding. The question of whether first to approach funding agencies for resources or to approach schools to solicit their participation is a classic chicken-and-egg dilemma. A project can be well conceptualized when resources are sought from foundations or government agencies, but the case may be stronger if the project has been ongoing for some time and can show results. Yet resources are needed to get a project started. Furthermore, government agency requests for proposals (RFPs) and program announcements usually have specific objectives, which may not fit ongoing projects. The structure of ongoing projects may have to be reorganized to fit those objectives. There may be a match with one aspect or focus but not the project in its entirety. Thus, there is a risk of funding some but not all of an ongoing project and jeopardizing its fundamental structure. Indeed this was the case when ETS secured funding for the STACI^N Project's science and mathematics teachers but not its social studies and humanities participants.

On the other hand, there are risks involved if the schools are solicited for participation prior to obtaining committed funding. The support could be delayed or worse never materialize, thereby creating logistical and ethical problems and diminishing the researcher's credibility with the schools. However, if the schools are selected before seeking funding, the project can be a truly collaborative effort, because the schools have the opportunity to provide input to the project's design and the proposal. They are not simply handed a *fait accompli* and asked to participate.

Support for longitudinal research in education is difficult to obtain and even harder to sustain. Federal administrations change, producing shifts in substantive foci and budgets. For example, when a new U.S. Secretary of Education was appointed some years ago, priorities changed; several RFPs were withdrawn and programs were canceled. Private foundations often change their agendas to incorporate the views of new trustees or senior officers. Peer review in federal funding agencies frequently favors more traditional or less risky approaches to problems. Innovative ideas simply may fall through the cracks and not get funded. The question then becomes the extent to which one reconciles or manipulates a project's objectives to bring them into alignment with the priorities of funding agencies. Too much adjustment may sacrifice the integrity and structure of the project. Insufficient accommodation might result in no funding. A possible but difficult solution is to try to write a proposal that both meets the funding agency's priorities and maintains the project's integrity.

Research Design Issues: Addressing the Research Objectives. General designs to examine the impact of curriculum innovations were discussed in chapter 2. In this section, some of the problems encountered in the design and implementation of research are described. These issues include the basic design, data collection procedures, treatment differences, comparability of data, informed consent, and dissemination of results.

Research designs for multifaceted projects such as STACI and STACI[N] are extremely difficult to develop. In the original STACI Project at BUHS, a quasi-experimental design that allowed for comparisons between naturally occurring control and treatment classes of the same courses was initiated. The fact that science courses formed a natural sequence made the design all the more appealing, because the progress of students as they enrolled in successive science courses could be traced over 3 years.

As mentioned previously, there were many reasons that the design did not yield the anticipated results. First, ETS staff began with the assumption that the project would examine the systems thinking approach's impact on student learning and transfer of knowledge across courses, with less emphasis on related components such as organizational impact and the process of implementation. The initial focus was premature and misdirected. The innovation's impact on learning was examined, assuming that there would be sufficient implementation. Although research in the STACI Project was not as informative as originally anticipated, ETS staff did gather a great deal of data that proved useful in planning the transition from STACI to the STACI[N] Project.

The original project at BUHS was thwarted because there was insufficient treatment or curriculum development, which meant that students were not exposed to a significant amount of materials infused with the systems perspective. The teachers did not really integrate the innovation into existing instruction so that students were able to make explicit ties between the innovation and traditional methods. Thus, the students perceived to some extent that systems activities were not mandatory, valued, or an important part of the curriculum.

In the students' view, systems thinking was separate from science. Systems, for most students, was not seen as a tool to help solve substantive problems. To some degree, the lack of connection escalated in the project's second year when systems concepts were reintroduced rather than reinforced. There are several lessons to be learned from the BUHS experience:

1. Explicit connections between the course content and systems thinking as an analytic tool must be built into the instruction.
2. Planned linkages between courses within a departmental sequence need to be developed to insure sufficient carry-over.
3. Students should be told explicitly about the generic use of models to solve problems and how models will be used in instruction.

The research design did not address the intended initial purposes of the project with sufficient directness and focus. Systems thinking is an analytic technique or problem-solving tool, not a content area whose acquisition can be assessed by a simple pretest/posttest design. Rather, as an analytic tool, it is likely to influence the cognitive processes by which learners approach tasks. This is not to say that systems thinking does not affect knowledge acquisition through the development of effective higher order cognitive processes. Because these processes often take substantial time to emerge, it is likely that the duration of the STACI Project provided an insufficient test of the approach's potentials.

The notion of using pretest/posttest comparisons of control and treatment groups was fundamentally inappropriate. As noted in chapter 2, Cronbach (1963) pointed out that the power of course evaluation is not found in formal comparisons of control and treatment groups' test data where real differences get lost amid the plethora of results. Rather, "it is clearly important to appraise the student's general educational growth, which curriculum developers say is more important than mastery of the specific lessons presented" (p. 674). Cronbach recommended small, well-controlled studies that enable researchers to examine alternate versions of the same course to study and produce results with explanatory value. The three STACI substudies attempted to address this need (Cline, 1989; Mandinach, 1988a, 1988b).

Several other peripheral issues also affect the conduct of projects like STACI[N]. When data are collected from individuals, it is necessary to obtain their prior approval. The two major requirements for this approval are the provisions of confidentiality and informed consent. Maintaining confidentiality can be complicated in schools where many assessment activities are normal and public parts of instructional procedures. One needs to distinguish between activities requested by research and those that are parts of regular instruction.

Obtaining informed consent in school-based research can be very difficult. Because students are minors, the informed consent must come from parents or legal guardians. It is the legal right of every parent or student to choose not to participate in any research project. There are two issues here. First, simply obtaining consent is difficult. ETS staff tried several approaches to obtain consent. The first approach at BUHS was to mail letters of explanation about the project along with letters of consent to be signed by each student's parents. Self-addressed stamped envelopes were enclosed. Less than half the parents returned the letters. However, one parent took the time and effort to return a form with consent withheld, accusing ETS and BUHS of conspiring to make her child into a human guinea pig.

In a second attempt, students were asked to carry home another copy of the letter and form. This attack yielded more returned forms. The youngest students seemed to experience more difficulty remembering to return the signed forms. Teachers tried several times to elicit signed letters from parents. Eventually the project had to contend with a consent rate of 86%. Consent was either withheld or forms were not returned for the remaining 14%. These students then were excluded from the research activities of the project.

The second issue concerning consent focuses on how to deal with students for whom consent was not obtained. In the control classes at BUHS, these students simply did not take the various tests that served as pre/post measures of ability and knowledge. The problem was more complicated in the treatment classes. The systems teachers had to contend with the fact that several students chose not to participate in the curriculum innovation. For the purposes of the STACI Project, a boundary was marked between research and instructional activities. These students did not participate in any activity that was requested solely for research purposes. They were, however, exposed to the curriculum innovation by virtue of the fact that they were assigned randomly to a class in which the treatment was being used. The systems approach was considered a normal part of the instruction of that class.

If assessment of an innovation's impact is to be made, there must be a measurable separation between treatment and control classes. Should teachers in the control classes adopt aspects of the innovation, there is no way to examine differences due to the treatment. Although evidence of this contamination might be considered as a positive sign that the innovation is spreading, it is a nightmare to the researchers. From the teachers' perspective, colleagues who express interest in and begin to use the approach are complimenting the original teachers for their work with the innovation. Although infusion of the innovation distinguishes treatment from control, the course content of the groups should be comparable. Otherwise it would be impossible to assess the innovation's impact if course content were not held constant.

The nature of the intervention also influences the design of research. Students must receive sufficient exposure to the new instructional materials and approach if the innovation is to affect achievement and learning. Thus, teachers must develop and implement sufficiently intensive and extensive modules of the new curriculum for effects to be realized. There is always a danger that research on learning outcomes will be conducted before the new instructional program is sufficiently implemented. It is difficult and inappropriate for researchers to assess an innovation's impact prematurely. However, there is a great deal to be learned from observing the innovation as it evolves and takes hold. This ultimately was what happened in the initial phase of the project. There were two very distinct research foci here: learning outcomes and implementation. Tracing the development and implementation of the innovation provides invaluable information as does the subsequent examination of impact on student learning outcomes, teaching activities, and classroom processes and procedures. Each research focus has a specific objective and time for appropriate application.

Another issue related to a research project is the need to disseminate information about the curriculum innovation and project. Schools must understand that it is the responsibility of the researchers to disseminate such information. However, the researchers must be concerned with protecting the anonymity of project participants. Whenever possible, draft documents should be reviewed by the school personnel, including teachers and administrators. Researchers and teachers must recognize that there is a purpose in providing and disseminating information about projects such as STACI and STACI[N].

As previously mentioned, when a project becomes more visible, inquiries about the project increase. These inquiries are directed to the research team as well as to the school personnel. Frequently the inquiries arrive by letter or telephone and are dispatched by providing information about the curriculum innovation. However, inquirers frequently want to visit the school, observe what is happening, and talk with the teachers. These requests take extra time and place additional demands on the teachers beyond ordinary requests and duties. They also interrupt normal academic activities. The ETS staff attempts to screen these requests, respond to them, and protect the teachers.

Also of concern is the issue of disseminating instructional materials developed in the project. On one side, the project staff wants to promote widespread use of the materials, yet teachers' ownership of the materials must be protected. Ownership is a growing concern as the teachers produce more materials that have potential marketability. As mentioned earlier, there is also the question of who actually owns materials produced under the auspices of the project. Individual teachers should be rewarded for producing good materials, yet much of the work is collaborative in nature. It is frequently the case that many teachers contribute to one curriculum module. There may be one primary author, but several teachers usually have advised and provided input. Thus, ownership becomes murky. Publication is an issue that challenges the project and continues as a point of discussion.

Research Design Issues: Assessment. A final category of research-related issues concerns the design, implementation, and practical constraints of assessing the impact of a curriculum innovation. Assessment is affected by the introduction of an innovation such as the systems thinking approach. Teachers themselves are also the targets of assessment in school settings. They are evaluated by department chairpersons, principals, and supervisors. Thus, the innovation also affects the evaluation of teachers' performance. Finally, the issue of accountability is addressed. Curriculum innovations change teaching and learning activities in fundamental ways. These changes may be diametrically opposed to existing standards of achievement maintained by teachers, schools, states, or the general public. There are many levels of accountability that a curriculum innovation can likely affect.

The systems thinking approach and similar computer-based learning environments create a need for new measurement techniques that can capture the cognitive activity that is ongoing and the product of such environments. These environments shift the focus of assessment from learning outcomes to the processes of learning. Correspondingly, they emphasize procedural as well as declarative knowledge. Procedural skills, such as self-regulation, metacognition, and general problem solving, are assumed to be generalizable across domains. Consequently, traditional measures do not adequately capture the products and processes resultant from the learning environment. Moreover, such systems provide the rationale and opportunity to integrate assessment with instruction and learning. No longer need there be distinctions between testing and teaching. Instead, testing and teaching can become interactive components merged to facilitate more effective and efficient learning activities for individual students.

New technologies are likely to stimulate a number of changes in measurement, particularly because they can facilitate the integration of instruction and learning with assessment. Computer systems enable teachers and researchers to focus not just on learning outcomes, but more critically on the cognitive processes engaged by the student in route to the solutions. Because there is not one exclusive solution path, both instruction and assessment of the results of the instruction are likely to change. This change in focus to a process orientation ultimately capitalizes on the interactive nature of the computer and its data collection and tracking capabilities. Thus, instructional activities can be used for measurement purposes and assessment procedures become embedded within instruction, making classroom activities more informative for both student and teacher.

A critical by-product of these changes is a necessary reformulation of the measurement techniques used to assess learning. Traditional techniques that are targeted to outcomes and single correct answers do not provide sufficiently informative feedback about the learning state of the student. Instead, measures are needed that are grounded in cognitive task analysis techniques, can focus on procedural as well as declarative knowledge, and are process oriented and sensitive to differential learning progress. A number of forward-looking projects have begun to address these issues (see Bunderson, Inouye, & Olsen, 1989; Snow & Mandinach, 1991). Much recent work focuses on a shift to authentic assessment, particularly portfolio development and performance assessment. Technology and new assessment techniques provide vehicles for reformulation of classroom processes and procedures.

A corollary of assessment is the accountability issue, which takes many forms in school settings. Schools are concerned that teachers and students meet the achievement standards mandated by various external sources. Achievement standards can be determined by the teachers or by department chairpersons in accordance with standards recommended by professional organizations. District, county, state, and national standards also must be met. These standards are reflected in large testing programs as well as in specifically prescribed curriculum objectives that must be met in individual classes. These recommended or mandated standards are likely to constrain the introduction of a curriculum innovation just as the innovation is likely to affect the degree to which those standards might be achieved.

Standardized test performance may be affected by the introduction of a curriculum innovation, at least in its early phases. As teachers experiment with how best to implement the new approach, they might sacrifice some valuable instructional time that normally could be used to teach content-specific knowledge on which the tests focus. Instructional time away from the objectives of a test might translate into lower test scores. As teachers become more efficient in their use of the innovation, this possible outcome should diminish and eventually disappear.

There is a very real tradeoff here. To some extent, teachers must teach to the test because the public demands to see results. There is little room in the already crammed teachers' curriculum objectives to ask that more be added to their courses. There simply is not sufficient time in school. To ask teachers to implement an innovation places many constraints and additional demands on them that may imperil their achievement of the objectives. On the other hand, the curriculum innovation may assist in the acquisition of long-term educational objectives that are not readily assessed on traditional paper-and-pencil, multiple-choice, standardized tests. Recall the scenario about the calculus teacher's dilemma with the advanced placement examination. However, also recall the promising outcomes from the AP Biology Examination.

Two other ways in which the introduction of a curriculum innovation might affect standard measurement practices are the teachers' assessments of students' progress and the administrators' or supervisors' evaluations of teachers' performance. As already discussed, the very nature of assessment procedures is likely to change because of the shift in focus of learning to a process orientation rather than simply an emphasis on outcomes. Assessment procedures and the actual methods by which data are collected also will change because of the increased capabilities new technologies make available to both researchers and teachers. The same technology that enables the researcher to study a learner's progress will enable teachers to conduct their own assessment of students' performance. The fact that instruction and assessment can be intimately linked is likely to change how teachers function in their classrooms and approach the concept of student evaluation.

Teachers also must be wary of how the innovation and its accompanying capabilities might affect the traditional assessment of students. The shift in emphasis to more long-term educational objectives, not just the more easily quantifiable content knowledge, will influence in-class testing procedures, learning progress, and comparisons to other classes that are taught traditionally. The potential initial trade-off between short-term gains and long-term benefits must be acknowledged and considered when planning student assessment within new learning environments. Authentic assessment such as portfolio collection and performance-based techniques may become the preferred methodology.

Similarly, administrators and supervisors must alter some of their procedures for observing and evaluating teachers participating in a curriculum innovation project. These teachers will use many pedagogical procedures that may not occur in a traditional classroom because of the fundamental changes in classroom processes and the teacher's role that result from the innovation. Thus, the evaluation of participating teachers must accommodate the changes in order to recognize their hard work and commitments to the implementation of the new approach.

The issue of teacher evaluation becomes all the more critical if there are young, untenured teachers among the project participants for whom the curriculum innovation could actually imperil their careers if misperceived and not evaluated properly. Such young teachers should be recognized for their efforts and altered evaluation criteria used on their behalf. The STACI[N] Project had several such new teachers for whom evaluations have occurred. In most cases, the administrators and supervisors recognized their achievements and they were evaluated appropriately. The ETS project staff worried about a few young, untenured teachers who initially expressed concerns that their participation in STACI[N] might have a possible negative impact on their tenure decisions and careers. These fears ultimately were eliminated by the reassurances of senior district administrators. Their careers are flourishing and they have blossomed under the auspices of the project.

SUMMARY

It is clear from the earlier remarks that the introduction and implementation of a curriculum innovation such as the systems thinking approach is a complex and labor-intensive enterprise for researchers and teachers alike. It takes commitment, sufficient resources, and cooperation from all participants in order to give a project a reasonable chance to succeed. The task is not easy, as participants vacillate between the peaks of elation and the depths of frustration. Participants need to be convinced of the curriculum innovation's value and the worth of their participation.

There have been and will continue to be many unexpected problems and issues that will be encountered as implementation occurs. Some are relatively trivial and easily handled. Others might threaten the project's continuation. It takes concerted efforts and collaborative problem solutions to rectify many of the these complicated issues. There are also many unanticipated benefits and advantages to participation in a project such as STACI^N.

Many problems and many successes have been experienced in the brief history of the STACI Projects. No problem has been so difficult that it could not be surmounted with the appropriate focus and effort. As researchers, ETS staff must maintain an unbiased perspective concerning the promotion of systems thinking, the GUI microcomputer, and modeling software. These components are the tools and foci of inquiry. However, their potentials to influence curriculum development, instructional strategies, and the processes by which learning and teaching occur are becoming increasingly apparent.

Conducting a project such as STACI^N necessitates fundamental role changes for researchers. This project is both a demonstration of the implementation process and a research project. Researchers in dual-purpose projects can not function simply as impartial and objective observers. Instead, they also must function as facilitators of and collaborators in the implementation process. Although this role change challenges some assumptions about traditional program evaluation, it opens infinite possibilities for rewarding and fruitful collaborations between schools and research organizations such as ETS. Such has been the case in the STACI^N Project.

5
Technology and Patterns of Teacher Adaptation

This chapter describes a theoretical perspective in which teacher performance and classroom procedures in computer-based settings can be observed and compared. The perspective can be used to classify the different modes of adaptation that teachers use as they implement technological curriculum innovations in their classrooms. The chapter uses as an example the systems thinking approach as implemented in the STACI[N] Project.

A conceptual matrix is proposed with two explicit dimensions. The first dimension in the matrix corresponds to teachers' level of proficiency with the technology, both in the sense of expertise with computers as well as the pedagogical processes required to support computer use. A developmental continuum of four stages is proposed, but the progression is not expected to be uniform. The second dimension corresponds to the type of application with the particular piece of software. In this case the STELLA simulation-modeling package is used as an example. Four categories of application describe how teachers use systems thinking and STELLA in their courses. Applications depend on course content, subject area, level of student competence, and educational objectives. On this dimension a developmental continuum in not implied.

The proposed conceptual matrix is based on the assumption that technology stimulates changes in the role of the teacher, classroom procedures, and more generally in teaching and learning activities. Before presenting the matrix, some of the research findings on technology's impact on teacher behavior are described. The matrix then is delineated. Finally, vignettes of selected teachers who have been classified within the matrix are presented.

CHANGING ROLE OF THE TEACHER

Curriculum innovations are likely to provide the impetus for a number of fundamental changes in the role of the teacher and the processes by which teaching and learning activities occur in classrooms. Once instituted, these changes are likely to permeate classroom procedures and influence behavior both with computer-based and off-line activities. Research findings are described from the STACI[N] (Mandinach & Cline, 1992) and two complementary projects, the recent survey of teachers completed by the Center for Technology in Education (CTE) (Hadley & Sheingold, 1993; Sheingold & Hadley, 1990), and the innovation and research projects of Apple Classrooms of Tomorrow (ACOT) (Dwyer, Ringstaff, & Sandholtz, 1991; Sandholtz et al., 1990).

Chapter 5

The Systems Thinking Approach

Changes affect classroom management, the role definition of the teacher, and how that role is executed. Teachers must have sufficient content knowledge for both traditional and innovative courses. However, with systems thinking, they also need to gain knowledge about its theoretical foundations, an understanding that is fundamentally different from declarative knowledge acquisition in traditional disciplines. The teachers need not become systems experts, rather they must have a sufficient working knowledge of and experience with the theory and the learner-directed pedagogical approach to implement it effectively.

The extent of knowledge acquisition might differ depending on how systems thinking is implemented. For example, in using causal-loop diagrams, teachers might be more reliant on off-line materials and less influenced by the underlying mathematics of STELLA. In contrast, when building STELLA models, teachers also must supplement their content-specific knowledge with a more thorough understanding of STELLA, and then apply that knowledge to preexisting, disciplinary expertise.

Observations indicate that some teachers need to be completely knowledgeable about the content area and feel confident of their mastery of the systems thinking approach in order to implement it effectively. These are necessary but not sufficient conditions to insure success in implementing the systems approach. As already mentioned, the teachers must be willing and able to share control of the classroom and learning process with the students. Using traditional methods, teachers can often anticipate the sorts of questions and responses students are likely to pose. Therefore, teachers' disciplinary expertise is an important instructional and classroom management tool.

The systems thinking approach changes these patterns of interactions substantially. As noted, there are generally many solution paths with the systems approach. It would be impossible for the teacher to anticipate all possible questions and alternate solutions that students might generate. With the increasing prominence of the technology, the teacher no longer is the information transmitter who functions with absolute mastery and control of content knowledge and instructional procedures. Learning becomes the responsibility of both teachers and students, with teachers functioning as facilitators of learning and students as more active participants in the classroom. These changes require teachers to relinquish deeply entrenched pedagogical behaviors, thus creating fundamental shifts in the way classrooms, teachers, and students function. Experience in the STACI[N] Project indicates that not all teachers are capable of or willing to explore and accept this evolving new role.

Center for Technology in Education Survey

Sheingold and Hadley (1990) conducted a survey of teachers who were attempting to integrate technology into their curricula. They compiled a list of over 600 public school teachers, Grade 4 through Grade 12, who made substantial use of computers in their classes. Over 80% of the respondents reported that the use of computers has changed how they conduct their classes. The authors reported three major areas in which the changes occur. The first area focuses on teachers' expectations of student performance. The teachers reported that they expect more from their students, in part because computers enable them to present materials of greater complexity. Such complexity can be seen in the emphasis on the use of technology to promote the acquisition of higher order thinking skills, as well as content-specific knowledge.

A second area of change involves individualization. Technology allows for more personalized work and greater attention to individual students. The teachers spend less time in lectures or whole-class activities and more time with small groups or individuals. However, such change can create problems in the classroom. As reported by the STACI[N] teachers, such individualization creates certain pedagogical difficulties in an environment in which teachers serve as sole facilitators to 15 or more computer stations. One STACI[N] teacher drew a parallel to a bee pollinating flowers. The teacher's role in this environment is to move from computer to computer troubleshooting students' problems just as a bee flies from flower to flower. It is a labor-intensive process in which teachers express the need for clones to assist in the individualization of instruction.

The third area of change focuses on the shift in the classroom from a teacher-directed to a student-centered environment. Classroom activities become more focused on projects rather than lectures. Students often work independently and in small groups. The teacher's role here becomes one of a coach or facilitator rather than a dispenser of information. To achieve this form of interaction, teachers report that they must devote considerable time learning how to function in this manner as it is different from traditional forms of pedagogy. Sheingold and Hadley reported that on average, teachers require 5 to 6 years of experience before they feel comfortable with the technology. Many of the survey's respondents reported that the integration of technology into their courses has caused them to teach differently and more effectively.

ACOT Findings

The second, complementary implementation and research activity is ACOT, a project in which many classrooms are thoroughly infused with technology to create a multimedia environment (i.e., computers, CD-ROM, videotape players, laser disks, scanners, modems, etc.) (Dwyer et al., 1991). The ACOT

Project is completely supported by Apple Computer, Inc., and managed by Apple employees. ACOT sites are provided with home computers for every teacher and student. However it is important to note that because ACOT sites are unique technology-based learning environments, the results are likely to have a more limited range of generalizability.

Dwyer and colleagues reported that many factors contribute to or impede a smooth transition to technology-based curricula. A first factor is teacher beliefs. The authors reported that ACOT teachers expected that technology would help them become more effective and efficient. They did not however anticipate that their pedagogy would change. They mention three pervasive shifts: (a) to a child-centered approach, (b) to a collaborative environment, and (c) to an active orientation. One of the most pressing impediments encountered by ACOT teachers is the "inflexibility" of the school environment. As was mentioned in earlier chapters, much of this inflexibility emanates from the pressure toward accountability. ACOT teachers, and educators in general, who are trying to innovate with or without technology, run the risk of pursuing long-term objectives that are counter to existing local, state, and national standards. They must struggle against these pressures and be committed in their pursuit of the innovation's goals. Commitment on the part of the teachers is a necessary but not sufficient condition for organizational change to occur. Cooperation on the part of administrators who are willing to provide support for the innovation is also needed.

The ACOT staff also reported that support can come in a variety of forms and is dependent on the phase of technology's implementation (see Dwyer et al., 1991). For example, during the early phases, it is important to provide hardware and software, requisite training, and maintenance of the technology. As technology becomes more deeply embedded, there is a need for the development of flexible scheduling, instructional strategies, and opportunities for further training. At the most advanced phases, support is necessary to acknowledge the need for alternate assessment strategies, instructional procedures such as team teaching, and professional development activities such as publishing, mentoring, and attending conferences.

Sandholtz and colleagues (1990) used their experiences with ACOT to outline a developmental scheme for categorizing the progression toward expertise in technology-based classroom management. They described three stages through which teachers pass as they implement technology in their curricula (see Table 5.1). The first is the *survival stage* in which the teachers struggle against the technology while attempting to maintain traditional classroom practices. They are overcome by the barrage of technical, physical, and classroom management problems that assail them and do not have the ability or experience either to anticipate or resolve the problems. Physical problems include those that were mentioned in chapter 4 such as room configurations, chalk dust, and cooling. Technical issues

TABLE 5.1
Teaching Activities Across Stages of Proficiency with Technology

SURVIVAL STAGE
Struggle with technology
Assailed by problems
Status quo in classrooms
Cannot anticipate problems
Teacher-directed
Unrealistic expectations
Management problems
Chaos

MASTERY STAGE
Developing coping strategies
Increased tolerance
New forms of interactions
Increased technical competence
Increased experience and confidence
More engagement

IMPACT STAGE
Infused technology
New working relationships and structure
Learner-centered
Teachers as facilitators of learning
Less threatened by technology
Technology enhanced curriculum coverage

include delays in equipment arrivals and repairs. From the standpoint of management, the authors highlight that the introduction of computers with most students working in small groups of two or three substantially increases the levels of noise and movement in the classroom. To most traditional teachers, a computer laboratory filled with actively engaged students looks like chaos. However, with experience the teacher will come to recognize that this usually is productive learning activity. Another issue that Sandholtz and colleagues raise is that students can create new forms of cheating with the introduction of technology. Teachers often cannot assign individual responsibility for group work. Of course, some novel cheating schemes can be expected. However, what may appear to be cheating to an inexperienced computer-using teacher is usually collaborative and productive small-group work products.

The second phase is the *mastery stage* in which teachers begin to develop strategies for coping with the problems they encountered during the previous stage. They become more tolerant of the newly created forms of classroom interactions and the environment more generally. With experience there is a corresponding increase in the teachers' level of confidence in their abilities to function effectively within the new classroom structure. The teachers become more technically competent and are at least able to avoid some of the earlier hardware and software problems. Similarly, classroom management creates an environment in which there is less or different student disciplinary problems. Students are more engaged in the instructional activities.

In the *impact stage* technology has become increasingly infused into classroom management activities and instructional procedures. Teachers are less threatened by the technology and realize that some students might be more knowledgeable than they about the computers, thus creating a different set of working relationships in the classroom. Instruction becomes more learner centered, with students serving as peer tutors. Teachers are no longer simply the dispensers of knowledge and sole experts in the classroom.

However, it is important to note, both from the ACOT and STACI[N] experiences, that not all teachers are capable of such role redefinitions, nor is the progression across stages uniform. Change comes slowly with regression to safe and more traditional procedures quite prevalent, thus necessitating a longitudinal approach to the application and examination of these deeply entrenched pedagogical behaviors.

CONCEPTUAL MATRIX FOR TECHNOLOGICAL APPLICATIONS

The Proficiency Dimension

Findings from STACI[N], CTE, and ACOT form the foundation for the proposed matrix for the use of technological applications. In particular, one dimension of the matrix is based on ACOT's three stages of survival, mastery, and impact. This dimension is termed the teachers' level of proficiency with the technology. ACOT's three categories are used, but a fourth is added which has been termed the *innovation stage*. The innovation stage is thought to occur when a teacher uses technology to move beyond the mandated scope of the curriculum toward a complete restructuring of teaching and learning activities. Technology forms the theoretical and methodological foundations for changing foci of course content, pedagogical processes and procedures, and instructional strategies.

Table 5.2 delineates across the four categories of the proficiency dimension the activities that occur in technology-based and systems-based classrooms. The first column lists activities identified from these studies that relate to general technology applications. These activities are also relevant when the systems thinking approach is implemented. The second column outlines activities specific to the systems approach.

The technology-based activities at the different ACOT stages have been described earlier. Attention here is focused on how the systems thinking activities are manifested across levels of proficiency. At the survival stage, teachers struggle to determine how to use the

TABLE 5.2

Teaching Activities Across Stages of Proficiency with Technology and Systems Thinking

TECHNOLOGY	SYSTEMS THINKING

SURVIVAL STAGE

Struggle with technology	Struggle to use systems
Assailed by problems	thinking
Status quo in classrooms	Need for constant hand-
Cannot anticipate problems	holding
Teacher-directed	Trial-and-error model
Unrealistic expectations	construction
Management problems	Stop and wait for expert
Chaos	assistance
	Textbook search for topics

MASTERY STAGE

Developing coping strategies	Less reliance on systems
Increased tolerance	experts
New forms of interactions	Sounder curriculum modules
Increased technical competence	Increased ability to trouble-
Increased experience and confidence	shoot student problems
More engagement	Increased use of modeling

IMPACT STAGE

Infused technology	No more funnels
New working relationships	Systems-infused curriculum
and structure	More varied use of systems
Learner-centered	applications
Teachers as facilitators of	
learning	
Less threatened by technology	
Technology enhanced curriculum	
coverage	

INNOVATION STAGE

Restructuring of curriculum	Curriculum revision based
and learning activities	on systems thinking

systems approach just as they struggle with the technology more generally. There is a constant need for hand holding, both for technical as well as systems thinking issues. Solutions to problems are sought externally. The teachers' systems model construction is a trial-and-error process. They work until they get stuck and then stop, waiting for an expert to troubleshoot and solve the problem. The teachers often remain stuck until a solution is given to them. They do not have sufficient knowledge to solve the problems on their own. Furthermore, they have difficulty identifying topics that are appropriate for the systems thinking approach. As the teachers look for applications that are amenable to systems, they frequently search their textbooks for problems to which systems can be applied. They have not yet developed a sense of what to look for, but they continue to search resource materials for possible applications. There is no typology for classifying or identifying models, topics, or items that are amenable to systems thinking.

At the mastery stage, teachers show less reliance on systems experts. They are better able to troubleshoot problems with their own models as well as those of their students. Teachers can readily identify parts of the curriculum to which systems can be applied. Their instructional modules are sounder and more complete, containing not just systems models but also ancillary materials. An increasing amount of systems thinking occurs in the classroom.

The impact stage reflects curricula that are infused with varied applications of systems thinking. These applications do not necessarily rely on on-line activities. Instead, there are portions of the curriculum that are based implicitly on systems theory and underlie the instruction, as well as those that are obviously systems-based. It is at the impact stage that teachers are less concerned with the accountability issues that usually accompany the implementation of a curriculum innovation. That is, they recognize that the use of the innovation will enhance successful achievement of educational objectives and standards. The students at the high school in Tucson term this the "no more funnels" phenomenon. These students are rejecting the system of education that uses teachers as the dispensers of knowledge, dumping information into students' heads for the purpose of regurgitating those facts onto tests, after which they promptly forget what has been "learned." Instead, instruction concentrates on the process of learning for which teachers serve as facilitators.

The final stage is *innovation*. This occurs when the entire curriculum is revised, using systems thinking as the underlying theoretical philosophy. Unlike the impact stage, where there remains a balance between systems- and nonsystems-based activities, the innovation stage consists of a transformed and all-pervasive systems learning environment. However, systems applications consist both of on-line and off-line activities. Many of the traditional classroom procedures and processes become transformed due to the introduction of the curriculum innovation. Instruction is constructivist and learner directed.

The Systems Applications Dimension

The second dimension of the matrix focuses on how the innovation actually is applied. It emphasizes what is done with a particular piece of software in a classroom setting. In the case of the STACIN Project, the focus is on specific forms of systems thinking implementations in the curricula. As mentioned in chapters 2 and 3, the technology of interest here is the systems thinking approach comprised of three elements: system dynamics, the STELLA software, and the GUI of the Macintosh computer. As with the stages of technology use, four categories of systems applications are identified. However, unlike the technology continuum, a developmental sequence is not implied (see Fig. 5.1). The categories include *parameter manipulation, constrained modeling, epitome modeling,* and *learning environments.* These categories reflect different ways of using the systems thinking approach. They are differentially appropriate depending on course content, subject area, level of student competence, and educational objectives. However, the application categories do differ with respect to predicted levels of cognitive complexity and anticipated outcomes. Cognitive complexity increases across the first three categories. Given their diverse natures, learning environments are more difficult to categorize with respect to cognitive complexity. There is a wide variety of possible applications that can be categorized as learning environments.

FIG. 5.1. Modes of teacher adaptation.

Systems Thinking Applications

		Parameter Manipulation	Constrained Modeling	Epitome Modeling	Learning Environment
	Survival				
Levels of Technology Proficiency	Mastery				
	Impact				
	Innovation				

The basis of the systems thinking approach is the creation and examination of models of complex phenomena over simulated time. Such phenomena are likely to contain many variables that are interconnected and form feedback loops. Rarely are they simple isolated events. Feedback loops imply circular causality rather than linear causality. Systems-based instruction can occur on-line, using STELLA, or off-line, using a variety of alternate activities. Teachers can develop models and then structure activities so that students explore the phenomena with varying degrees of assistance. Alternately, students can develop their own models.

The first category of systems application is parameter manipulation. Teachers generally construct a systems model and develop fairly structured worksheets as ancillary materials. The worksheets can vary in the degree to which they focus the students' examination of the model. In the most structured case, the worksheets step the student through every phase of the model, each variable, their parameterization, and the model's operation. These activities generally require students to manipulate the numerical parameters that define the variables and observe the effects on the system as the model is run dynamically over time. Students are asked to form hypotheses, run the model to test them, and revise the hypotheses according to test results. The teacher's role is to develop the systems model and ancillary materials that form a complete curriculum module. In most instances, the teacher will present the model to a class using a computer projection system, then let the students work through the ancillary materials in small, collaborative groups at each computer station. The teacher serves as a resource person and troubleshooter, moving from one group to another as students encounter difficulties. These problems could be substantive, systemic, or operational with respect to STELLA or the Macintosh. These exercises require students to apply the systems approach to existing substantive knowledge. Topics on which parameter manipulation applications have been developed include enzyme balances, groundwater supply cycles, ozone depletion, and the greenhouse effect.

The second category is called constrained modeling. Large systems models containing hundreds of variables, interactions, and equations are rarely useful for instructional purposes at the precollege level. Instead, these students need models that contain a manageable and limited number of variables whose interactions can be examined systematically. These instructional models are constrained, in that the number of variables are limited by the phenomenon under examination. Such constrained models are often found in textbook problems. Teachers generally assign such a problem to the students, who in turn construct a model based on the problem's specifications. Depending on how the teacher structures the activity, students may solve the problem using traditional methods, they may choose to construct a systems model, or they may do both. For example, the exercises found in most high school physics textbooks such as the acceleration problem described in chapter 1, are frequently used for constrained modeling. Students who used constrained modeling gained a deeper understanding of the phenomena than those who solved the problems using traditional methods (Mandinach, 1988b).

A cross between parameter manipulation and constrained modeling also has been observed but does not form a separate category of the dimension. This form of application is termed *structural manipulation*. Instead of changing numerical parameters, students are asked to manipulate structural components of a model. They may be asked to add or delete variables or change the interrelations among variables. This task is somewhat more complex than simply altering the numbers that define the variables. It requires students to have a more advanced understanding of modeling and the nature of interrelationships among variables within a system. Teachers generally structure this activity as they would parameter manipulation. However, there are cases when students construct a model and perform such structural manipulations. Both structural and parameter manipulation are forms of model manipulation, a step preliminary to more complex model construction.

The third category of the application dimension is called epitome modeling. Here complex systems with many variables are examined through model construction. The model simulates the essence or epitome of the phenomenon to be examined. Examples of epitome modeling in the STACI[N] Project have included acid rain, drug interdiction, and various historical conflicts, revolutions, and wars. In almost all instances, students develop original models, using primary research as the foundation for their understanding of the phenomena. Teachers serve as coaches, resource persons, and facilitators of the modeling process. They may guide the students to appropriate references relating to substantive issues, and they may also provide troubleshooting expertise on systems thinking and the use of STELLA. But the cognitive work of model construction is done by the students as they accumulate information, begin to understand the interrelatedness of the variables within the system, and construct a representation of those interactions.

The fourth and final category is learning environment. Here systems thinking becomes the philosophical foundation for all instructional activities. A learning environment may take many different forms, and teachers' roles will differ accordingly. Activities here do not necessarily require the use of the hardware and software. In fact, many of the learning environments observed in STACI[N] involve off-line activities. For example, one mathematics teacher begins his class with a complex theoretical question that is systems based. The teacher's instructional objective is for the students to understand the mathematical concepts within the more general context of the world, using systems thinking to provide the interconnectedness. Two middle-school teachers collaboratively have created several multiweek units on various topics, including wolves, owls, the environment (see Crawford & Molder, 1992a, 1992b). They used many different, cross-disciplinary activities that are systems based to triangulate on the subject. An on-line example of a learning environment has been created in chemistry. One teacher created a large computer database on the periodic table to serve as a multipurpose reference tool. There are several systems-based tools within the database, including models for many elements.

Patterns Across the Matrix

Figure 5.2 presents the matrix with the distribution of the project teachers across the two dimensions: level of proficiency and form of application. As can be seen in Fig. 5.2, the 35 teachers represented in the matrix are distributed unevenly across the proficiency dimension. Four teachers were classified as at the innovation stage, 12 at the impact stage, 9 at the mastery stage, 4 are borderline mastery and survival, 4 at the survival stage, and 2 who did not even approach the survival stage.

FIG. 5.2. Distribution of STACI^N teachers across the conceptual matrix.

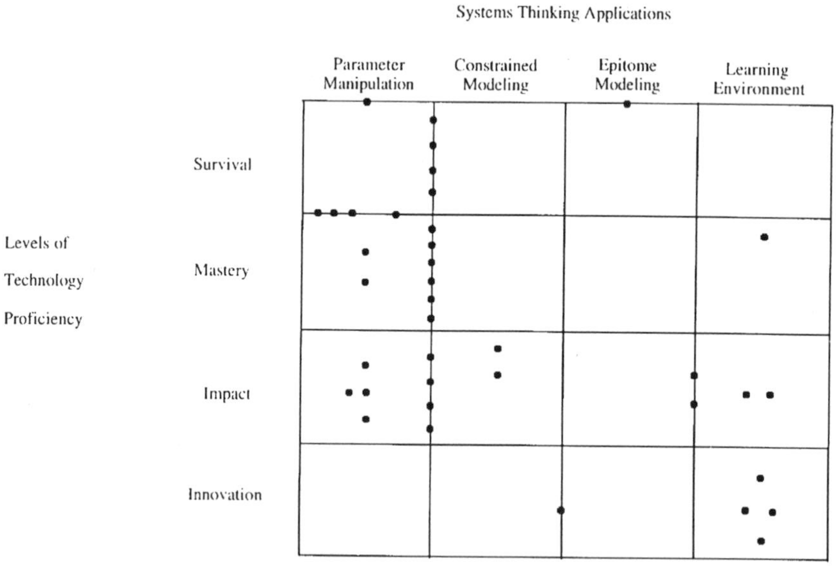

The application dimension is more complicated, because many teachers use several types of applications depending on the courses and students involved. Eight teachers use only parameter manipulation; 14 combine this form of application with constrained modeling; three others alternate between learning environments and parameter manipulation. Only 2 teachers solely use constrained modeling. One person combined constrained with epitome modeling. Pure epitome modeling was found in only one classroom, but was combined with learning environments in two other instances. Lastly, learning environments were created by 4 teachers.

A number of interesting patterns emerge from the placement of the teachers within the matrix. First, note that there are no teachers in the innovation by parameter manipulation or innovation by constrained modeling cells. By definition of the innovation stage, it seems highly unlikely that curricula would be restructured by the use of these two types of applications. Instead, these two cells reflect adaptation of the systems thinking approach to more traditional classroom activities. Also according to definitions, all but one of the teachers implementing learning environments are among the most sophisticated users of technology. It is notable that the four teachers who are creating the most pervasive and innovative learning environments are also those who rely more on the philosophical perspective of systems thinking than on extensive use of the hardware and software. Many of their activities are done off-line using systems as the underlying philosophy. The teachers are, however, proficient computer users. The computer becomes one of many learning tools and activities and not the driving force of the curriculum.

The students served by the teachers who implement learning environments fall into two distinct categories. In the case of those at the innovation stage, three teachers deal with quite able middle school students. The fourth teacher in this cell serves an at-risk, primarily minority, high school population. All but one of the other individuals using learning environments also teach at both ends of the spectrum of students, either the most gifted or those at risk. Only one of the teachers serves an average student group.

Also notable is the one teacher who lacked sophistication in the use of technology, but perhaps implemented the best example of epitome modeling. This individual knew nothing about the computer, yet he could direct students to appropriate resources to support their systems models and projects. The teacher provided the substantive and pedagogical guidance, whereas peer tutors served as computer experts in the class, making up for the teacher's lack of technical knowledge. Students were able to develop extremely complex systems models as long as there were peers who could provide the computing expertise.

Perhaps the most obvious finding is that the majority of the systems applications are either parameter manipulation or constrained modeling, the two forms of applications that are most easily fit into existing curricula.

Teachers must contend with accountability pressures from the school board, parents, and the public to cover the specified curriculum. There also is a focus on their students' performance on standardized tests. Thus, there is pressure to minimize disruption to the status quo. Parameter manipulation and constrained modeling are alternate methods for teaching traditional topics. They do not revise the curricula as much as epitome modeling or learning environments. Instead, they provide innovative instructional strategies for accepted topics. Additionally, individuals who teach more advanced courses or deal with older students often shift away from parameter manipulation to more cognitively complex applications of constrained or epitome modeling. A recent trend is for teachers, particularly those serving the at-risk populations, to move toward off-line, systems-based activities, using the technology less than originally anticipated.

A final pattern that emerges is that in time, most teachers become increasingly adept at dealing with the challenges the technology imposes on their classrooms. Some individuals struggle more than others, but they eventually all become familiar and comfortable with the technology. The impact stage is the stage to which most teachers aspire and will reach. However, with appropriate conditions, there is a level beyond impact, the innovation stage, in which technology serves as a tool for the restructuring of both the curriculum as well as the role of the teacher. Yet, it appears that a special set of circumstances, course objectives, and pedagogical style are necessary for the innovation to evolve to that stage.

In addition to level of proficiency and form of application, it is also possible to classify the teachers according to how they use the systems thinking perspective. This classification also has four categories: *builder, user, creator,* and *facilitator.* As the STACI[N] Project has progressed over the years, it has become apparent that some teachers are primarily builders of systems models or curriculum modules. Other teachers are primarily model users. However, these patterns are not mutually exclusive. Some teachers both build models and use ones developed by others. Teachers can also create learning environments in which they do not build models or ancillary materials, but they instead construct situations in which students are free to explore phenomena using the systems thinking approach. The final type of usage is facilitation in which teachers make possible the use of systems either for students or other teachers, taking the role of mentor or coach. There are different levels of expertise within the categories of the usage dimension. Some teachers are adept at building systems models or using them in creative and effective ways, whereas others are not as adept and struggle with these activities. Simply being a good model builder does not ensure that a teacher can effectively teach with the systems-based materials. Pedagogical expertise merged with subject expertise and experience with the systems thinking approach are all critical for maximum effectiveness.

In the STACI^N Project thus far, model building is the predominant form of use. Fifteen teachers have been categorized as model builders, whereas 9 both build and use previously existing models. Four teachers only use models built by other project participants, whereas another 4 create activities that either require innovation or are learning environments. Creation may not be possible with the more structured applications, parameter manipulation, and constrained modeling. The 3 remaining teachers engage in combined patterns of usage: one builds and creates; one builds and facilitates; the third builds, creates, and facilitates. The distribution of the teachers by the classification and type of use bears little relationship to either level of proficiency or form of application at this time. Therefore, it is not displayed in Fig. 5.2. However, these patterns will continue to be monitored, for such relationships may emerge in the future.

SELECTED VIGNETTES

To provide more detailed descriptions of how technology affects performance in the STACI^N classrooms, six vignettes of selected teachers now are provided. There are vignettes of three individuals, two pairs, and one trio of teachers. They are drawn from several different parts of the matrix to provide a variety of illustrative scenarios (see Table 5.3). Among the vignettes, two focus on teachers at the innovation level of proficiency, two at the impact stage, one at mastery, and one at the borderline of survival and mastery. Along the application's dimension, two vignettes report constrained modeling and parameter manipulation usages, two are learning environments, one is parameter manipulation, and one a combination of parameter manipulation and learning environments. Teachers in three vignettes build their applications, two create them, and one both builds and uses systems materials.

Longest Participating Project Member

The first vignette is of the teacher who has participated in the project for the longest period of time. When the project started he taught both general physical science and physics, but now he teaches only the latter. He is classified as being at the impact stage on the proficiency dimension, and he builds parameter manipulation and assigns constrained modeling applications. Increasingly he uses constrained modeling, because he teaches the more advanced science students, and physics is more amenable to problem-based solutions. He now is attempting to teach two forms of physics, which include one with a mathematical orientation and another with a conceptual orientation, both of which use systems thinking as the underlying instructional strategy.

TABLE 5.3
Matrix Dimensions Represented in the Vignettes

	Matrix Dimension	
Vignette	Technology Proficiency	Systems Applications
1	Impact	Constrained Modeling/ Parameter Manipulation
2	Mastery	Constrained Modeling/ Parameter Manipulation
3	Innovation	Learning Environment
4	Impact	Parameter Manipulation/ Learning Environment
5	Survival/ Mastery	Parameter Manipulation
6	Innovation	Learning Environment

Key:
1= Longest participating project member.
2= Departmental chairman and project adviser.
3= Applied mathematics.
4= Professional development.
5= Social studies amid science and mathematics.
6= Integrated curriculum.

This teacher has always used the Socratic method in the classroom, rarely providing direct answers. His goal is to improve his ability to ask the right questions of his students that will stimulate learner-directed, cooperative learning activities. The questions are used to elicit explanation, discussion, and further learning on the part of the students. He also is adept at facilitating laboratory interactions among students in the context of traditional science curricula. From all observations, the teacher is very comfortable with a learner-directed classroom where students take an increasing amount of responsibility for their own instructional activities. This teacher now functions as a mentor, guide, and coach, rather than a transmitter of information.

The transition from the traditional curriculum to the systems thinking approach has been gradual and at times admittedly difficult for this teacher. He initially identified a few topics within his courses that he thought were amenable to the systems approach and constructed mostly parameter manipulation modules for those topics. His early perceptions were that he was spending a great deal of time and making little progress. As his expertise with systems thinking and the technology increased, he began to see many more general applications that could be implemented. Much of his current classroom activities involve constrained modeling and in-depth exploration of physics concepts using the systems approach. The teacher's stated objective is to have both his mathematical and conceptual physics courses completely infused with systems, and he is well on his way to accomplishing that goal.

It is safe to say that this teacher has become the project's intellectual leader from the standpoint of systems thinking implemented within the constraints of the existing curriculum. He has found a comfortable fit for the systems thinking approach in course content and accepted curriculum objectives. He is the person from whom other project members most often seek advice. He is also the most frequently cited STACI[N] curriculum developer as reflected in the project's report books collected three times each year. He serves as the local project director in his school and has mentored several colleagues. Because of his mentoring activities, this teacher has developed a strong, collaborative working group in his school with whom he can exchange ideas and materials. The importance of this support group is in stark contrast to his earlier experiences when he had no colleagues with whom he could work. The working group has facilitated both curriculum development and intellectual growth for the project teachers in this school.

The systems thinking approach has enabled this teacher to find an instructional strategy that helps him to accomplish many of his educational objectives. Professionally he has flourished with the approach. Along the proficiency dimension, he has progressed from limited experience using technology, short of science laboratory procedures, to a sophisticated user of most aspects of the technology.

Department Chairman and Project Adviser

An interesting contrast can be found in the teacher who has become the project's most senior adviser and administrator. This outstanding teacher is the science department chairman and the STACI[N] local project director for his school. The teacher is at the cutting edge of educational practice and research as he participates in many nationally recognized curriculum innovation and research projects. Thus, his advice to STACI[N] emanates from a global perspective on education nationally as well as within his own school. By his own admission, he is a late bloomer in the project with respect to the use of technology and the systems thinking approach. In his role as departmental chairperson and local project director, his first efforts were directed to facilitating the progress of other teachers to insure that the project became established in the culture of the school and district. Given the pressures for accountability that many teachers encounter, this was a wise decision. Only later did he allow himself the time to begin developing and implementing systems in his own courses. He regrets not having developed his technical proficiency sooner. Thus, he is classified at the higher end of the mastery stage, bordering on impact.

This teacher builds and uses constrained modeling and some parameter manipulation in introductory and advanced biology classes. He collaborates with other biology and chemistry project teachers, attempting to bridge the conceptual gap between these two disciplines. This group brings together teachers from several schools and disciplines to produce stronger cross-disciplinary applications. Many interesting systems models and curriculum modules have been developed jointly and shared among this collaborative working group. The teacher, in conjunction with his colleagues, is now developing some of the most sophisticated applications in the project. One such model for which he had primary responsibility is on recombinant DNA, a topic not generally taught at the high school level. In fact, this teacher is one of the few who has been trained in the topical area and is certified to teach it.

According to the teacher, one of the most important strengths in the STACI^N Project is the networking component. Teachers working together in such collaborative groups tend to produce materials that have greater transportability than curriculum modules developed in isolation. The materials are based on multiple perspectives and therefore have greater applicability across classrooms. The teacher anticipates that the same benefits that are gained from the teachers' collaborations will also be observed when students work in small-group settings.

As the department chairman, the teacher also anticipates that the use of the systems thinking approach will create a sequence of science courses that will become increasingly learner directed and capitalize on the ability of the technology to promote higher order thinking skills. Through participation in the project, the school has gained access to some of the latest technology that can be integrated into existing curricula to help students learn more effectively across disciplines. These were the primary incentives for recommending that his school participate in the project. They were such strong incentives that more teachers than ETS could support expressed their intention to participate in the project. Because of his experience, wisdom, and administrative responsibilities, the teacher has been able to secure otherwise unavailable resources, such as extra hardware, projection equipment, and supplies.

From the perspective of his teaching duties, he recognizes the many possible systems applications in his own discipline. He also understands that there are external constraints imposed by the mandated curriculum. Because the teacher began the STACI^N training as a technology novice, he also understands the frustrations of learning systems thinking from the viewpoint of both a teacher and a student. He expressed frustration about not being able to be the very best at something, and recognized that there was so much to know before he could consider using the approach in his classroom. Yet, he also recognized that the collaborative working groups and the technology promote the learner-directed environment, and that the acquisition of higher order thinking skills would help to compensate for his perceived inadequacies. Additionally, he makes effective use of the expertise among his students with respect to technology, including peer tutoring, lab assistants, and the creation of a learner-centered environment. By the teacher's own admission, his frustrations have been productive, because they have forced him to think more fruitfully about how to present certain topics and lessons. This individual serves as eloquent testimony to the continuing professional development of an excellent teacher through the use of an instructional strategy that presents new opportunities for curriculum enhancement. This individual has worked hard to become a productive developer and teacher of systems-based materials, but he has also functioned in important administrative and advisory capacities. The teacher and reciprocally the project have benefited immensely from his participation.

Applied Mathematics

A third example is a mathematics teacher who teaches in a school where three-quarters of the students are at-risk and only a small percentage pursue further education immediately after graduation. He teaches the spectrum of mathematics courses, including remedial, pre-algebra and calculus. It is difficult to convey the energy and love of learning that this teacher infuses in his courses and students. The classroom is a whirlwind of activity, and he has an intense dedication to achieving his objectives. This includes often staying at school until 8:00 p.m. to work with interested or needy students. That same commitment also can be frustrating to administrators who may present impediments to his work.

The teacher goes well beyond the average in executing his professional responsibilities. He not only stimulates the students' intellectual development, but he also focuses on their social and interpersonal skills, which are so critical to their success in daily life. This teacher does not believe in answering questions directly. Questions are redirected into procedures for seeking solutions. He has one of the most effective and unique classroom management and pedagogical styles observed in the project. This is all the more remarkable given the challenges presented by his particular group of students and the environment in which he must function.

This teacher is always looking for more effective and engaging ways of presenting materials and ideas to his students. He never conveys facts to the students, instead instilling in them a need for control over their own learning. The teacher serves as a facilitator of the learning process. The students are constantly in motion, actively engaged in a variety of creative activities, many of which are small-group projects.

The teacher does not believe that mathematics should be taught in isolation or in the abstract. His goal is to make mathematics come alive and have it make sense in terms of concrete applications in other disciplines. He wants students to open their minds to alternate solutions, and cross-disciplinary applications. Systems-based activities are being extended to the humanities and science departments. Systems thinking is the means by which he accomplishes these objectives. He opens every class with a question of no apparent relevance to mathematics, then begins to tie the issue to mathematics and other disciplines. He asks the students to focus on the global nature of the daily problem.

The point of these activities is to show students that much of mathematics and their everyday world are interconnected, requiring examination of complex variables and their interactions. Students learn mathematics as part of the problem-solving process, using the systems thinking approach as a resource. The teacher creates an innovative, systems-based learning environment, in which there are no easy answers but many creative problem-solving strategies. The teacher rarely relies on the computer to create this learning environment. However, he does use STELLA and the Macintosh as an instructional tool to enhance particular parts of the curriculum. The innovation and learning environment really occurs in the creative mix of systems theory, technology, mathematics, and the extension to cross-disciplinary applications. Most recently, he has begun collaborating with a humanities teacher to integrate mathematics and systems thinking into that domain.

The teacher has also provided the impetus for an outgrowth of his work with systems thinking, namely an independent, extracurricular activity known as the Sunnyside Systems Thinking Club. He is the club mentor and advisor. The club brings together interested students throughout the school who want to learn more about systems thinking and the uses of the approach in everyday activities. The club has a membership of some 40 students who gather at all hours of the school day to work on simulations and discuss issues. The students have made presentations at national conferences and have established internships with local industry. The students are making concrete use of their knowledge of systems in real-world settings and on relevant activities.

This teacher takes risks in his classroom, enthusiastically trying innovative pedagogical and instructional approaches with his students. The welfare of the students is always primary. The teacher considers this a moral issue as he has been entrusted with a mandate from parents and the public to provide the best possible education for the students. The innovations often run counter to accepted rules and standards. The teacher relies on his department chairman to serve as a buffer against the pressures of accountability. It is fortunate that the chairman also is a member of the STACI[N] Project.

Without the efforts and resolve of this teacher, systems thinking would never have been introduced at this school. In fact, the teacher worked in isolation for 2 years with only his personal computer and over 40 students before STACI[N] Project resources could be obtained to help support his activities. The teacher and department chairman had to exert substantial pressure on the district administration to be allowed to join STACI[N] and expand their work with systems thinking. The systems thinking approach has now become an established part of the mathematics department's curriculum, with the expressed objective that students must take charge of their own learning. Systems thinking has not only changed how this teacher functions in the classroom, but it now has expanded to influence other teachers within and outside of the mathematics department.

Professional Development

The next example is comprised of two young teachers, one male and one female, who also teach at-risk students. In fact, there are some 27 languages and dialects spoken in their school. It has the second most diverse student population in the country. Few students go on to higher education; many drop out. The teachers frequently get new students with limited English language skills. The composition of classes constantly is in flux. These teachers function in a district where the curriculum is strictly mandated and pressures for accountability and material coverage run high. It also is a district that has had a severe financial crisis for several years. Thus, there are limited resources, few incentives, and consequently a morale problem. Teachers frequently leave the district to take better paying jobs elsewhere.

When they joined the project, these two teachers candidly expressed concern that systems thinking might interfere with the curriculum and therefore be detrimental to their chances for tenure. In the ensuing years, the mandates relaxed a bit with changes in the school administration, and both teachers have since been granted tenure. In fact, the teachers have been able to use the project as a springboard to produce remarkable professional development.

Their teaching responsibilities are vast, covering life science, earth science, biology, and chemistry. They work closely together, and with two other science teachers who also participate in the project from their school. These two teachers have shared responsibility for project direction and curriculum development, and also have served as mentors to other project members. They are quite expert with the technology, both being classified at the impact stage. The male teacher has taken on the added responsibility of serving as part-time computer technician and supervisor of the computer laboratory. He has a district mentorship to fund these activities. He may be only slightly more advanced with respect to the computers, although both teachers are equally expert at using the systems thinking approach as a teaching tool.

Their use of systems thinking varies according to the course, level of student, and educational objectives. In most instances, the teachers have developed well-conceptualized, parameter manipulation modules with structured worksheets. This format makes sense, given the nature of their students. Many students' proficiencies with textual materials are severely limited. They cannot effectively read a textbook. The teachers' goal is to expose the students to various scientific concepts by stepping them through the thought processes engendered in systems thinking until they are able to carry out such cognitive activities on their own.

With class sizes often exceeding 40, this means that the teachers must move among some 15 to 20 computer stations troubleshooting students' questions. In their weaker moments, the teachers candidly hope for absences so they can function more effectively among the students present in the computer laboratory. The teachers report that this enterprise is absolutely exhausting, but that students are more likely to be on task and learn more deeply. Teachers must be alert and constantly be "on-call" to function effectively in this very different form of learner-directed environment. The computers do not eliminate work for the teachers, but in fact, create more and different forms of demands in terms of classroom management, assessment, patterns of interaction, and pedagogical procedures. Laboratory aides, team teaching, or paraprofessionals are desperately needed to address at least the classroom management issues. These teachers are beginning to devise coping strategies in which pairs of teachers cover for one another in the classroom to free up someone who can assist in the laboratory.

These two teachers also have done some work with learning environments, one of which is a modeling activity of earthquakes. Students study various aspects of plate tectonics, geology, and architectural building codes. Their objective is to build a house that can withstand earthquakes of various magnitudes. Students select building materials and plots of land with specific geological characteristics. The learning environment then simulates the earthquake and its aftermath. Although the teachers built the model, the students are free to explore the environment, which functions in the manner of a game-like simulation.

Most recently, one of the teachers has begun to supplement instructional activities with off-line, systems-based exercises. For example, newspaper articles relevant to content are being used as the impetus to stimulate systemic thinking and writing. Such off-line activities are being devised as alternatives to the overcrowding problem in the computer laboratory.

These two teachers are prime examples of how the integration of technology into their curricula has changed dramatically their classroom dynamics, their educational objectives, and their professional development. The teachers have most effectively used the STACI[N] Project as a vehicle for professional development. When they first joined the project in 1988, they were insecure in their positions, and the administration was not supportive. They have since blossomed into self-confident and superb classroom teachers despite the demanding environment in which they function. The new administration recognizes the excellence of their contributions. The teachers also have become intellectual leaders, mentors, and model project participants. By their own admissions, the project has helped them to grow professionally. When the district failed to reach contractual agreement several years ago, all teachers were ordered to give up all extra activities. These two teachers refused to give up the only activity that provided them intellectual and professional development opportunities. They report it is the only activity in which they are truly recognized as professionals.

The teachers acknowledge that the use of systems thinking has not only changed their classrooms, but also has influenced their ability to teach. Systems thinking has stimulated improvement in their understanding of their own disciplines, as well as the learner-directed pedagogical processes. Participation in the project has helped the teachers to succeed, just as these teachers have facilitated success in STACI[N].

Social Studies Amid Science and Mathematics

The final two vignettes contrast two sets of middle and junior high school teachers who function quite differently with respect to systems thinking, given the structural characteristics of middle and junior high schools. The first set is comprised of three experienced, junior high (now middle) school social studies teachers. They are unique in the STACI[N] Project due to their disciplinary affiliation (i.e., almost all the other teachers are in mathematics and science). Their task of integrating systems thinking into social studies is made difficult for at least three reasons. A first issue is substantive. Although there is a natural fit between social studies and systems thinking, model building is quite challenging because of the need to quantify many qualitative variables. Furthermore, the models produced in social studies are large and complicated, making the teachers' instructional task more difficult regardless of who is constructing the models.

Second, much of the success of the project can be tied to the collaborations among the teachers. These three teachers work together but have no other social studies colleagues in the project to whom they can turn for assistance. Therefore, they must rely on their own experience and expertise. All three were novice computer users when the project began, and none had a substantial background in mathematics. This problem was initially alleviated by the school's project director, an experienced mathematics and computer teacher. She served as an invaluable mentor for the first 3 years. However, she resigned for personal reasons from the district and a suitable replacement is not yet available.

A third reason for the difficulties experienced by these teachers concerns the structure of the junior high school. There are formal departmental boundaries and a great deal of pressure toward accountability and standards in their school. Although the teachers are committed to using systems thinking, they are constantly faced with pressures to improve test scores and to cover the mandated curriculum. The pressure still exists even though the department chairman is a member of the project. The accountability pressure emanates from the district. It will be interesting to observe what happens as this school shifted to a middle school format in the 1992/1993 academic year.

Movement along the proficiency continuum has been difficult for these teachers. None had any experience with computers before the project began. All three voluntarily sought out several additional computer courses in an effort to become more knowledgeable and comfortable with the technology. They are progressing toward their goal of technology proficiency, but it takes time. They have been classified as borderline cases between the survival and mastery stages, primarily because most of their work has been in curriculum development rather than classroom applications. Only recently have they begun to introduce their students to systems thinking in the computer laboratory. Observations indicate that with experience, their skills and levels of confidence in the computer laboratory are improving rapidly.

The systems applications used by these teachers are parameter manipulations. Their objectives are to use these materials to create environments that promote students' acquisition of higher order thinking skills and content knowledge. The teachers have devoted vast amounts of time and energy constructing models and ancillary materials. Generally they work together. Earlier they often required intensive assistance from HPS or the local project director. The need for such assistance has decreased substantially, as they are able to build models now with less guidance. Their models include immigration, health issues, water consumption, and the like. These topics are particularly relevant to the students. For the most part, students are engaged by and interested in the models. Because the students are so young, the teachers feel the need to step them through the modules in fairly structured sequences. The students are gaining a deep understanding of the content and are acquiring valuable experience with the technology. The objective is to provide the students with more flexibility in using the technology as they gain experience with systems thinking.

Although these three teachers have struggled throughout the duration of the project, they also have worked extremely hard to compensate for their lack of expertise and experience with the technology. Their disciplinary affiliation and the fact that the project's emphasis is on science and mathematics has made the provision for substantive expertise quite difficult. Yet, the three teachers continue to be enthusiastic, productive, and valued members of the project. As their school shifts to a middle school core curriculum, fundamental changes in the structure and functioning of the school are influencing how systems thinking can be applied. The core curriculum should provide much more freedom from departmental accountability so that the teachers can pursue cross-disciplinary applications. Although the transition has created some pressing management problems (e.g., overcrowding, the use of the laboratory as a classroom, general disorientation), it is anticipated that the organizational changes on a long-term basis will provide a substantial number of opportunities for new applications of the systems thinking approach that will further enhance the work of the three social studies teachers.

Integrated Curriculum

The final set of two teachers works at a small, middle school with an academically able and relatively homogeneous student population. These teachers were engaged in team teaching until the 1992/1993 academic year. The structure of team teaching and the cross-disciplinary emphasis of the middle school enables these two teachers to try some truly innovative activities with their classes. Initially, these teachers approached the middle-school curriculum as several distinct disciplines. However, they quickly realized that the key to using systems thinking was to consider the curriculum as one unit into which the approach could be integrated.

Systems thinking forms the theoretical foundation for their activities. As mentioned, the teachers have created systems-based curriculum units that operate for several weeks. They attempt to bridge disciplinary boundaries by selecting thematic units around which students build extended projects. For one unit, they selected environmental issues. The students developed independent research projects on various topics, such as dolphin preservation, deforestation, acid rain, nuclear power, and Arctic oil drilling. Systems thinking was the thread that tied all the projects together. Students also prepared a science museum based on their work with environmental issues. Small groups of students created long-term projects on topics such as water, nutrient cycles, pesticides, biomagnification, and decomposition. Their work on the "Keepers of the Earth Museum" was reinforced through field trips, invited speakers, and other relevant activities. Another unit focused on an endangered species, the spotted owl. The teachers integrated science, mathematics, literature, and social studies to explore the population dynamics of the owl. They conducted a similar unit on wolves, based on the assumptions of predator/prey population models. Other units that these teachers produced include a simulated journey on the Amazon River, the Mayan culture studied through the genre of a mystery, and a comparison of the Bubonic Plague and AIDS epidemic.

According to the teachers, the typical middle-school student's view is limited and self-centered. They perceive their own actions as independent and isolated events, rather than interconnected sequences of influences and outcomes. Therefore, these teachers prepared a workbook of common activities that forced the students to consider the antecedents and consequences of their actions. The actions selected were particularly relevant to the students' everyday activities. The theme of the workbook is that nothing occurs in isolation. All actions have causes and consequences, for which students must assume responsibility. For example, if a student decided to stay up until 1:00 a.m. watching television, they were asked to hypothesize about causes and consequences of this action. Why did the student do this? What effect would such an action have on performance in school the next day, disciplinary actions, and the like? The scenarios are relevant to students' lives, thereby stimulating engagement in the problems and in-depth analysis.

The curriculum for the 1992/1993 academic year for the entire school focuses on *Seeds of Change*, an exhibit at the Smithsonian Institution. The concept of the dynamics of change has been integrated into all courses at the school to celebrate the quincentenary of Columbus' discovery of America. These two teachers and one other nonproject teacher attended a workshop at the Smithsonian on the program. They, in turn, trained the entire faculty. All members of the faculty are involved so that the topic of change can be addressed from multiple perspectives.

The teachers' are using *Seeds of Change* to explore topics such as demographic trends, cultural interchange, political transformations, economic and agricultural transformations, dietary changes, and the redivision of world labor. Their goal is to provide a context into which students can place the significance of the Columbus voyages, showing how the discovery relates to many historical, political, and social events that occurred before and after 1492, not just in this country but in the entire world. Their intent is to show how one event can have such a profound effect on the rest of the world and its future. They also anticipate that the program will help students to recognize the relevance of the events of 1492 to current events in their own lives, as well as contemporary issues that face the country today. Thus, the theme, *the interdependence of the world*, is an ideal topic for the systems thinking approach. Because these teachers no longer team teach the core curriculum, they are serving different function in the *Seeds of Change*. One individual has maintained her role as a seventh-grade core teacher; the other now divides her time between teaching the eighth-grade core and curriculum administrative duties.

Although most of the student activities created by these teachers do not require the computer, they can be enhanced by the technology. The teachers are adept at identifying when and when not to use to the computer as an instructional tool. The innovation in their classes is the philosophy of systems thinking that permeates all activities. Thus, these teachers have restructured many conventional activities into innovative and engaging systems-based modules that have served to restructure both the content and delivery of the curriculum.

DISCUSSION AND EDUCATIONAL IMPLICATIONS

This chapter has described a conceptual perspective in which teacher performance, classroom processes, and instructional procedures were observed and compared. The systems thinking approach was used as an example for classifying the modes of adaptation teachers use as they implement technologically based curriculum innovations in their classrooms. A matrix was proposed in which the proficiency with technology and the type of application form its two dimensions. STACI^N Project teachers were classified along these dimensions. Patterns across the matrix were noted and vignettes of selected teachers described.

These dimensions have facilitated a better understanding of how teachers use technology and how the technology affects the role of the teacher, professional development, classroom procedures, and instructional strategies. Some of the numerous ways that technology has impacted the STACI^N teachers have been described. Technology in the case of STACI^N refers not only to the GUI of the Macintosh computer and the STELLA software, but also to the theory of system dynamics. Thus, when the impact of technology is discussed, it includes the theoretical perspective as well as the hardware and software. These three components that comprise the systems thinking approach have altered the professional activities and performance of teachers participating in STACI^N. The structure and functioning of the classroom and the role of the teacher have been transformed in many fundamental ways as a result of the implementation of technology.

The ACOT continuum for mastery of teaching with technology outlines many of the developmental changes one can expect to occur as teachers begin to introduce and integrate technology into their classroom procedures. The STACI^N Project has extended that continuum by one stage to include technology's role in the restructuring of curricula and the classroom. That is, given the right set of circumstances, some teachers can use technology as a stimulus to design innovative learning environments that change fundamentally the way teaching and learning activities occur. Such innovation is analogous to the hackers who understand computer games so well that they can go beyond the explicit rules and find creative solutions. Similarly, these teachers often stretch the implicit and explicit rules of the classroom to implement innovative and challenging computer-based and off-line applications. This requires a high level of pedagogical expertise as well as a great deal of insight into the classroom.

Such an innovation also requires a high degree of administrative support to relax or adjust the accountability standards. The innovations reported here span the range of schools, from the most elite to the most needy.

141

What these cases have in common is that the department chairpersons, principals, superintendents, and school boards are all supportive of the teachers' innovative efforts. They often must explain and actively defend their work to curriculum supervisors, parents, and the public. Effective innovation requires such administrative support. This need is created, in part, because the use of technology requires time, a rare and thus highly valued commodity in schools. Time taken to implement a computer-based program is time taken away from an already filled curriculum. Only an administrator can protect teachers from the accountability pressures.

Finally there are two interrelated and noteworthy observations from the STACI[N] Project thus far. The first, mentioned briefly earlier, concerns assessing the changes in the classroom environment. When a supervisor visits a teacher's class both in its traditional setting and in the computer laboratory, it is likely that two distinct classrooms will be observed. The traditional class might look quite orderly, with students listening or working quietly and alone at their desks. In the computer laboratory, students rarely work alone. There are usually dyads or triads of students at each computer, and other students wandering around, looking over one anothers' shoulders, comparing solutions, and the like. There is constant activity as the students are actively engaged in their work. The room is abuzz with activity. It is often noisy and chaotic. An observer might assume that this chaos is unproductive, off-task behavior. Actually, it is just the opposite. Supervisors must recognize and understand the classroom management differences that are created with the use of technology.

A second issue is the emerging need for new student assessment procedures. Because students interact collaboratively when using technology, it is often difficult to determine who is doing what portion of the cognitive work. Is one student doing everything, or is there shared responsibility for the learning? What often happens is that students work in groups on-line, but they are assessed off-line without the aid of the technology and on an individual basis. There remains some implicit assumptions that collaborative work is tantamount to cheating and that assessment can only be done at the individual level. This is unfortunate because most real-world work environments require more collaborative than individual efforts. There is a need to recognize that students are given mixed messages about when collaboration is acceptable behavior in terms of work and assessment.

Assessment procedures also need to change to incorporate the emphasis on the processes of learning, not just the outcomes of instruction. Many computer activities focus on how the students attain solutions in addition to the gains in specific declarative knowledge. The increasing emphasis on the processes and procedures of learning change the nature of assessment, and run counter to most traditional assessment techniques. These are not issues that classroom teachers can change. But they are factors of the environment in which they must function.

As technology becomes more deeply entrenched in the classroom environment, teachers and students will begin to develop more effective strategies that enable integration into pedagogical and instructional practice. The teachers in the STACI[N] Project span the range of expertise in the extent to which their efforts have been effective. With time, these teachers have made substantial progress in implementing the systems thinking approach and with technology, more generally. It is anticipated that there will continue to be progress as they find new and improved ways of using the perspective in their curricula and classrooms.

6
Future Research and Policy Implications

The previous chapters have amply documented the fact that the design, implementation, and evaluation of curricular innovations, particularly computer-based efforts, are complex enterprises requiring input from many sources. This volume has reviewed how one such innovation, the STACI^N Project, evolved over a 6-year period. Many individuals and organizations have provided various inputs, without which STACI^N could not have survived. The earlier chapters have chronicled these contributions as well as the many problems, concerns, and issues that must be addressed to sustain a project's successful operation.

As with the theoretical foundation that supports the STACI^N Project, the issues that influence a curriculum innovation form a complex system of interacting variables. To understand the factors that either contribute to or hinder a curriculum innovation, it is inadequate to examine each of these variables in isolation. By now the reader should recognize such thinking as laundry listing. Such a procedure is analogous to using individual t tests when an F test and interaction analysis are more appropriate. Instead, there is a need to trace how the sequences of variables interact to form complex feedback loops.

Appendix B contains a multivariate, multilevel model proposed for a computer-based curriculum innovation such as systems thinking. Indeed, it uses systems thinking to analyze the object of the STACI^N Project. As such, it represents a new and hopefully productive perspective to view a phenomenon that is observed with increasing frequency in schools throughout the nation. It is intended that this model should prove useful from at least two perspectives. First, it should point to those areas where additional research is needed to expand and specify further the model. In the description accompanying the model in the Appendix, many such suggestions for future research are noted. Second, the ongoing model building activities should point to policy implications for all those involved in computer-based curriculum innovations similar to the STACI^N Project. These two topics, future research and policy implications, are the issues discussed in this final chapter.

FUTURE RESEARCH

As noted in chapters 1 and 2, most of the efforts in the first 6 years of the STACI^N Project have been devoted to design and implementation issues. Everyone involved in the project has been surprised at how long it has taken for the innovation to be implemented in the participating schools. As the innovation begins to take root, the focus of the project is giving increased attention to expanding the research activities. As with all other activities in the STACI^N Project, the research will be a collaborative effort among the teachers and the ETS staff. Using the objectives and goals for participation in the project stated by the teachers, four general categories of research topics were identified. Four corresponding research task forces consisting of teachers and ETS staff have been organized. The task forces have designed research projects addressing these general topics, and data collection activities began at the beginning of the 1992/1993 school year. The four categories are defined here.

The first category is curriculum, instruction, and teaching. The object here is to document how subject matter is taught differently as a consequence of using systems thinking. Matters such as course content, scope, and sequencing need to be observed and recorded. In addition, more needs to be learned about changing classroom dynamics, including interactions among teachers and students. In many respects, teachers and their behaviors are the object of inquiry here. Therefore, an important part of the methodology will require the teachers to observe and record their own classroom activities. Some of this work was started by the ETS staff in earlier classroom observations and teacher interviews. This research is fundamental to all other investigations, for it will document the extent to which systems thinking has been implemented in the project classes. The issue of precisely what data will be collected and how they will be analyzed will be a continuing issue for this research task force to resolve. As with all systems, it is anticipated that the focus of this and all research task forces will shift and evolve over time. The reader who finds that last sentence to be a logical statement is undoubtedly a systems thinker.

The second research task force will focus on learning and declarative knowledge, or what teachers usually assess in examinations. This group will address the issue of the most effective ways to measure content knowledge acquisition. It will have to determine the question of relevant comparisons. For example, if the claim is made that students learn biology "better" using systems thinking, what is the implied comparison here? Is it with students who learn biology without systems thinking? Or is it implied that these students learned biology better than they would have using traditional methods? Clarity needs to be gained on these questions, and the research designs for the task force need to reflect that clarity. This task force must certainly avoid some of the traps that educational evaluations have encountered in the past. One perspective that will undoubtedly be employed here is the collection of information on student performance over many years, perhaps from middle school through high school. Multiyear portfolios documenting student performance will be created. Appropriate methods for research on learning and declarative knowledge will take several years to develop, and they also will undergo continuous refining.

Problem solving and systems thinking will be the focus of the third research task force. As already noted, this is frequently called procedural knowledge. This task force will be particularly interested in the application of systems thinking to the kinds of problem-solving tasks students encounter in their classes. For instance, this task force might create a test of systems skills similar to the one used early in the STACI Project at BUHS. Alternately, they might devise model-building exercises that require the application of systems principles and skills for successful solution. For example, students might be asked to write a short essay on a topic that requires systems thinking. Their capacity to analyze a situation and apply systems skills could be measured. Comparisons could then be made between a student's essay before and after a systems thinking curriculum module has been used in class. These essays also might be accumulated in the portfolios to document long-term growth.

Student motivation is the topic addressed by the fourth research task force. As in the draft model described earlier, motivation here also refers to a variety of concepts, including attitude, self-concept, achievement orientation, aspiration, and other affective variables. This topic might be approached in several ways. First, traditional, self-report, paper-and-pencil measures might be employed. However, many investigators question the validity of these instruments. Also, respondents might manipulate their answers so that misleading profiles are created. A second method that might be used would identify behaviors that reflect motivation in classrooms. For example, one can look at attendance or disciplinary measures as indicators of interest or motivation. This task force will devise other creative ways to assess these concepts. The questions of which variables to study and how to collect indicators of them will be the ongoing issues addressed by this task force.

The four research task forces periodically will review their work collectively to insure that important substantive questions relevant to the impact of the curriculum innovation are not being overlooked. Future reports of the STACI^N Project will be richly informed by the data collected and analyzed by these research task forces.

POLICY IMPLICATIONS

Turning finally to the issue of educational policy implications, it has been noted several times that technology-based innovations such as the systems thinking approach have the potential to change the fundamental nature of teaching and learning activities. However, due to their extremely complex and complicated structures, such innovations require longitudinal perspectives for both their implementation and research components. It is virtually impossible to attempt to understand the structure and functioning of a curriculum innovation by examining several variables in isolation.

Instead, a systemic perspective that recognizes the interactions among many variables is a more appropriate way to understand factors that contribute to the success or failure of an innovation.

This volume has described at length one such innovation, its inception, implementation, and evolution. Operation of the STACI^N Project will continue for at least the next 2 years with funding from the U.S. Department of Education. All those involved in the project, including the teachers, administrators, HPS staff, and ETS, intend that the project will continue for many years. During this time, the project will continue its foci on the effects of the curriculum innovation on organizational structure and functioning, classroom activities and dynamics, and student learning processes and outcomes.

At this point in the history of the STACI^N Project, it is possible to draw out implications for educational policy in only one of the three areas of research, classroom dynamics. As yet, not enough research has been accomplished in the organizational change and student learning outcome areas to support the derivation of relevant policy recommendations. Therefore, comments in this last section will be directed only to the classroom level. Future publications reporting on the STACI^N Project will include research results and policy implications in all three areas. The comments here focus on the transitions that appear to result from the implementation of the computer-based curriculum innovation. Several separate yet interrelated classroom processes have been observed to change thus far. These changes are likely to become more pronounced as the innovation continues to take hold and evolve. Some of these changes have been elaborated in earlier chapters. Here they are juxtaposed as transitions from the present, traditional classroom to the future classroom that is infused with the computer-based curriculum innovation. These changes have relevance for the future of the teaching profession.

The traditional classroom is one in which the teacher is in control. It is a teacher-directed environment in which the instructor (who purportedly knows the most about a topic) stands in front of a class of students (who purportedly do not know the content) and bathes them with knowledge. The teacher generally feels compelled to know as much as possible about the topic and tries to anticipate all questions students might ask. The teacher does not want to be put in the position of not knowing the answer to a student's question. The teacher's goal is to impart or transmit information to the students, most frequently in a didactic manner. Students sit passively and receive information while the teacher talks at them. The content of such traditionally taught courses frequently focuses on declarative knowledge, rote learning, and abstract concepts.

This portrayal is, of course, a caricature. Most classes are not so rigid, and few teachers are so dictatorial. However, many classes still operate primarily in the traditional manner with the teacher assuming complete control and sole responsibility for the learning process. Learning can be an interactive enterprise with teachers and students sharing responsibility for the processes and outcomes of instruction.

The inception and implementation of a computer-based curriculum innovation such as the systems thinking approach shifts classroom control and responsibility for learning to a shared process. Learning becomes learner-directed as students are required to participate actively in classroom activities. The innovation facilitates more interactive learning, rather than espousing a didactic method of instruction. Thus, students can assume more responsibility for their own learning as active participants. Correspondingly, the role of the teacher shifts to one of facilitator of learning, rather than transmitter of information.

In the learner-directed environment, the focus of instruction is on procedural knowledge and general problem-solving skills, rather than on declarative knowledge and rote learning. Furthermore, environments such as those created by the systems thinking approach shift the focus of instruction to real-world applications and problems. In doing so, learning is concretized, rather than dealing with abstractions that have little apparent relevance to anything. Finally, a computer-based curriculum innovation project can diminish "teacher talk" and provide students with opportunities for individual and group intellectual exploration.

All these changes in the processes and dynamics of the classroom produce a very different set of activities involving both students and teachers. Furthermore, they require a very different set of behaviors, skills, and abilities from teachers. These changes have implications for the preservice and continuing education of teachers. They also suggest that the greater emphasis in teacher evaluations may need to be placed on such characteristics as tolerance of ambiguity, management of organized chaos, and comfort with technology driven change. Successful teachers in the future will behave very differently and will require preservice and in-service support structures that are only beginning to become clear.

SUMMARY

A major theme of this book has been that technology has the potential to change fundamentally the ways in which teaching and learning activities occur. The STACI[N] Project begins to examine some of the changes that result from implementing one such technology-based curriculum innovation. The systems thinking approach makes accessible to students and teachers modeling capabilities heretofore found only on very expensive computers. Such modeling broadens the range of cognitive representations and instructional strategies students and teachers can bring to bear to solve problems. The systems approach enables students and teachers to develop and implement dynamic models of systems by using a variety of abstract representations to explore many phenomena and make them concrete. The integration of this learning environment into all curricula has the potential to produce students who have a greater capacity to understand the interrelated and complex nature of phenomena that they will encounter in their daily lives. Technology-based curriculum innovations such as the systems thinking approach provide opportunities to examine how technology can enhance the fundamental nature of teaching, learning, and assessment activities.

The STACI[N] Project represents a case in which technological advances provide an opportunity to implement an instructional perspective and collect data that will inform learning processes, teaching activities, and implementation issues. The goal is to use technology to assist in the development of innovative instructional strategies by which to teach content knowledge as well as general problem-solving skills. However, many implementation issues, such as course sequencing, integration, curriculum development, teacher training and support, and the changing role of the teacher, need to be addressed in greater detail.

Furthermore, this volume has provided a draft systems thinking model for the STACI[N] Project. The model provides a conceptual foundation for examining the implementation and impact of computer-based curriculum innovation projects. It espouses a means for examining a curriculum innovation systematically, exploring how the variables interrelate and form

FIG. 6.1. Traditional education.

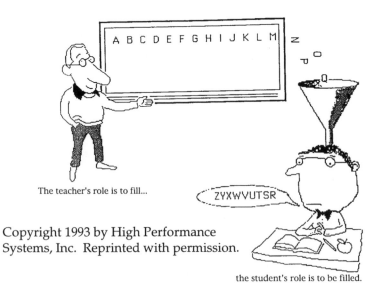

The teacher's role is to fill...

ZYXWVUTSR

Copyright 1993 by High Performance Systems, Inc. Reprinted with permission.

the student's role is to be filled.

feedback loops that subsequently influence other factors in the system. The dynamic and ever-changing nature of schools requires such a systemic approach to stimulate problem resolution and organizational change.

Figure 6.1 serves as a concluding comment for this volume. This cartoon is a caricature of traditional education as described in chapter 4. The teacher's role is to distribute facts, and the students' role is to accept and reproduce those same facts. The systems thinking approach has so irrevocably changed the teachers in the STACI[N] Project that they are no longer content to sustain the old model of education. Figure 6.2 portrays what the students at Sunnyside High School have created for the official project logo with the motto "NO MORE FUNNELS". The systems thinking approach and the use of the technology have created the need for a different form of education. The project's teachers, administrators, and many of the students now acknowledge and support that need for change. They refer to themselves as the "FUNNEL BUSTERS".

FIG. 6.2. A logo for innovative education.

NO MORE FUNNELS

Source: Systems Thinking Club, Sunnyside High School, Tucson, AZ. Reprinted with permission.

Appendix A

EVOLVING CASE STUDIES

Case studies of each school provide global perspectives of how the technological innovation is impacting the schools as organizations. Through repeated interviews and observations, information is being continuously elicited from a variety of people at each school to provide valuable insights into the extent to which the use of technology has influenced performance, activities, and educational philosophy. Preliminary indications of how such impact is evolving can be found in the following section, which describes the implementation of the systems thinking approach at the eight schools.

To date, BUHS has been observed for over 7 years, the California schools for over 5 years, and Sunnyside for more than 3 years. Many changes and events have occurred that provide useful information about the schools and the functioning of the project at those sites. Information about the eight schools is presented here to provide insights into potentially important characteristics, events, or personnel that either facilitate or hinder the implementation of a project such as STACI[N]. The case studies describe administrative support, personnel, level of commitment, productivity, turnover, computers and physical facilities, and other tangible factors that might influence the structure and functioning of the project.

BUHS

Because a longer time has been expended working with and observing at BUHS, there are naturally more events to report that have shaped the nature of the project. BUHS is distinct from the other project schools in several ways. First, it is a rural school that serves five small New England towns. It was BUHS that originally conceived the idea to implement systems thinking in the school. This conception was created by two community members, a husband and wife, with children at BUHS. They initiated the early training and fund-raising activities. In fact, on behalf of the BUHS teachers, they wrote the proposal to the Secretary's Discretionary Fund. Although the idea to use systems thinking was generated internally, it is likely that the efforts would have succeeded less rapidly without the help of ETS, ETC, and Apple, who made the delivery of a classroom set of computers possible.

There were no Macintosh computers at BUHS before systems thinking was introduced. As already noted, three computers to support instruction with systems thinking were acquired before ETS arranged for the donation of the laboratory set of Macintoshes. Additional hard disks were purchased by allowing the computers to be used for an adult education desktop publishing course. BUHS does not use a laboratory arrangement for the computers. Instead, it was decided that the computers would be transported from room to room as needed by individual teachers. The computers are used primarily by the systems thinking group and therefore are usually resident in the science wing. A second laboratory of Macintosh computers was provided by the District and is housed in the classroom of one of the project teachers. The loan of the machines to teachers and students for weekends and holidays is strongly encouraged.

There were four original teachers at BUHS who undertook the implementation of systems prior to ETS's involvement. Three teachers were in the science department. The fourth teacher who conducted the experimental social studies course was a member of the mathematics department. The teachers had the complete support of the administration, at the levels of both the superintendent and the principal. The superintendent, who has since died, was publicly supportive of the project's efforts but was never actively involved in project activities. The new superintendent is intrigued by the project's potentials and has pledged his full support. As an ardent Macintosh user, he immediately requested copies of models so that he could better understand the objectives of the project. Despite the principal's decision to maintain a hands-off policy in the project's daily operation, he has been completely supportive of the teachers and the use of systems thinking. He prefers to let the responsibility remain with the teachers and particularly the project directors. He has, however, interceded in project matters when organizational and managerial assistance has been necessary.

The original project director was an experienced teacher who had been recognized nationally for his professional excellence. In 1988, he was named the state teacher of the year, one of several prestigious awards received during his career. The other teachers spanned the continuum of experience. One was approaching retirement, one quite experienced, and the third a fairly young but excellent teacher. Each of the teachers themselves provided interesting case studies because they approached the use of systems thinking in such diverse ways. The extent to which these approaches are representative of the larger group of teachers is still unclear.

One teacher saw ways to use the computer and systems thinking as a natural adjunct to his regular instruction. He immediately began to integrate systems modules and problems infused with systems into his classes. The transition and connections appeared to be quite smooth and explicit. His ultimate goal has been to infuse his course more fully with modules that use the systems approach. The only constraint has been the labor intensive limitations on his time to devote to this effort. This teacher eventually assumed the role of project director when the original project director resigned. He not only provides mentorship for the other teachers at BUHS, but he has emerged as the intellectual leader for all project participants and produced a wealth of curriculum modules in the area of physics.

A second dedicated and hard-working teacher attempted to use systems as an adjunct learning tool, but without taking advantage of the opportunities provided by computer use. The teacher spent inordinate amounts of time preparing elaborate systems models that were presented to students in a lecture format. These models were so complex that he often sought assistance from HPS. Yet he expected his students to grasp both the substantive topics and systems principles.

The teacher failed to make use of the computer as an interactive teaching tool. It was relegated to the role of audio-visual equipment. The students watched the teacher demonstrate modeling. They rarely if ever had the opportunity to have hands-on experience manipulating models on the computer. Because the teacher spent so much time on model preparation, there was a great deal of psychological investment on his part. He had extremely high expectations for what the systems approach could accomplish with his students. These expectations were unrealistic in that they were both premature and overly ambitious. His focus was on measurable student achievement, not necessarily on learning or thinking. This is an important distinction because, to him, evidence that the innovation worked was good performance by the students on the tests he developed, which were extremely difficult in both content and systems thinking. How the students approached problems or course content was inconsequential. Thus, the teacher set himself up for disappointment and failure, which took the form of a roller coaster of emotions over a 2-year period of time. During this time, he resigned from the project several times, frustrated at his students' inadequate performance. He ultimately withdrew from project activities and was replaced by another teacher.

The other two teachers also experienced the successes and frustrations of implementing the innovation. The original project director used a sabbatical to take a systems course at Dartmouth College before the project began. It was at this time that he began to develop what he thought were reasonable expectations about the use of systems in his classes. However, he soon discovered that modeling a number of phenomena in chemistry was far too complex, not only for his students but also for himself. Consequently, he had to modify his expectations and find a more contained way of using systems thinking. Following the lead of another project member, they determined that a more effective instructional strategy was to blend constrained modeling and guided inquiry within the course content. The approach was not widely infused in the curriculum as the teacher sought appropriate topical areas. However, once he began to collaborate with some of the California chemistry teachers, a number of potential applications became apparent. Here is a prime example of a temporarily stalled teacher who gained new insights and renewed enthusiasm simply by collaborating with other project members in the same discipline. Despite his renewed commitment to the instructional perspective, this teacher decided several months later to withdraw from the project. His tenure as state teacher of the year provided insights into how he wanted to spend his final years of teaching. He chose not to give priority to systems thinking and therefore, regrettably, resigned. He does however continue to support and participate informally in project activities.

The fourth original teacher, a prototypical Renaissance man, proposed the experimental social studies course to provide advanced mathematics students the opportunity to pursue in-depth historical research to which a systems perspective could be applied. He was intrigued with the idea of exposing high-school students to a college-like seminar, bringing in experts from around the country. Despite being quite scholarly, the teacher never acquired a working knowledge of the Macintosh and STELLA, a problem that severely limited the extent to which he could assist his students. Consequently, the teacher needed continuous assistance from the systems experts at MIT. In the project's first year, there were several students in the class who were experienced with the computer and STELLA who served as peer tutors. In Year 1, the class drew heavily upon these student computer experts and the teacher's content knowledge. However, in Year 2, the teacher's lack of technical knowledge prevented the class from making effective use of the approach's intellectual rigor. The teacher has since retired and was replaced by the science department chairman who wanted to understand more fully the potential of the approach in his department.

The purpose of these four scenarios is not to place blame or laud any particular teacher. All four worked extremely hard on this ground-breaking and labor-intensive endeavor. The intent here is to highlight certain characteristics of the teachers that may have facilitated or prevented them from making effective use of the technology and intellectual approach. It was clear from the project's outset that none of the teachers or researchers recognized just how labor intensive and intellectually demanding the undertaking would be. The teachers not only had to learn much more about systems thinking but also needed to familiarize themselves with the computer and software.

Three of the teachers readily admitted that they did not feel comfortable with computers and were skeptical about their educational applications. This was observable by their failure to use the computer in an effective manner. Perhaps more important were the pedagogical strategies employed by two of the teachers that really limited the extent to which they could implement the systems approach effectively. These teachers used a pedagogic style, which made them reluctant to relinquish control of their classes and let the students assume some responsibility for their own learning. They felt that before they got up in front of their classes with a new curriculum module, they first had to have complete command of the entire body of knowledge. This meant anticipating every question a student possibly could ask. However, with the systems thinking approach, there are often many possible answers and solutions paths, and an infinite number of questions that might be raised in seeking those solutions. Students actively can offer information from which other students and the teacher can benefit. The theoretical model espoused here is constructivist in nature, one of active participation and interaction among students rather than passive reception of information. Unfortunately, the class structures and processes were not conducive to this interactive and learner-directed type of learning environment. The first physics teacher mentioned here uses guided inquiry with his classes, an approach that is likely to be a more effective implementation of the innovation. Although the War and Revolution teacher espoused guided inquiry among his students, his effectiveness was severely limited by his lack of technical knowledge. The teachers who maintained strict classroom control found the approach problematic and frustrating. The teacher who allowed for inquiry and took advantage of the technology benefited from the systems approach.

It also is important to note that these four teachers worked in disciplinary isolation (i.e., without interaction with substantive colleagues). Two of the BUHS teachers made constant use of the systems expertise at MIT and HPS, but they did not have other educators with whom to collaborate. In fact, the teachers rarely used one another as potential resources. It was difficult to determine if this was a result of different content areas or more personal, pedagogic, and stylistic differences. When the network was introduced, the BUHS teachers were initially somewhat reluctant to participate. The distance and lack of familiarity with other participants was to some degree responsible for this hesitance. Only two of the original BUHS teachers took advantage of the opportunity to attend the early California training sessions. In each instance, they found colleagues with whom they shared ideas and collaborated. Although they both renewed their interest and enthusiasm, in one case the teacher's motivation ebbed after the training session ended. Collaboration increased when they began to make use of the electronic mail facility to exchange ideas, models, or questions with other project teachers. They also seemed reluctant to provide the project staff with information about their activities. Their reaction was almost one of drawing territorial rights. They saw that other teachers had implemented effective uses of the approach whereas they could not; thus it appeared that they quietly chose to maintain a distance from the project that had its roots in their own institution. There are mutually beneficial advantages that can result from interactions among all the schools in the network. It was hoped that BUHS would begin to take advantage of the expertise and potential collaborations made possible through the network.

Fortunately this wish has come to fruition, due primarily to the changing composition of the project participants. Upon the retirement of the mathematics teacher and the resignation of the frustrated biology teacher, the science department chairman and another science teacher joined the project. The configuration consisted of four committed science teachers whose objective was to infuse the systems thinking approach into the departmental curriculum. Having the department chair as not only a supporter but also a participant strengthened that commitment. The junior high-school computer coordinator also expressed interest and began to work informally on the project. His involvement was facilitated by the fact that the junior high and high school occupy different sections of the same building.

Because the new teachers joined the project at the beginning of the school year, it was imperative to provide some intensive training to bring them up to speed in systems thinking. It was impractical to rely solely on the mentorship of the two experienced members of the group. HPS conducted an intensive training session during the fall semester, and both new teachers were strongly encouraged to attend the next training in California. Only the department chair was able to come to Stanford, where he gained new insights into how the perspective could be used effectively in science.

During the spring semester of 1990, the original project director resigned, and the physics teacher agreed to assume that role. The junior high-school computer coordinator who had also been assigned to teach mathematics for Team Nine (a group specializing in core instruction for the at-risk freshmen) became the fourth member of the project. All but the science department chairman attended the summer training at Stanford in 1990. It was clear that these three (physics, general science, and Team Nine) young, enthusiastic, and creative teachers formed a successful, collaborative working group. They were striving toward the development of curriculum materials that would engage at-risk as well as the most gifted students. The project director began serving as mentor while the two new and less experienced members provided fresh ideas about potential applications. The computer coordinator also brings technical expertise to the project, which is vital due to the large number of computers of varying vintages. These three teachers have infused new life into the project at BUHS. They see many applications for the approach and are eager to implement their models across the curricula and for a variety of students. They have the full support of the science department chairman, who realized after administrative duties prevented him from attending the summer training, that he would best serve the project in his administrative capacity rather than as a full participant. Thus, STACI^N at BUHS has never been in better shape or in more capable hands.

With the appointment of the junior high-school teacher came access to a second Macintosh laboratory. The district had supplied the junior high school (which is located in the same building) with a complete set of Macintoshes for which the teacher has responsibility. Although the hardware is to be used for a variety of instructional purposes, the new machines certainly contribute to meeting project objectives. The BUHS teachers collaborated to offer the project's first course in systems thinking in the first semester of the 1991/1992 academic year.

Hillview Middle School

The first of the project California sites is a middle school located in the affluent community of Menlo Park. As the principal noted, the school serves the community with the highest per capita income in the country. When first contacted, the school enrolled approximately 400 students in Grades 5 through 8 and employed about 20 faculty. In the 1989/1990 academic year, Hillview merged with another middle school and became an institution serving Grades 6 through 8. Students generally come from upper-middle-class, professional families where there is a great deal of active interest in their children's education. Thus, there is usually substantial public and parental input and participation in the school's activities.

Hillview has had a change in superintendents since the project began. The first superintendent was neutral to the project and generally did not interfere with activities as long as they did not cost any additional money. The second individual was an assistant superintendent in another of the project's districts. She fully understands and supports the project. However, the district is small and has limited discretionary financial resources. Although she is enthusiastic about the project, she generally defers to the building principal for operational matters. The principal has been supportive of and helpful to the project, has taken an interest in what his teachers are doing in STACI^N, and has appeared at many project activities to show his support. He also suggested the need to convene a meeting of project principals to discuss STACI^N's impact on their schools. This meeting was held in June, 1992. The principal has left project management decisions to the local project director and ETS, choosing not to get involved in some rather delicate personnel matters. In conjunction with the project director, the principal did assist in setting up a functional and secure computer laboratory for the project computers. He also has provided resources to allow project members to attend professional conferences related to their STACI^N activities. The Hillview project director has been a major asset to STACI^N. He is an experienced science teacher who is also a certified Macintosh computer technician. He has served as the project's resident technical expert.

The two other original Hillview teachers remain heavily involved with the project. These two individuals have been completely committed to infusing the systems approach into their team-taught, cross-disciplinary curriculum. Despite one person's maternity leave, these two dedicated teachers have developed and implemented extensive materials that cross disciplinary lines, with the common thread being systems thinking. They combine science, mathematics, social studies, and literature, and organize the curriculum modules around common themes to which the systems perspective is applied. They also wrote a workbook that all project teachers can use to introduce systems to their students. This workbook has been used for all seventh- and eighth-grade students as an introduction to systems thinking. These two teachers plan to revise the entire seventh- and eighth-grade curricula with systems thinking as the underlying philosophy. In the 1992/1993 academic year, these two teachers were given separate teaching assignments that will further spread systems thinking throughout the school. One is teaching the seventh-grade core curriculum. The other is now in charge of administering and teaching the eighth-grade core curriculum.

A fourth teacher was an original member of the project but had to resign when she assumed the role of computer coordinator at a local private school for the gifted. For 2 years, she continued her work with systems thinking as an unofficial project member. Upon mutual agreement, she resumed her role as an official participant in the project to the benefit of Hillview and her own institution. She recently moved to southern California and has been replaced by an experienced eighth-grade core curriculum teacher.

The most recent systems-infused activity at Hillview is a program that is ongoing during the entire 1992/1993 academic year, entitled *Seeds of Change*. The program focuses on the quincentenary of Columbus' discovery. It involves the entire school population and faculty. The premise of the program is that the discovery of America should not be considered an isolated event. Rather, there were important antecedents and consequences of the voyage that can be analyzed from a systems perspective. Three teachers, including two members of STACI[N], attended a workshop at the Smithsonian Institution and then mentored the rest of the faculty. The curriculum has been altered to infuse this program throughout the school year.

Students at Hillview are generally high achievers for whom teachers and parents hold rigorous standards. The teachers and parents view the project as an excellent way to provide a rich learning environment for the students, with the assumption that it does not interfere with standards and achievement. When students graduate from Hillview, they enter Menlo-Atherton High School, another of the project schools.

Menlo-Atherton High School

Menlo-Atherton High School (MA), is an institution with a bimodal student population that results in a host of challenging problems. MA is located in Atherton, an exceedingly wealthy community. It serves two very distinct populations. About 70% of the students are from the affluent, primarily White communities of Menlo Park and Atherton. The remaining 30% are

Black, Hispanic, and Pacific Island students from the poverty stricken city of East Palo Alto. These latter students are generally low academic achievers. MA is fortunate to have a supportive administration and excellent teaching staff. The superintendent has been an ardent supporter of the STACI^N Project, appearing at training sessions and other project activities. He not only visits the training classes but also attends the workshops as a student. The project has benefited from the leadership of the local project director and a responsive administration. The first principal was an active proponent of STACI^N from its inception, even assisting in fund-raising activities and helping to construct the well-secured and equipped computer laboratory. Her support and enthusiasm for the project provided important stimulation for the project teachers. Although she has retired, she continues to support the project and its work. The new principal is less involved in STACI^N, leaving responsibility to the project director.

STACI^N is extremely fortunate to have an excellent teacher serving as local project director at MA. Although he did not have a great deal of computer experience before undertaking the project, he is an experienced administrator, science department chairperson, respected educator (teacher of the year, numerous advisory boards, and research projects), and an individual dedicated to making the project work. He and the first principal worked to select teachers whose students and courses would benefit most from the systems approach. The outcome was a cadre of seven teachers, six in the sciences and one in economics. Rather than eliminate interested persons, the teachers agreed to split the stipends, the same amount provided in lump sum to the other schools that each nominated five teachers, and share the five dedicated computers. Not only did MA function with two extra teachers in the 1988/1989 academic year, but they added two mathematics teachers in the following year, who were mentored by the original participants.

There has been some turnover in personnel at MA, although four of the original teachers remain in the project. The project went from a high of nine teachers in the summer of 1989 to a low of six in 1991, when two teachers transferred to other high schools in the district, one retired, and a fourth resigned due to an over committed schedule. There are now seven participants, including the retired teacher who has returned to STACI^N and serves in a special capacity described later.

MA has an interesting composition of teachers, all of whom are extremely dedicated individuals trying to make the innovation work. All participants are trying to find appropriate applications for systems. However, the degree of success varies across the courses. The general science teachers have viewed the approach as an effective tool for remedial, at-risk students, where most other attempts have failed. They report that students who have been completely turned off by textbooks and school have found the work with the computer interesting and engaging. They are more likely to attend classes when the systems approach is being used. These students are being trusted with valuable computer equipment and are responding to that responsibility. Currently there is only one teacher using the approach in general science. She is a second-year teacher who joined the project when she arrived at MA in 1991. The approach was complementary to her pedagogical style, achieving success in the general course as well as in her chemistry courses.

At the other end of the spectrum, a second chemistry teacher is using the systems approach as a way of stimulating her chemistry and advanced chemistry students. Advanced students undertake independent research using STELLA. Both chemistry teachers are combining systems with collaborative, 2-week problem-solving tasks that require students to make interesting applications of the systems approach to the domain. A physics teacher also is using the approach for an enriched method of solving problems. The two other teachers are fairly new to the project and are attempting to integrate systems into various mathematics courses.

An interesting lesson can be drawn from the case of a former project teacher who had resigned due to health problems and has since returned to the project. This individual had hoped to move out of the state, but continue working informally on the project. When the move failed to materialize, he asked if he could be brought back into the project despite the fact that he would not be teaching full-time. MA rehired him so that he could provide support and expertise to the project. He frequently serves as a substitute teacher for the science department, especially when one of the systems teachers is absent. He serves as a laboratory resource person, a team-teacher, and a mentor to newer project participants. His special status in the project has facilitated the use of systems thinking in other teachers' classes, as well as collaborative teaching and curriculum development. He is contributing substantially to his own professional development as well as that of others because he has more time to spend on the project. He also has taken on the task of compiling and producing the project's periodic newsletter, *The Stock Exchange*. This is a task that will continue even after he moves from California, an indication of his dedication and commitment to the project's objectives. Thus, the project continues to thrive with four science teachers, two mathematics teachers, and this special resource person.

MA is a success story. But there is the sense that almost any project placed into an environment with a supportive administration and dedicated faculty would succeed. MA is by no means a utopia, as it suffers from overcrowding, fiscal constraints, racial tension, and other problems. However, the school does foster freedom and responsibility among the faculty so that they may provide their students with an excellent and stimulating learning environment. The systems thinking approach has helped to further that perspective.

Mountain View High School

Mountain View High School is a multiethnic institution serving one of the northernmost communities in the Silicon Valley. The district was attractive initially because of the widely known and highly respected superintendent. Indeed, all interactions with the superintendent proved informative, helpful, and supportive. He was an excellent administrator who was completely straightforward concerning funding and staffing issues. He actively pursued funding for the project, not just for his own staff, but for all the teachers in the project. He showed fiscal support for his own faculty by providing funding without hesitation for the nonscience teachers and resources for a well-equipped laboratory for the project computers. The superintendent retired and was replaced by a young, innovative educator who believes strongly in the potential of computers. His 10-year plan focuses heavily on technology, thereby providing a direct connection between district and project objectives. The superintendent has asked for research manuscripts and regularly attends the project workshops. It is clear that the superintendent is committed to the project and will continue to support it in every possible way.

The first principal at Mountain View attended 1 week of the initial summer training so that he would have a better understanding of his teachers' activities, after which time he remained uninvolved. The new principal has been much more involved, even helping to raise funds to upgrade the computer laboratory. Most of the project administration has been left to the local director, a physics teacher, who has handled substantial computer repair problems, scheduling issues, and personnel changes. The initial approach to problem resolution was to seek assistance from ETS and Apple. This tactic was compounded by the fact that this school had many maintenance problems. It also was affected by personnel turnover in the district financial management office on which the project relied for timely repair and replacement of equipment. Eventually, the school accepted responsibility for all subsequent maintenance and repair problems.

Progress with the systems approach at Mountain View was slow in developing. This is partially the result of some unique personnel issues. One teacher who has been writing a textbook tried to participate in the project while meeting her writing deadlines. She wavered about her participation until she finally realized she was over-committed and withdrew, leaving open the possibility of returning at a later date. She continues to use systems in her biology classes and is working with the project director to integrate systems into the required freshmen science course. She was replaced by a mathematics teacher who has been doing some superb work applying systems in his courses. The systems thinking approach has been totally infused into his advanced algebra and precalculus courses. Another teacher abruptly resigned her teaching position at the end of the 1990/1991 academic year on the first day of the project's summer training. It was impossible to replace her at that late date. A new mathematics teacher was appointed at the beginning of the next academic year, but it was too late for the individual to take advantage of the summer training.

Part of Mountain View's uniqueness is also its primary problem. Project teachers represent a diverse set of disciplines (physics, geology, mathematics, social studies, and at one point humanities). This disciplinary spread has allowed an estimated 80% of the senior class to be exposed to the systems thinking approach. Each of the teachers worked in isolation; they have not made much use of the substantive task forces by communicating with colleagues at other schools. For the most part, they work either alone or among themselves rather than with teachers from other schools. With the appointment of a second mathematics teacher, collaboration within the Mountain View faculty is beginning.

One of the original Mountain View teachers was a humanist. He was the only one in the entire project and was obviously isolated. To add to his difficulties, he lost his entire home in the October 17, 1989, Loma Prieta earthquake. Systems thinking was not necessarily the most salient factor in his life for a period of time. When HPS announced that they no longer would support STELLAStack, this teacher decided that his participation would be severely limited without the HyperCard interface and subsequently resigned from the project. One of the original project participants, a chemistry/physics teacher, attempted to work with the chemistry task force and experienced difficulties and frustrations because the nature and structure of her course differed substantially from the other chemistry courses. She preferred to work alone, stressing outcomes rather than the processes of learning. Because she also taught physics, a more effective forum for systems, she chose to collaborate with the other Mountain View physics teacher rather than use the application in chemistry. Mountain View boasts the only remaining high-school social studies teacher in the project. As a history/economics teacher, he continues to develop some interesting applications, particularly in his history courses.

The underlying theme at Mountain View has been isolationism. The teachers participating in the project are certainly excellent, experienced, and busy professionals. These teachers rarely collaborate with project members from other schools, a problem due partly to time. Several Mountain View teachers have been varsity coaches, a position which demands substantial portions of their time. However, in the training sessions, they rarely interact with people from other schools. An acknowledged strength of STACI[N] has been its ability to allow teachers to cross previously imposed barriers such as departmental or school boundaries. However, the Mountain View teachers are now beginning to take advantage of this opportunity to interact with other dedicated professionals.

Part of the early problem in communication was attributable to a computer virus that prevented the Mountain View teachers from using the electronic mail network for almost a year. It was nearly impossible to get a message through the school's switchboard. Consequently, all project participants had difficulty maintaining contact and obtaining the needed information about what actually was happening at the school. The communication issue has been resolved, and it is now anticipated that sharing with other project participants will begin to evolve.

South San Francisco Unified School District

Three of the STACI^N Project's schools are located in the South San Francisco Unified School District, which serves a multiethnic, working-class population. As a large district, it faces certain unique problems, but it also can provide certain services that are impossible for smaller districts. The project has had continued contact with several administrators who have facilitated and supported the effort from its inception. The first superintendent was a continual source of support, even helping to seek funding for the project from local foundations. He generally deferred to the assistant superintendent for secondary education and the special projects director when it came to matters of project administration and personnel. However, there were a few times when it was necessary for the superintendent to use his leverage and intercede on behalf of the project. There was no reticence on his part to come to the assistance of STACI^N. He retired at the end of the 1989/1990 academic year. His replacement understands the philosophy of the project but cannot devote much energy or resources to STACI^N because his primary concern is to balance the budget. Although he has pledged his support, he is reluctant to do anything that might cost the district money. The administrative support continues at the level of the assistant superintendent and the new special projects director, who recognize the project's worth to the district, especially because one of the schools, El Camino High School, has received national media coverage for its superb work with the curriculum innovation.

The assistant superintendent has taken the lead in resolving problems that arise in any of the three schools. He is the person who provides the final arbitration. This pattern has occurred several times in resolving some delicate issues concerning the selection of new personnel and the replacement of stolen equipment. Some financial and equipment problems have been resolved jointly with the district office.

The individual who has served as intermediary among administrators, teachers, and ETS is the director of special projects. This person has provided a valuable service both to ETS and the project teachers. He functioned as a project administrator across the three schools, organizing meetings, providing resources (i.e., disks, paper, etc.), orchestrating repairs, and dealing with ordinary problem resolution. He also has written proposals and contracted with agencies in an effort to seek additional monies for project efforts. His successor is continuing the supportive tradition.

Although the district has encountered severe financial difficulties, it has in the past found the resources to assist its teachers in their work on the project. The district has provided funds for additional training sessions taught by one of the project teachers on such topics as HyperCard, STELLAStack, and general Macintosh training. It has awarded mentor teacher funding to several project teachers to provide them with extra money. An award was made to the district by a local foundation to be used to defray some of the project's cost, with the stipulation that matching monies also had to be obtained. ETS provided the matching funds. These monies were critical because one school has three social studies teachers for which ETS cannot use government money for stipend payment.

The district also paid stipends to teachers for attendance at the February, 1989, training, while the project was seeking funding. No other district provided stipends for their faculty; consequently there were both positive and negative implications of this reward system. There is no doubt that the stipends given to the teachers for participation in the project are inadequate. They simply cannot be reimbursed sufficiently for their time and efforts. However, every little bit helps, especially when time and resources are so limited. Yet, when some people are paid stipends and others are not, different messages are being sent by the administrations. For South San Francisco, the message was that the administration supported the teachers' efforts. It was clear that some teachers could not or would not have continued their participation without these payments. From the perspective of the other schools who were not paid, these stipends could be construed as subtle bribes. Teachers in three California schools were not paid stipends. In the first, such payment was considered unnecessary, as the teachers believe that project activities are professional development. The second school simply did not have the resources to pay stipends. Teachers in the third school expressed some jealousy. The general point here is that these payments provided interesting insights into the motivations and resources of both teachers and administrators. The project will never know how many South San Francisco teachers would not have continued to work on the project at that early stage if there were no monetary incentives.

Another interesting yet contradictory incident concerning stipends but also commitment to the project occurred a year later. The district and teachers failed to come to terms on a contractual arrangement. The teachers were instructed by their union to do no work other than teach their classes and leave campus promptly at the close of each school day. No extracurricular activities were allowed except coaching duties. STACIN teachers ignored this advice, stating that the project was the only activity worth pursuing for purposes of professional and intellectual development. Against union advice, they refused to give up their work with systems thinking, demonstrating their commitment to the project.

The district recently has suffered severe financial problems. Many experienced teachers and high-level administrators have been forced to resign. The district has been in a state of turmoil and the staff is completely demoralized. One project school principal took early retirement; another was reassigned to a middle school. A third principal, a graduate of that school, left the district to accept a better paying position in a neighboring district after 22 years of service. A senior project director's request for a leave of absence was denied. The assistant superintendent's job has been redefined and is now titled director. Several project teachers were forced to seek better paying jobs in neighboring districts. ETS was told that the district would be unable to continue to cover any project-related costs, including stipends for the social studies teachers. Yet, through these difficult times, teachers report that participation in STACI[N] is the one motivating factor that maintains their sense of professionalism.

Westborough Middle School

Westborough is one of three middle schools in the South San Francisco Unified School District. Originally a junior high school, Westborough converted to a middle-school core curriculum in the 1992/1993 academic year. Approximately half the students feed into El Camino High School and half into South San Francisco High School. Westborough's first principal was a supporter of the project from its inception. He left primary responsibility for the project in the experienced hands of the local project director, a senior mathematics and computer science teacher. Jointly, they designed the computer laboratory and managed some rather delicate issues when changes occurred in the composition of teachers. Neither of these individuals returned for the 1991/1992 academic year. The principal took early retirement, and the project director resigned from the district due to an illness in her immediate family. The new principal is an ardent supporter of the project, who established his interest by attending training sessions to understand better the activities of his teachers. He is trying to protect systems thinking while restructuring the school into a core-curriculum format, adding a grade, and experiencing a severe space shortage.

The original cadre consisted of two mathematics, two social studies, and one science teacher. Except for the local project director, none of the other teachers had any computer experience. The two social studies teachers rapidly became captivated with the technology and made every effort to seek opportunities for additional training. The other two teachers were less enthusiastic. One of these teachers resigned in January, 1989, when he decided to retire. He was replaced with another social studies teacher who immediately formed a close working group with his substantive colleagues. The other teacher resigned in the beginning of the 1989/1990 academic year after he failed to appear at the summer training. In fact, he was asked to resign because of his lack of performance. He had no intention of making use of the systems thinking approach. The timing of these events was unfortunate because he neither attended the summer training nor made it possible for his replacement, another mathematics teacher, to attend the training, thus delaying this new teacher's first real exposure to the perspective until the following February.

Another interesting personnel issue arose when the project director decided to take a 1-year sabbatical because of illness in her family. This teacher had served a vital role at the school. Because her social studies colleagues were inexperienced computer users, she functioned as the technology expert and intellectual leader. The teachers had formed a close working group whereby the project director served as organizer and mentor. When she requested the leave of absence, the district expected that she would also withdraw temporarily from the project. ETS staff and the other Westborough teachers felt that the project and the working group would suffer greatly without the intellectual mentorship the project director provided. After much deliberation with administrators, it was decided that she could continue her participation in the project despite being on leave from the district. The outcome was that she devoted more time to the project and the working group than if she had continued her teaching responsibilities. There has been a thriving and collegial working group at Westborough, mixed with mathematics and social studies teachers who are developing materials that provide cross-disciplinary uses of the systems approach. This form of participation continued during a second sabbatical year, which unfortunately could not be extended for a third year, at which point she resigned from the district

Westborough added a fifth teacher to its ranks in the fall of 1991. This individual teaches an introductory computer course and industrial science. This is the project's first experience with the latter discipline, which allows for an extension of the systems approach to the many systems that are taught in the course. The extension also helps to facilitate a more cross-disciplinary approach that serves as a precursor to the school's transition to a middle-school core curriculum in the 1992/1993 academic year.

Many changes will occur at Westborough as it makes the transition from a departmentally organized junior high-school to the middle-school core curriculum. There are many uncertainties as to how the changes will affect STACIN. The project's experiences in one junior high school and one middle school provide some clues as to the possible impact. An initial speculation is that the transition will facilitate more collaboration among the project participants and more extensions of systems to other non-project teachers due to a decreased emphasis on departmental structure. There is likely to be more exchange of ideas and curriculum materials, greater flexibility in the use of systems thinking, and more innovative applications of the perspective. It will be interesting to observe Westborough as it undergoes the transition over the next few years.

South San Francisco High School

South San Francisco High School, called South City, is one of two high schools in the district participating in the STACI^N Project. The first principal here was not at all involved in project activities, a problem acknowledged by several of the project teachers who lamented the lack of professional recognition. All responsibilities for project administration, orchestration, and the computer laboratory centered on the local project director. Not only has this individual served as administrator and intellectual leader for South City, but he also was hired by the district to conduct a series of in-service training sessions on HyperCard, STELLA, STELLAStack, and more generally, the Macintosh. He also was hired by the project to conduct similar sessions for the South Bay schools as well and by HPS to assist in the all-project training sessions. Thus, this teacher has become a valuable resource for the teachers at the school as well as those in collaborating institutions. He has served as a mentor to new teachers, particularly at South City, as they struggle to learn the systems thinking approach.

The current cadre of participants includes three teachers currently at South City and two who were former members of the faculty. The group went through several participants until it found the right composition of members. Unfortunately, the school lost an excellent participant when the chemistry teacher moved out of the district after the first year of the project. She was replaced by a mathematics teacher who, working in collaboration with the project director, also a math teacher, has produced a number of applications for their courses. A biology teacher, in collaboration with the biology task force, has developed what HPS considered some extremely sophisticated and applicable models of biological phenomena. This individual currently is teaching middle-school science in a neighboring district and continues to work on the project. An economist and a social studies teacher who were original project members encountered problems similar to those of the other social studies task-force participants and ultimately decided to withdraw from the project. They were replaced by an enthusiastic young science teacher whose courses include chemistry, physics, and geology. This teacher was trained and began working with the project in February, 1990, as an official member of the El Camino High School group, thereby establishing a cross-school collaboration that bridged institutional barriers. After two resignations at South City, he became a member of his own school's group, but continued to maintain the collaboration with El Camino's science teachers. He, too, has left the district for a science job at a high school in a neighboring affluent community and continues to be a valued contributor to the project. A PhD-level chemistry teacher joined the project in the 1991/1992 academic year. She rapidly acquired knowledge of systems and has begun using the approach effectively in her classes.

Early in the project, one got the impression from the teachers at South City that they were overwhelmed, underpaid, and not sufficiently appreciated. The first principal generally took a hands-off approach to the entire enterprise. It was difficult to gauge how much internal support he gave to the project teachers. It was apparent that the teachers came immediately to either the special projects director or ETS when needs arose. South City's approach to the project seemed to be a direct result of the disinterested school administration, not a district-wide condition. Despite this situation, the majority of the South City teachers produced outstanding curriculum materials.

Two events at South City recently changed the structure and functioning of STACI^N at the school. First, a new principal was appointed during the summer of 1991. Because she has served in a variety of counseling and administrative capacities in the district for many years, she is well known and highly respected by most of the South City faculty. She has positively changed the ambiance of the school and created a supportive environment in which projects like STACI^N can thrive. Despite her brief tenure as principal, she has shown substantial interest in and enthusiasm for the project. She joined the two other project principals at a school board meeting as a sign of support and has been extremely helpful with respect to fund raising. The teachers have acknowledged that her support is much appreciated and makes a difference.

A second event that affected South City and STACI^N was the resignation of two project teachers during the summer of 1991. These individuals felt compelled to take positions at neighboring districts with higher pay scales. Both teachers were extremely productive members of the project who had established collaborations particularly with teachers at other schools. They both had expressed interest in continuing their work with the systems thinking approach and STACI^N. The project's policy had always been that if teachers left the district, their formal participation in the project ceased because ETS's contractual arrangements were with the districts, not individual teachers. The project was faced with losing two people who were committed to using systems thinking at their new schools and who were important contributors to several working groups. The project resolved the issue by offering the two teachers 1-year consulting contracts equivalent to the stipends. These contracts will be reviewed annually to determine their viability. If ETS thinks the relationships are advantageous to the project and the teachers perceive them to be professionally functional, the arrangements will be continued. To date, these teachers continue to be productive members of the project, assisting in the activities at South City as well as other STACI^N schools. Both teachers are initiating systems thinking activities in their own schools.

El Camino High School

El Camino is a veritable ugly duckling story, reflective of the fact that it started as a major problem school and was transformed into a wonderful success. The transformation was due, in part, to a change in administrations. When first approached to join the project, El Camino was managed by a traditional principal who employed an authoritarian leadership style. He had been at El Camino for many years and was widely feared by many students and faculty. He was not particularly interested in innovations and eschewed technology. His hostility toward the STACIN Project was evident from the first meeting in which he expressed his opinion that computers would be of little value in teaching and learning. Nevertheless, he agreed to allow the project into his school. Needless to say, the hostile attitude he presented in front of selected faculty did not instill confidence that the project would be supported appropriately. He also suggested to his faculty that participation in the project would be personally profitable because each teacher would be given a computer and "lots of money."

During the first year, the principal did nothing blatantly harmful to the project, nor did he make things easy. He grudgingly approved a room that could be used as a computer laboratory. The room was poorly lighted, had little ventilation, few chalkboards, and inadequate facilities (i.e., armchair desks in rows). The room was not dedicated solely to computer use. Other classes used the room and abused the computers. Moreover, the room was on the first floor of a school building in a high-crime neighborhood. There were 15 computers there for anyone who could break into the room and foil an obviously inadequate security system. This is precisely what happened in March, 1989, and again in July, 1990. ETS staff were not informed of the first theft of two project computers until two teachers inadvertently mentioned it at the subsequent summer training, some 3 months after the incident. Security was a hard lesson to learn; the computers grudgingly were replaced at the district's expense, only after the superintendent interceded to require that an assistant purchase the new hardware.

The second theft of three computers really created problems for the district. Not only the computers but also the projection system and the overhead projector were stolen, both of which had been purchased by the district. A new superintendent had just arrived. The district was in severe financial difficulty with an enormous projected deficit. The last thing they needed was to replace $10,000 in equipment, despite the stipulation in the contract with ETS. External Research at Apple again came to the rescue. They promised to replace the computers as a one-time supplementary "gift," with two explicit conditions. First, there would be no consideration of replacement computers unless the district replaced the projection equipment. Second, the laboratory had to be moved to a more secure second-floor location. These conditions were met before the opening of school.

About this time, a fortuitous event occurred. The principal decided to retire, and a forward-thinking successor was appointed. The new principal believed in supporting his faculty and was a strong proponent of the use of technology in education. The change in social climate at the school was immediate and obvious to anyone who visited the campus. There was an open door policy and a feeling of respect for the faculty's professionalism. The principal thoroughly supported the project and the teachers' involvement in STACI^N. Although responsibility for the project rested with the project directors, the principal provided valuable input into personnel selection and the physical plant. In conjunction with the special projects director, he made sure that the replacement computers from the second theft were delivered before the opening of school. Whiteboards were installed to replace the chalkboards in the laboratory. The room was dedicated primarily to STACI^N Project use and exclusively to computer classes. Security measures were improved to minimize the possibility of further theft. Perhaps the biggest and most striking change has been the motivation, support, and responsibility the new principal instilled in his faculty, staff, and students. The change made El Camino a vastly improved environment in which to teach and learn. A neighboring district lured this principal away at the end of the 1991/1992 school year. Fortunately, he was replaced by a woman who shares many of the same values and objectives. It is likely that the project will continue to thrive under the new administration.

The first principal influenced the initial selection of teachers and created a difficult atmosphere in which the project had to function. It was particularly threatening for three young and untenured teachers, who perceived that their careers might be in jeopardy. The faculty originally selected for participation in the project were at both ends of their careers and thereby were more or less affected by the principal. The project director was an experienced social studies teacher who maintained a nonconfrontational manner. He resigned from the project at the end of the first year. The principal then appointed a business teacher whose nomination ETS vetoed because there would be no colleagues with whom he could work, further evidence that the principal did not understand or take interest in the project. The other experienced teacher also taught social studies and apparently was not influenced by the administration. He, too, resigned at the end of the first year because of other commitments. He was replaced by another social studies teacher who also found he was overcommitted and resigned in the middle of the second year. Of the three young teachers, one was a mathematician who never really gave the project a chance and resigned after failing to attend the second summer training. These teachers were replaced by two extremely enthusiastic science teachers.

Of the original group, the two young teachers who had expressed the most concern about the possible negative effects on their careers not only continue to participate in the project, but have thrived and developed professionally. Serving now as co-project directors, they have mentored their new colleagues, shown limitless enthusiasm, and produced and implemented some outstanding curriculum modules, particularly for at-risk students. These individuals instruct primarily in biology and life sciences, but also teach chemistry and earth science. They took the initiative, applied for, and received an award from a local foundation and obtained money from the district to purchase additional computers, memory upgrades, and hard drives for the laboratory.

Collaboration among the four science teachers at El Camino is enhanced by the fact that they all teach the same courses. They also have established a collaboration with another science teacher formerly from South City and now at a high school in Marin County. Initially the project directors were concerned that having only four teachers at El Camino might reflect badly on their school. They were assured that it was better to have a strongly committed foursome. A fifth teacher eventually would be appointed when an appropriate person could be identified. Instead, they opted for the appointment of the colleague from South City with whom they could work on substantive matters. This collaboration worked well; the new South City teacher took it upon himself to obtain training and came to the February, 1990, workshop armed with ideas and well-developed models. He bridged what heretofore has been considered a tension-filled gap between the two high schools. Thus, there was a cohesive cadre of teachers, working together across science courses to integrate systems into their classes.

These teachers readily acknowledge that having the support of the principal makes a great deal of difference. They also acknowledge that participation in the STACI^N Project is one of the most important professional activities in which they are currently engaged. Given the dire fiscal condition of the district, the teachers report that STACI^N is the only activity that provides intellectual challenges and motivation. In fact, these teachers crossed picket lines during contract negotiations so that they could continue their work on the project. The progress made by these teachers and the successes they have experienced show what is possible when dedicated professionals have an opportunity to flourish. It will be most illuminating to monitor the evolution of the work at El Camino as these teachers become more experienced with the systems thinking approach.

Sunnyside High School

Sunnyside High School in Tucson, Arizona became the eighth and final school in the STACI^N Project in the spring of 1990. Although Sunnyside joined the project in an official capacity in 1990, it had important ties to project activities dating back to the first summer workshop at Stanford in 1988. A mathematics teacher attended that training as an invited guest. He was accompanied by four teachers from other schools in Tucson. Subsequently, a group of 10 teachers from various Tucson schools attended the first winter workshop, some of whom continued to work with systems thinking on their own. However, the Sunnyside mathematics teacher continued to collaborate with STACI^N Project participants. In fact, he asked to attend at his own expense the next summer workshop. This teacher continued using systems in his classes and created a Sunnyside High School Systems Thinking Club. With only his personal Macintosh, this teacher had over 40 primarily minority students involved with systems thinking.

Sunnyside, with only one teacher, one Macintosh, and no support, made fantastic progress using the approach with a large number of at-risk students. ETS staff visited the school several times and became increasingly impressed with the systems activities accomplished with limited resources. It became clear that STACI^N and Sunnyside High School would benefit mutually by obtaining the hardware and software necessary to expand the project to include an eighth school.

As mentioned in chapter 2, the director of Apple External Research sought a teacher from the project who could address a national conference on the education of at-risk students in the spring of 1990. Sunnyside High School, led by the mathematics teacher, was an ideal representative. The teacher managed to negotiate the participation of several students who ultimately made the conference presentation. Following the conference, Apple donated a laboratory of hardware for use at the high school. The donation of the computers made possible the expansion of systems thinking to other teachers, a full-blown implementation of the approach, and participation in STACI^N. Fortunately, ETS was able to raise additional funds from the U.S. Department of Education to support the activities at Sunnyside and bring them formally into the project.

Computers were delivered to Sunnyside in May, 1990, and three mathematics teachers attended the summer training the following month. The teachers quickly gained a good working knowledge of systems thinking, aided by their collaborations with other project participants, their existing expertise with computers, and the original teacher's experience with the systems approach. The three STACI^N Project participants have been mentoring two other mathematics department colleagues in the use of systems thinking. Several teachers in other departments have already expressed interest in the approach. In fact, a humanities teacher joined the project in 1992 in time for the summer training.

The teachers are fortunate to have complete support from the principal and assistant principals. The principal is an ardent Macintosh user who is interested in learning what the teachers are trying to accomplish with systems thinking. He has expedited several presentations about systems thinking at Sunnyside for the school board, the public, and at national computing conferences.

Initial contact with district-level administrators proved frustrating. ETS staff were advised that most communication should occur with the assistant superintendent for curriculum. The district administration's first reactions were very skeptical, for they were experiencing severe financial problems and could not consider any activity that would require money from their budget. They also expressed concern that the systems approach might negatively affect their existing curriculum. ETS staff assured the administration that there would be no interference with their curriculum nor would there be any expectations for an immediate monetary outlay. The original superintendent remained uninvolved. A new superintendent has been appointed and briefed about the project.

It was the students who managed to convince the administration of the worth of the systems approach. Several students were asked to give a presentation at a school board meeting. Prior to the meeting the students rehearsed before the assistant superintendent. ETS staff watched her become completely enthralled with the approach during the rehearsal. From that time, she became a staunch supporter of the project. The presentation to the school board, the public, and other administrators only served to further reinforce the merits of the systems approach.

Appendix B

DRAFT MODEL OF A COMPUTER-BASED CURRICULUM INNOVATION

In this appendix a model will be developed. It will be a first draft of a model of computer-based curriculum innovations that can be generalized to other projects similar to STACI[N]. However, the experiences of the systems thinking projects will be used as the specific exemplars. In stepping through the various phases of model development, this appendix first will identify the primary variables that are likely to be salient in a curriculum innovation effort. The key variables that influence the implementation and evolution of a curriculum innovation will be identified. How these factors combine to influence one another and interact with other variables then will be examined.

Models and Maps

The first phase in developing a model of a computer-based curriculum innovation is to define the key variables. Specification of key variables in modeling is a highly subjective decision. The modeler selects among a theoretically infinite number of possible variables to describe adequately the phenomena and processes of interest. The delineation of boundaries for the model also is subjective, for the specification of endogenous and exogenous factors represents the modeler's perception of reality. Consequently, the acceptance or rejection of any particular model depends on the degree of verisimilitude attributed to it by others, as well as the goodness of fit with any available empirical data. As in all the chapters in this volume, the focus continues to be on three primary areas that have guided the STACI[N] Project's inquiry: student learning, classroom processes, and organizational change. Therefore, the draft model of a computer-based curriculum innovation presented later is offered as the authors' characterization of the systems involved at three levels of social organization: the student, the classroom, and the school. Consequently, the model is presented in three analogous levels, using the STELLA mapping mode.

    A STELLA map is a convenient way of portraying a first draft of what eventually will become a STELLA model. The software package permits two basic modes of operation: mapping and modeling. The former is preliminary and does not require the same detailed specification of variables and interrelationships. The latter produces the differential equations that permit running the model over simulated time to observe patterns of relationships and the outcome values of variables. The first draft of the model for a computer-based curriculum innovation is presented as a STELLA map. The same four STELLA building blocks described in chapter

3 are used in constructing a STELLA map. The building blocks are: (a) stocks, which function as accumulators; (b) flows, which add to or delete from the stocks; (c) converters, which express relationships between variables; and (d) connectors, which establish logical linkages among model elements. Due to the fact that a computer-based curriculum innovation is comprised of such a multitude of complex, interrelated variables, it is not yet possible to create a working model. Rather, the intention here is to present a map of a computer-based curriculum innovation to invite comments and suggestions from colleagues for the revision and expansion and eventual model construction.

Student Learning Level

Turning first to student learning, Table B.1 lists the major relevant domains and variables, and Fig. B.1 is a printout of the corresponding STELLA map. The student learning resulting from instruction is the major focus here, and the domains of motivation and assessment are portrayed as salient factors. Instruction is portrayed in the map as exogenous flows into two stocks that accumulate learning. One stock accumulates procedural knowledge; the other accumulates declarative or content knowledge. Procedural knowledge refers here to problem-solving skills using systems thinking, and it accumulates primarily as a consequence of instruction in and experience with systems thinking. This accumulation is portrayed in the map with an arrow from the flow of systems instruction to procedural knowledge.

TABLE B.1

Major Domains and Variables for the Student Learning Level

Instruction
        Curriculum-systems instruction
        Curriculum-traditional instruction
        Procedural knowledge
Student Motivation
        Self concept
        Need for achievement
        Attitudes
        Aspiration
        Perceived benefits
        Willingness to use computers
Assessment
        Standards
        Performance
        New techniques
        Integration with instruction
        Accountability

FIG. B.1. Student learning level.

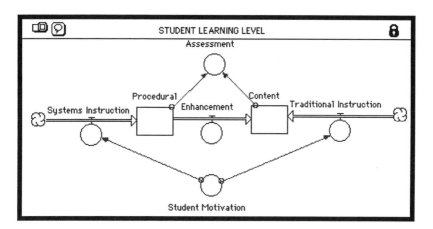

Declarative or content knowledge in fields such as biology, chemistry, or physics accumulates primarily as a consequence of instruction in these areas. Correspondingly, it is portrayed in the map with an arrow from the flow of traditional instruction to declarative knowledge. In STELLA, the arrows indicate the direction of influence or causality. In many instances, the flow might operate in both directions, indicating a reciprocal relationship. However, in the interest of clarity and parsimony, all arrows in this draft map will be limited to one direction.

It is a major assumption of the model as well as the STACIN Project that the acquisition of subject knowledge is substantially enhanced as a consequence of the use of both traditional and systems thinking instructional techniques. In the future, the STACIN Project will be able to examine this as our empirical data. This enhancement of learning is portrayed in the map as a flow with the arrow pointing from the procedural knowledge stock to the declarative knowledge stock. Here one could cogently argue that the arrow should point in both directions, for the acquisition of declarative knowledge could easily enhance the acquisition of procedural knowledge. However, to preserve simplicity at this point, the enhancement as portrayed in Fig. B.1 remains unidirectional. A future model will have to take into account a bidirectional or reciprocal relationship. In the model, this enhancement will be stated as an exponential growth relationship. The map also recognizes the critical importance of student motivation and its impact on learning of both procedural and declarative knowledge. Motivation is portrayed as a converter. Through its connection with both types of instruction, it regulates or controls the amount of learning that accumulates.

Note that Table B.1 lists a number of noncognitive factors under the category of student motivation, including self-concept, need for achievement, attitudes, aspirations, perceived benefits, and willingness to use computers. All these factors are relevant for student motivation, and all exert some influence on both procedural and declarative knowledge learning. However, for two reasons they are not all specified in this map. First, it is necessary to constrain the size of the map for the purpose of this introductory explanation. Second, further empirical research is needed to provide a basis for hypothesizing the nature of the relationships between all the factors listed under the domain of student motivation and the accumulation of learning in the two stocks of interest. An important characteristic of all modeling and simulation activities is the fact that they are never finalized. All models are constantly under revision and expansion. It is anticipated that future versions of this model of a computer-based curriculum innovation will greatly expand on the rudimentary beginnings presented here. For example, all the factors listed under the domain of student motivation, and most likely other factors as well, will be included as stocks, flows, or connectors in subsequent versions of this model.

The same pattern of simplification is repeated in the domain of assessment, which in Table B.1 includes the following factors: academic standards, performance, new measurement techniques, integration with instruction, and accountability. All these factors are influenced by procedural and declarative knowledge learning. However, they are not each included in the map portrayed in Fig. B.1. Nevertheless, they are listed in Table B.1 to convey the authors' contention that, based on their field work in the STACIN Project, these variables are relevant and interrelated.

The map in Fig. B.1 represents one particular perspective on student learning. It is a simplified version of what has been observed in the STACIN Project field work. As such, it has some unique features, such as the distinction between the input flows to procedural and declarative knowledge acquisition. However, this model is not all that different from those proposed by others (see Salomon, 1990, 1991). The value of the perspective proposed in this volume will become clearer when the map is extended to include the other two levels, classroom processes and organizational change. Perhaps what makes this proposed model unique are the hypothesized interrelationships among variables across the three levels.

Classroom Processes Level

Turning to the classroom processes level, Table B.2 lists the major domains and associated variables; Fig. B.2 portrays the corresponding map. The proposed model is somewhat more complex at this level. At the student learning level there were three domains, but, as Table B.2 shows, at the classroom processes level there are five: instruction, curriculum, resources, support, and accountability. As in the student learning level, the domain of greatest interest here also is instruction, which is composed of four factors: two stocks, interactive learning and learner-directed learning; and two flows, technology, and student and teacher role changes. Like the two stocks at the student learning level of the model, the stocks at the classroom processes level also accumulate learning. However, the types of learning are different. Here the emphasis is on interactive and learner-directed learning, the two hallmarks of computer-based curriculum innovations.

TABLE B.2

Major Domains and Variables for the Classroom Processes Level

---

Instruction
     Technology
     Interactive learning
     Student and teacher role changes
     Learner-directed learning
Resources
     Hardware and software
     Laboratory
     Networks
     Stipends
     Release time
     Paraprofessionals
Support
     Training
     Technical assistance
     Subject expertise
     Administrative commitment
Curriculum
     Theoretical foundation
     Topic selection
     Sequencing
     Integration
Accountability
     Students
     Groups
     Class
     Teachers

Interactive learning is greatly facilitated, of course, by the microcomputers. The immediate feedback from the machines makes a new and potentially more effective learning environment possible, which is characterized by rapid responses to student inputs or queries. The technology functions as a dedicated tutor, allowing students to progress through the materials at their own pace. Furthermore, the feedback is tailored to student

FIG. B.2. Classroom processes level.

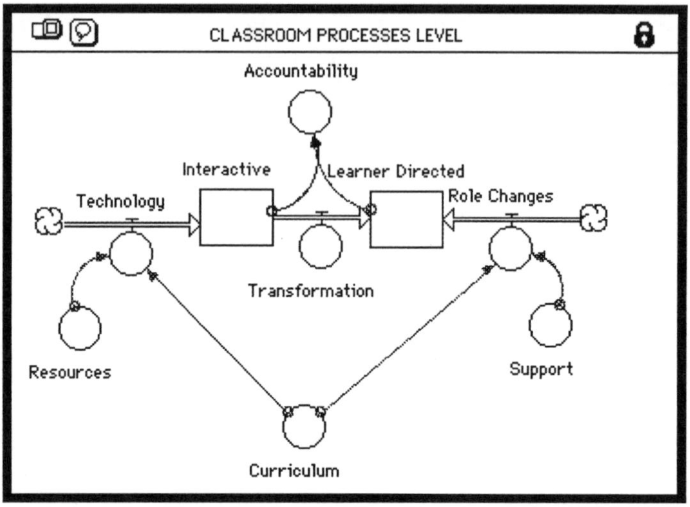

input, and this type of interactivity produces individualized instruction. There is a second, derivative connotation to interactivity in computer-based curriculum innovation projects. Because very few schools can afford to purchase enough microcomputers to provide one for each student, most students work on computers in groups of two or sometimes three. As already noted, this type of computer laboratory arrangement promotes group work and problem solving. Consequently, group learning emerges from the interactions among the students. Therefore, technology is portrayed as an external flow which feeds into the stock, interactive learning.

Likewise, the learner-directed learning is also portrayed as a stock, but its accumulation is directly affected by the role changes experienced by both teachers and students in a computer-based curriculum innovation. This relationship is depicted in Fig. B.2 by the arrow from the flow role changes to the stock learner-directed learning. As noted in the chapters, students take greater responsibility for their own educational activities in the learner-directed classroom. The teacher is no longer the sole or primary dispenser of knowledge. Students become more active in the processes of teaching and learning. They function as both the instructors and the instructed for themselves, for other students, as well as for their so-called teachers. Thus, learner-directed learning is depicted as a stock and the external flow of role change most directly affects its accumulation.

Note that Fig. B.2 denotes a relationship between interactive and learner-directed learning with the flow arrow going from the former to the latter. This portrayal reflects the assumption that the interactive learning environment created by the technology facilitates the transformation of the classroom from a teacher-directed mode of operation to a learner-directed format. This relationship is analogous to the enhancement observed at the student learning level between procedural and declarative knowledge acquisition. In the model it also will be expressed as an exponential or rapidly increasing relationship.

The domains included in the classroom processes level of the model that influence instructional activities also are portrayed in Fig. B.2. Look first at the resources converter on the right-hand side of the figure. This converter regulates the level of technology available and used in the classroom. Now look at Table B.2 that lists several key factors. First, and obviously most critical, are the hardware and software necessary to implement the computer-based curriculum innovation. As mentioned in chapter 4, the computers, peripheral equipment, and programs must be housed in a suitable and secure classroom setting. Various configurations of fixed and mobile laboratories are possible. If the innovation includes several schools, an electronic networking capability can greatly facilitate resource sharing among participating teachers and students.

In addition, several other resources directed at giving greater capacity and flexibility to the teachers can enhance the level of use of the technology. These include stipends for the teachers to compensate them partially for the enormous amount of extra time they must devote to curriculum development activities. Of course, as the innovation spreads throughout the school and district, stipends cannot be provided for all teachers involved in the effort. However, in the early stages of such a labor-intensive project, stipends can provide an extra incentive. In the STACI[N] Project, teachers repeatedly expressed the opinion that stipends were not the primary reason for participating, but they certainly did help and were much appreciated. They also recognized that the stipends could not be continued indefinitely.

The lack of sufficient discretionary time in the overcrowded schedules of teachers also influences the extent to which technology is used in classrooms. The theme most frequently mentioned in teacher interviews in the STACI[N] Project is the lack of any discretionary time to integrate anything new in their classes. Once school starts in the fall each year, the teachers are so heavily scheduled and programmed that they report having very little discretionary time even to consider anything innovative. Therefore, release time and the use of paraprofessional staff to accomplish the many nonteaching duties assigned to teachers can greatly facilitate the level of effective technology use in the innovation.

Turning to the support connector that regulates the accumulation of learner-directed learning, Table B.2 lists four factors. The first and paramount issue is initial and continuing teacher training activities. All too many computer-based curriculum innovation projects fail because inadequate training is provided in the effective use of the hardware and software. A common error in such projects is to invest most of the available resources in equipment and virtually ignore the need to allow teachers to become comfortable and competent with the hardware, software, and the pedagogy implicit in the innovation (see Cline, Bennett, Kershaw, Schneiderman, Stecher, & Wilson, 1986). Rarely is it sufficient to provide training just prior to the implementation. Rather, regularly scheduled and frequent sessions are needed to supplement the initial training. These subsequent sessions should be organized as workshops, allowing time for teachers to work collaboratively and learn from one another. Indeed, the structure and format of these sessions should mirror the interactive and learner-directed learning environments the teachers are creating in their own classrooms.

In addition to regular and frequent training workshops, the accumulation of learner-directed learning can be further enhanced by other types of support, including technical assistance, subject expertise, and administrative commitment. Particularly during those stages of the innovation when the teachers are working with new hardware and software, they need ready access to technical assistance for eliminating bugs and resolving equipment problems. In addition, as teachers make progress with their curriculum innovations, they frequently find that they need to consult experts in their subject matter to resolve substantive questions. Teaching old topics in new ways frequently makes one aware that subject mastery may not be as comprehensive as previously conceived. Therefore, access to someone else with expertise in the subject can expedite progress with the innovation. Frequently, this expertise can be located among immediate colleagues or perhaps with a faculty member in a neighboring school or district. On occasion, it may be necessary to seek assistance elsewhere, perhaps in a university or industrial setting.

In the long run, the type of support that may be most critical is that received from the school and district administration. It is essential to the success of any innovation program in any organization. In the STACI[N] Project, this type of support is referred to as *command commitment*. A great deal of effort has been devoted in this project to gaining the acceptance and support of the innovation among senior administrators. Periodic visits are made and reports are provided to building administrators, district supervisors, and school board members. Furthermore, meetings of the project principals have been convened to discuss STACI[N] and view firsthand the activities of the teachers in training workshops. Similar gatherings are planned for district personnel. The interaction of the four support factors, training, technical assistance, subject expertise, and administrative commitment, all enhance teacher and student role changes and thereby facilitate learner-directed learning.

Figure B.2 portrays the converter representing curriculum as influencing both stocks at the classroom processes level of the model. These relationships reflect the view that several curricular issues directly affect both interactive and learner-directed learning. Table B.2 lists these issues. First and conceptually most important is the theoretical foundation of the innovation. Many computer-based innovation projects are very weak with respect to any theoretical foundation. In fact, all too many projects have only computer use as the objective and foundation. As described earlier, systems thinking is the theoretical foundation for the curriculum innovation in the STACI[N] Project.

It has been pointed out previously that computers are not mandatory for teaching the theoretical foundation. Systems thinking can be used quite effectively in the classroom without computers. Indeed, at Hillview Middle School the Macintosh computers are not critical for the project. However, in most instances, the use of systems thinking in teaching substantive topics in biology, chemistry, mathematics, and physics is greatly enhanced by the implementation of models and simulations on the computers. The objective of the curriculum innovation is not to use computers in the classroom. Rather, the objective is to introduce students to systems thinking, an important problem-solving tool that is particularly useful in dealing with dynamic phenomena. In most but not all instances, the computer facilitates achieving that objective.

Given the existence of a theoretical foundation, the curriculum issues of topic selection and sequencing are derivative. They each follow from the theory being expounded. In the STACI[N] Project, the teachers work in groups or task forces on the curriculum issues of topic selection and sequencing. Collaboration increases productivity here. The task-force members select the substantive topics that they think can be taught more effectively using systems thinking. They then divide the labor among themselves to produce the curriculum modules. They also determine where in the course sequence to use the module and how to integrate it in the overall curriculum objectives.

The issue of integration raises another interesting question relevant to many computer-based curriculum innovation projects. On the one hand, integration refers to the inclusion of new curriculum modules into the instructional sequence. But integration can also take on another connotation: the integration of instruction and assessment. Many teachers in the STACI[N] Project have noticed that in the interactive and learner-directed classroom the distinction between teaching and testing becomes somewhat blurred. The computer provides rapid and specific responses to student inputs. If properly programmed, those responses can provide feedback in the form of assessment, diagnosis, and the specification of the next appropriate individualized instructional sequence. Therefore, it is possible that computer-based curriculum innovations could radically change the structure and functioning of most classrooms.

Fundamentally, teaching has been practiced in much the same manner for several thousand years. The person who presumably knows the subject matter being taught stands in front of those who either want to learn or are required to be present and dispenses the knowledge. Periodically the teacher stops the lecturing and gives some type of test or examination to see if the learners are absorbing the material.

Of course, there are many very exciting deviations from this pattern, but most teaching and learning activities in the nation's schools still adhere to this basic form. Introduce the interactive and learner-directed environments, however, and the potential for changing the dynamics of the classroom and enhancing the effectiveness and efficiency of educational practices is enormous. Immediate feedback makes it possible to use assessment for diagnostic purposes as well as accountability. The computer-based classroom can then integrate instruction and assessment in the same system. This integration has not yet been accomplished in the STACI^N Project, but it is on the agenda for future development.

The last converter portrayed in Fig. B.2 is accountability, which is influenced by both the interactive and learner-directed stocks. Accountability at the classroom processes level of the model corresponds to assessment at the student learning level. This representation at the classroom processes level reflects the authors' contention that both types of learning represented by the stocks affect the manner in which accountability operates. The instruments and procedures employed to gauge performance are necessarily different in a computer-based curriculum innovation project. The major reason for these differences is the fact that so many of the instructional activities take place in groups, and the methods of assessment of collective learning are not very well developed in the profession of education.

In the accountability domain, the model contains four factors, which are listed in Table B.2. The accountability factors correspond to different levels of measurement, including individual student learning and group and class performances. Also included is the teachers' performance, as indicated by both their students' learning and direct assessments of their classroom activities.

Organizational Change Level

The third level of the model is organizational change. At this level, the primary focus is also on learning. However, the learning is of a different nature. The emphasis here is on the capacity of the school as a formal organization to sustain and renew itself as a learning entity. This perspective is an outgrowth of the theoretical framework of systems thinking. It has recently been formulated by Senge (1990), a former student of Forrester at MIT. Senge proposed systems thinking as the vehicle for organizational sustenance and adaptation to its constantly changing environment. He

TABLE B.3
Major Domains and Variables for the Organizational Change Level

Students	
	Motivations
	Role changes
Teachers	
	Accountability
	Role changes
Administration	
	Accountability
	Commitment to change
Community	
	Support
	Involvement
	Resources

coined the phrase "learning organization" to connote an organization that uses simulation or microworlds to enhance its capacity for continual renewal and growth.

Table B.3 lists the major domains and associated variables for the organizational change level, and Fig. B.3 portrays the appropriate map of this section of the model. It should be pointed out that the model at this level is specified in less detail than at the student learning or classroom processes

FIG. B.3. Organization change level.

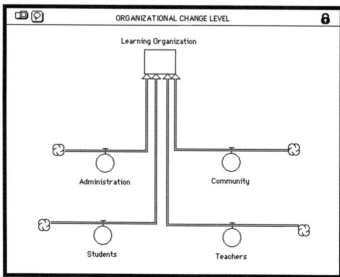

levels. This lack of detail in model specification results from the fact that the authors have thus far in the STACI^N Project devoted less time and resources to studying the organizational change level. It is anticipated that in future versions of the model organizational change will be at least as thoroughly specified, if not more so, than the other two levels.

Although there are four domains, there is only one stock, the learning organization, at the organizational change level. There are four flows, students, teachers, administration, and community, each representing the sources of accumulation for the learning organization stock. This representation reflects the perception that these collectivities are the major contributors to the organization's ongoing development of its capacities to achieve its goals. In the case of the schools, the primary goal is to provide quality education for all students to prepare them for future education, employment, and satisfying personal and professional lives.

Interlevel Linkages

Having portrayed and described each of the three levels of the first draft of a model of a computer-based curriculum innovation project, it is now time to turn attention to the various explanatory links among domains across the levels. Figure B.4 depicts a first approximation of these links. First, it should be pointed out that only a few of the most obvious links across levels are portrayed in Fig. B.4. This oversimplification of the three-level model is done for the purpose of demonstrating the heuristic value of the mapping mode in the STELLA software. To show all possible relevant links with STELLA connectors would make the figure extremely difficult to read and thus unintelligible. In the interests of making the point of the utility of the systems thinking approach and the STELLA mapping mode for the analysis of complex, multilevel changes in schools, the map is at this point kept to a sparse, yet understandable, minimum structure.

To facilitate the discussion of linkages across levels, the following terminology will be used in the remainder of this appendix: Level 1 refers to student learning, Level 2 refers to classroom processes, and Level 3 refers to organizational change. Returning to Fig. B.4 now and looking first at the connectors between Levels 1 and 2, note that the model specifies that both procedural and declarative learning at Level 1 have direct effects on the curriculum domain at Level 2. Again, one could argue that the direction of causality here is unclear, and subsequent versions of the model should consider this a reciprocal and feedback relationship. However, in this first draft of the model, unidirectionality is assumed for all connectors between all stocks, flows, and converters.

The other links between Level 1 and 2 shown in Fig. B.4 depict the influence of assessment of student learning at Level 1 on three connectors at Level 2, curriculum, resources, and support. It is clear that results from a variety of assessments of student learning are used to fine tune or change

FIG. B.4. Three-level model.

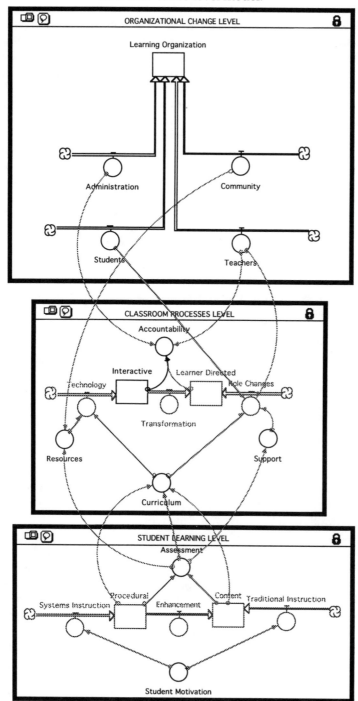

the curriculum. In fact, one of the most common processes employed by most teachers is to change the curriculum for the next year based on their evaluations of how students fared with the current curriculum. Frequently, these assessments are based on test scores and teachers' evaluations of how students performed on some compilation of homework assignments, quizzes, projects, and course examinations. Sometimes curriculum modifications are brought about by other factors, such as advice from other teachers or district mandated changes. These factors are not yet included in the model, but they will need to be in future editions.

Turning finally to the linkages between Levels 2 and 3, note that the pattern is not as symmetrical as that between Levels 1 and 2. In part, the asymmetry reflects the oversimplification of the model at this early stage of development; but it also reflects the complexity of the multifaceted, multilevel reality of computer-based curriculum innovations. Guided primarily by heuristic concerns, Fig. B.4 reflects only one connector between Level 2 for each flow at Level 3. The connectors selected for portrayal reflect the authors' perception of the most salient relationships observed in the almost 6 years of field research thus far in the STACI^N Project. Note also that in this draft version of the model all connectors flow from Level 3 to Level 2, reflecting the assumption that characteristics of the organization affect the dynamics of the classroom. For example, both students and teachers as flows at the organization have the major effect in determining the nature and extent of role changes in the classroom.

The third cross-level connector in this part of the model depicts the effect of the community on the resources made available to provide the technology that promotes interactive learning. The relationship can operate in a general way in that a community whose members are less affluent will not be able to provide a tax base adequate to produce the financial resources for the hardware and software. More specifically, a community may be able to obtain hardware or software through the personal generosity or corporate affiliations of residents of the district. It is also possible that this relationship might operate in the opposite direction as well. Affluent families or those with appropriate corporate ties might find it attractive to move to technology-rich school districts, resulting in the "haves" getting more.

The fourth and final cross-level connector in the model depicts the relationship between the school and district administration at Level 3 and accountability at Level 2. The assumption is that the administration monitors the output of the interactive and learner-directed stocks on a regular basis and makes a wide array of administrative, curricular, and personnel decisions based on these performance indicators. This monitoring takes many forms, including standardized test results, teacher evaluations, and students' performance after leaving school. Teachers are acutely aware of this monitoring and its impact on their professional careers. Consequently, the accountability pressures are most salient in the daily lives of most teachers. Again, one could argue quite cogently that this relationship between the administration and accountability is bidirectional. It is true that the accountability data flow upward from Level 2 to Level 3. However, the more powerful influences on the entire system as observed in the STACI[N] Project are clearly as portrayed in Fig. B.4.

Appendix C

PAST AND PRESENT PARTICIPATING TEACHERS AND PROJECT DIRECTORS

Brattleboro Union High School
Brattleboro, Vermont

Chris O'Brien*
Eric Achenbach
Charles Butterfield
David Clarkson
James Maland
Jake McDermott
Larry Richardson

Hillview Middle School
Menlo Park, California

Ken Capie*
Lynn Crawford
Susan Krumbein
Sharron Molder
Millie Niemeyer
Mark Schack
Kristen Thomas
Rich Wohlstadter

Menlo-Atherton High School
Atherton, California

Stan Ogren*
Maria Duraj
Robin Gregg
Kim Hansen
Roger Heathcote
Denis Lose
Margo McAuliffe
Charlotte Monteith
Joe Miller
Audrey Oka-Klein
Susan Schultz

Mountain View High School
Mountain View, California

Mike Harding*
Charlotte Dalton
Dennis Devine
Jim Forthoffer
Carol Gontang
Jim McGuirk
Larry Vilaubi

El Camino, High School
South San Francisco, California

George Kodros*
Joy Schermer*
Richard Arias
Robert Garrett
Rene Herrerias
Jolene Jordan
Ernest Koney-Li
Robert Nicolopolus

South San Francisco High School
South San Francisco, California

Gregg Whitnah*
John Heron
Roberta Hollier
Stan Johnson
James Marshall
James Orlich
Eileen Reilich
David Sondheim

Westborough Middle School
South San Francisco, California

Donna Czarnecki*
Ann Ban
Doug Harik
Jerry Lewis
Joslyn Negherbon
Joe Neynaber
Larry Olsen
Jack Rauch

Sunnyside High School
Tucson, Arizona

Doug Cardell*
Paul Dye*
Gene Hendricks
Jay Winslow

* Denotes current project director

References

Alderman, D., & Mahler, W. A. (1973). *The evaluation of PLATO and TICCIT: Educational analysis of the community college components* (PR-73-49). Princeton, NJ: Educational Testing Service.

Alpert, D., & Bitzer, D. L. (1970). Advances in computer-based education. *Science, 167*, 1582-1590.

Anderson, J. R. (1982). Acquisition of cognitive skill. *Psychological Review, 89*, 369-406.

Anderson, J. R. (1987). Skill acquisition: Compilation of weak-method problem solutions. *Psychological Review, 94*, 192-210.

Ansoff, H. I., & Slevin, D. (1968). An appreciation of industrial dynamics. *Management Science, 14*, 383-397.

Ball, S., & Bogatz, G. A. (1970). *The first year of Sesame Street: An evaluation.* Princeton, NJ: Educational Testing Service.

Ball, S., & Bogatz, G. A. (1971). *The second year of Sesame Street: A continuing evaluation* (Vols. 1 and 2). Princeton, NJ: Educational Testing Service.

Becker, H. J. (1983). *School uses of microcomputers* (No. 3). Baltimore, MD: The Johns Hopkins University, Center for Social Organizations of Schools.

Becker, H. J. (1984a). *School uses of microcomputers* (No. 4). Baltimore, MD: The Johns Hopkins University, Center for Social Organizations of Schools.

Becker, H. J. (1984b). *School uses of microcomputers* (No. 5). Baltimore, MD: The Johns Hopkins University, Center for Social Organizations of Schools.

Becker, H. J. (1984c). *School uses of microcomputers* (No. 6). Baltimore, MD: The Johns Hopkins University, Center for Social Organizations of Schools.

Bransford, J. D., & Vye, N. J. (1989). A perspective on cognitive research and its implications for instruction. In L. B. Resnick & L. E. Klopfer (Eds.), *Toward the thinking curriculum: Current cognitive research* (pp. 173-205). Alexandria, VA: ASCD.

Brown, A. L., & DeLoache, J. S. (1978). Skills, plans, and self-regulation. In R. Siegler (Ed.), *Children's thinking: What develops?* (pp. 3-35). Hillsdale, NJ: Lawrence Erlbaum Associates.

Bunderson, C. V. (1975). The TICCIT project. Design strategy for educational innovation. In S. A. Harrison & L. M. Stolurow (Eds.), *Improving instructional productivity in higher education* (pp. 91-111). Englewood Cliffs, NJ: Educational Technology.

Bunderson, C. V., Inouye, D. K., & Olsen, J. B. (1989). The four generations of computerized educational measurement. In R. L. Linn (Ed.), *Educational measurement* (3rd ed., pp. 367-407). New York: Macmillan.

Campbell, D. T. (1969). *The impact of Headstart.* Springfield, VA: U.S. Clearinghouse for Federal Scientific and Technical Information.

Campbell, D. T., & Stanley, J. C. (1963). Experimental and quasi-experimental designs for research on teaching. In N. L. Gage (Ed.), *Handbook of research on teaching* (pp. 171-246). Chicago: Rand McNally.

REFERENCES

Cline, H. F. (1989). *What happens when a school starts using a micro-computer laboratory?: The impact of a science micro-computer program on the structure and functioning of a high school* (TR89-4). Cambridge, MA: Harvard Graduate School of Education, Educational Technology Center.

Cline, H. F., Bennett, R. E., Kershaw, R. C., Schneiderman, M. B., Stecher, B., Wilson, S. (1986). *The electronic schoolhouse: The IBM secondary school computer education program*. Hillsdale, NJ: Lawrence Erlbaum Associates.

Cognition and Technology Group at Vanderbilt. (1992). The Jasper Series as an example of anchored instruction: Theory, program description, and assessment data. *Educational Psychologist, 27*, 291-315.

Corno, L., & Mandinach, E. B. (1983). The role of cognitive engagement in classroom learning and motivation. *Educational Psychologist, 18*(2), 88-108.

Crawford, L., & Molder, S. (1992a). *America: A universal nation within an interdependent world: Preparing for the Columbia Quincentenary*. Unpublished curriculum plans. Menlo Park, CA: Hillview Middle School.

Crawford, L., & Molder, S. (1992b, April). *Innovation in an integrated middle school curriculum*. Paper presented at the annual meeting of the American Educational Research Association, San Francisco.

Cronbach, L. J. (1963). Course improvement through evaluation. *Teachers College Record, 64*, 672-683.

Cuban, L. (1986). *Teachers and machines: The classroom use of technology since 1920*. New York: Teachers College Press.

Dalbey, J., & Linn, M. C. (1985). The demands and requirements of computer programming: A review of the literature. *Journal of Educational Computing Research, 1*, 253-274.

Duschel, R. A., & Gitomer, D. H. (1991). Epistomological perspectives on conceptual change: Implications for educational practice. *Journal of Research on Science Teaching, 28*, 839-858.

Dwyer, D. C., Ringstaff, C., & Sandholtz, J. H. (1991). Changes in teachers' beliefs and practices in technology-rich classrooms. *Educational Leadership, 48*(8), 45-52.

Eastwood, L. F., & Ballard, R. J. (1975). The PLATO IV CAI system: Where is it now? Where can it go? *Journal of Educational Technology Systems, 3*, 267-283.

Fetterman, D. M. (1989) *Ethnography: Step by step*. Newbury Park, CA: Sage Publications.

Flavell, J. H. (1976). Metacognitive aspects of problem solving. In L. B. Resnick (Ed.), *The nature of intelligence* (pp. 231-235). Hillsdale, NJ: Lawrence Erlbaum Associates.

Flavell, J. H. (1979). Metacognition and cognitive monitoring. *American Psychologist, 34*, 906-911.

Flavell, J. H. (1981). Cognitive monitoring. In P. Dickson (Ed.), *Children's oral communications skills* (pp. 35-60). New York: Academic Press.

Forman, G., & Pufall, P. B. (Eds.). (1988). *Constructivism in the computer age*. Hillsdale, NJ: Lawrence Erlbaum Associates.

Forrester, J. W. (1961). *Industrial dynamics*. Cambridge, MA: MIT Press.

Forrester, J. W. (1968). *Principles of systems*. Cambridge, MA: MIT Press.

Forrester, J. W. (1969). *Urban dynamics*. Cambridge, MA: MIT Press.

Forrester, J. W. (1971a). Counterintuitive nature of social systems. *Technology Review, 73*, 53.

Forrester, J. W. (1971b). *World dynamics*. Cambridge, MA: Wright-Allen Press.

Forrester, J. W. (1991). System dynamics: Adding structure and relevance to pre-college education. In K. R. Manning (Ed.), *Shaping the future* (pp. 118-131). Cambridge, MA: MIT Press.

Freeman, H. F., & Rossi, P. (1980). *Handbook of evaluation research*. San Francisco, CA: Jossey-Bass.

Gitomer, D. H., Grosh, S., & Price, K. (1992). Portfolio culture in arts education. *Arts Education, 45*, 7-15.

Hadley, M., & Sheingold, K. (1993). Commonalties and distinctive patterns in teachers' integration of computers. *American Journal of Education, 101*, 261-315.

Haney, C., Banks, W. C., & Zimbardo, P. G. (1973). Interpersonal dynamics in a simulated prison. *International Journal of Criminology and Penology, 1*, 69-79.

Harel, I., & Papert, S. (Eds). (1991). *Constructionism*. Norwood, NJ: Ablex.

Howard, D. C. (1987). *Metacognitive questionnaire*. Burnaby, British Columbia: Simon Fraser University.

Jones, R. M. (1986, Sept.). Macmodeling. *Macworld*, pp. 109-111.

Kershaw, D. (1976). *Final report of the graduated work incentive experiment* (Vol. 3). New York: Academic Press.

Larkin, J. H., & Chabay, R. W. (1989). Research on teaching scientific thinking: Implications for computer-based instruction. In L. B. Resnick & L. E. Klopfer (Eds.), *Toward the thinking curriculum: Current cognitive research* (pp. 150-172). Alexandria, VA: ASCD.

Lesgold, A. (1988). Problem solving. In R. J. Sternberg & E. E. Smith (Eds.), *The psychology of human thought* (pp. 188-213). New York: Cambridge University Press.

Linn, M. C. (1985). The demands and consequences of programming instruction in classrooms. *Educational Researcher, 14*(5), 14-16, 25-29.

Mandinach, E. B. (1988a). *Self-regulated learning substudy: Systems thinking and curriculum innovation (STACI) project* (TR88-25). Cambridge, MA: Harvard Graduate School of Education, Educational Technology Center.

Mandinach, E. B. (1988b). *The war and revolution case study: Systems thinking and curriculum innovation (STACI) project* (TR88-26). Cambridge, MA: Harvard Graduate School of Education, Educational Technology Center.

Mandinach, E. B., & Cline, H. F. (1990). Applications of simulation and modeling in precollege instruction. *Machine-Mediated Learning, 3*, 189-205.

Mandinach, E. B., & Cline, H. F. (1992, April). *The impact of technological curriculum innovation on teaching and learning activities*. Paper presented at the annual meeting of the American Educational Research Association, San Francisco.

Mandinach, E. B., & Linn, M. C. (1986). The cognitive effects of computer learning environments. *Journal of Educational Computing Research, 2*, 411-427.

Mandinach, E. B., Linn, M. C., Pea, R. D., & Kurland, D. M. (Eds.). (1986-1987). The cognitive effects of computer learning environments [Special issue]. *Journal of Educational Computing Research, 2 & 3*.

Mandinach, E. B., & Thorpe, M. E. (1987). Caveats and realities in technological curriculum innovation for researchers and teachers. *Technology and Learning, 1*(4), 1-3, 7, 9.

Mandinach, E. B., Thorpe, M. E., & Lahart, C. M. (1988). *The impact of the systems thinking approach on teaching and learning activities* (TR88-31). Cambridge, MA: Harvard Graduate School of Education, Educational Technology Center.

Marshall, H. H. (1987). Building a learning orientation. *Theory into Practice, 26*, 8-14.

Marshall, H. H. (1988). In pursuit of learning-oriented classrooms. *Teaching and Teacher Education, 4*, 85-98.

Marshall, H. H. (1992). Preface. In H. H. Marshall (Ed.), *Redefining student learning: Roots of educational change* (pp. ix-xvi). Norwood, NJ: Ablex.

Mattessich, R. (1982). The systems approach: Its variety of aspects. *Journal of the American Society for Information Science , 33*, 383-394.

Meadows, D. H., Meadows, D. L., & Randers, J. (1992). *Beyond the limits: Confronting global collapse and envisioning a sustainable future*. Post Mills, VT: Chelsea Green.

Meadows, D. H., Meadows, D. L., Randers, J., & Behrens, W. W. (1972). *The limits to growth*. New York: New American Library.

Miller, F., Jr., Dillon, T. J., & Smith, M. K. (1980). *Concepts in physics*. Orlando, FL: Harcourt Brace Jovanovich.

Morris, L. V. (1989). Finding time for teachers to learn: Routine activities of teacher work. *Technology and Learning, 3*(5), 1-4.

National Council of Teachers of Mathematics. (1989). *Curriculum and evaluation standards for school mathematics*. Reston, VA: Author.

Newman, D. (1990). Opportunities for research on the organizational impact of school computers. *Educational Researcher, 19*(3), 8-13.

Papert, S. (1991). Situating constructionism. In I. Harel & S. Papert (Eds.), *Constructionism* (pp. 1-11). Norwood, NJ: Ablex.

Pea, R. D., & Kurland, D. M. (1984). On the cognitive effects of learning computer programming. *New Ideas in Psychology, 2*, 137-168.

Pea, R. D., & Sheingold, K. (Eds.). (1987). *Mirrors of minds: Patterns of experience in educational computing*. Norwood, NJ: Ablex.

Polya, G. (1957). *How to solve it* (2nd. ed.). Princeton, NJ: Princeton University Press.

Pugh, A. L. (1973). *DYNAMO II users manual*. Cambridge, MA: MIT Press.

Quality Education Data, Inc. (1986). *Microcomputers in schools, 1985-1986*. Unpublished manuscript.

Raven, J. C. (1958). *Advanced progressive matrices* (Set I). New York: Psychological Press.

Raven, J. C. (1962). *Advanced progressive matrices* (Set II). New York: Psychological Press.

Redfield, C. L., & Steuck, K. (1991). The future of intelligent tutoring systems. In H. Burns, J. W. Parlett, & C. L. Redfield (Eds.), *Intelligent tutoring systems* (pp. 265-284). Hillsdale, NJ: Lawrence Erlbaum Associates.

Richmond, B. (1985). *STELLA* [Computer program]. Lyme, NH: High Performance Systems.

Richmond, B. (1993). Systems thinking: Critical thinking skills for the 1990's and beyond. *System Dynamics Review, 9*, 113-133.

Richmond, B., & Peterson, S. (1988). *STELLAStack* [Computer program]. Lyme, NH: High Performance Systems.

Richmond, B., & Peterson, S. (1990). *STELLA II* [Computer program]. Lyme, NH: High Performance Systems.

Richmond, B., Peterson, S., & Vescuso, P. (1987). *An academic user's guide to STELLA*. Lyme, NH: High Performance Systems.

Rieken, H., & Boruch, R. (1974). *Social experimentation*. New York: Academic Press.

Robinson, S. B. (1986, Dec.). STELLA: Modeling and simulation software for use with the Macintosh. *Byte*, pp. 277-278.

Salomon, G. (1990). Studying the flute *and* the orchestra: Controlled vs. classroom research on computers. *International Journal of Educational Research, 14*, 37-47.

Salomon, G. (1991). Transcending the qualitative-quantitative debate: The analytic and systemic approaches to educational research. *Educational Researcher, 20*(6), 10-18.

Sandholtz, J. H., Ringstaff, C., & Dwyer, D. C. (1990). *Classroom management: Teaching in high-tech environments: Classroom management revisited first-fourth year findings* (ACOT Report #10). Cupertino, CA: Apple Computer, Inc., Advanced Technology Group, Apple Classrooms of Tomorrow.

Scriven, M. (1977). *Evaluation thesaurus* (3rd. ed.). Inverness, CA: Edgepress.

Senge, P. (1990). *The fifth discipline: The art and practice of the learning organization*. New York: Doubleday.

Sheingold, K., & Hadley, M. (1990). *Accomplished teachers: Integrating computers into classroom practice*. New York: Bank Street College, Center for Technology in Education.

Shulman, L. S., & Keislar, E. R. (Eds.). (1966). *Learning by discovery: A critical appraisal*. Chicago: Rand McNally.

REFERENCES

Snow, R. E. (1980). Aptitude processes. In R. E. Snow, P-A. Federico, & W. E. Montague (Eds.), *Aptitudes, learning, and instruction* (Vol. 1, pp. 27-63). Hillsdale, NJ: Lawrence Erlbaum Associates.

Snow, R. E., & Mandinach, E. B. (1991). *Integrating instruction and assessment: A research and development agenda* (RR91-8). Princeton, NJ: Educational Testing Service.

Suchman, E. A. (1967). *Evaluative research.* New York: Russell Sage Foundation.

Swinton, S. S., Amarel, M. A., & Morgan, J. A. (1978). *The PLATO elementary demonstration educational outcome evaluation* (PR-78-11). Princeton, NJ: Educational Testing Service.

Zimbardo, P. G., Haney, C., Banks, W. C., & Jaffe, D. (1973, April 8). The mind is a formidable jailer: A Pirandellian prison. *The New York Times Magazine,* pp. 38-60.

Author Index

A

Alderman, D., 57
Alpert, D., 56
Amarel, M. A., 57
Anderson, J. R., 92
Ansoff, H., 51

B

Ball, S., 38
Ballard, R. J., 56
Banks, W. C., 19
Becker, H. J., 58, 81
Behrens, W. W., 53
Bennett, R. E., 183
Bitzer, D. L., 56
Bogatz, G. A., 38
Boruch, R., 38
Bransford, J. D., 92
Brown, A. L., 14
Bunderson, C. V., 56, 112

C

Campbell, D. T., 38
Chabay, R. W., 16
Cline, H. F., 22, 91, 108, 115, 183
Cognition and Technology Group
    at Vanderbilt, 92
Corno, L., 15
Crawford, L., 125
Cronbach, L. J., 38, 108
Cuban, L., 56, 59

D, E

Dalbey, J., 1
DeLoache, J. S., 14
Dillon, T. J., 11
Ducshel, R. A., 41

Dwyer, D. C., 83, 91, 115, 117, 118
Eastwood, L. F., 56

F

Fetterman, D. M., 38
Flavell, J. H., 14
Forman, G., 92
Forrester, J. W., 3, 4, 8, 49, 50, 51,
    52, 53, 56
Freeman, H. F., 38

G, H

Gitomer, D. H., 41
Grosh, S., 41
Hadley, M., 115, 117
Haney, C., 19
Harel, I., 92
Howard, D. C., 16

I, J

Inouye, D. K., 112
Jaffe, D., 19
Jones, R. M., 67

K

Kershaw, D., 38
Kershaw, R. C., 183
Keislar, E. R., 14
Kurland, D. M., 1

L

Lahart, C. M., 8
Larkin, J. H., 16

Subject Index